The Invisible Threads

The Invisible Threads

Independent Soviets Working for
Global Awareness and Social Transformation

by

Gale Warner

Seven Locks Press
Washington

From ALMOST AT THE END by Yevgeny Yevtushenko. Copyright © 1987 by Yevgeny Yevtushenko. Translation copyright © 1987 by Antonina W. Bouis, Albert C. Todd and Yevgeny Yevtushenko. Reprinted by permission of Henry Holt and Company, Inc.

Library of Congress Cataloging-in-Publication Data

Warner, Gale.
    The invisible threads: independent Soviets working for global awareness and social transformation / Gale Warner.
        p. cm.
    ISBN 0-932020-88-7:
    1. Soviet Union—Description and travel—1970–   2. Warner, Gale—Journeys—Soviet Union. 3. Peace movements—Soviet Union. 4. Peace movements—United States. 5. Soviet Union—Relations—United States. 6. United States—Relations—Soviet Union. I. Title
DK29.W37 1991
303.48′247073—dc20
                                            90-8915
                                          CIP

For more information, write or call:

Seven Locks Press
P.O. Box 27
Cabin John, MD 20818
(301)320-2130

for Zhenya

A Verse from "Fuku"

In every border post
        there's something insecure.
Each one of them
        is longing for leaves and flowers.
They say
        the greatest punishment for a tree
is to become a border post.
The birds that pause to rest
        on border posts
can't figure out
        what kind of tree they've landed on.
I suppose
        that at first, it was people who invented borders,
and then borders
        started to invent people.
It was borders who invented police,
        armies, and border guards.
It was borders who invented
customs-men, passports, and other shit.
Thank God,
        we have invisible thread and threadlets
born of the threads of blood
        from the nails in the palms of Christ.
These threads struggle through,
        tearing apart the barbed wire,
leading love to join love
        and anguish to unite with anguish.
And a tear,
        which evaporated somewhere in Paraguay,
will fall as a snowflake
        onto the frozen cheek of an Eskimo.
And a hulking New York skyscraper
        with bruises of neon,
mourning the forgotten smell of plowlands,
dreams only of embracing a lonely Kremlin tower,
but sadly that is not allowed.
The Iron Curtain,
        unhappily squeaking her rusty brains,
probably thinks:
        "Oh, if I were not a border,
if jolly hands would pull me apart
and build from my bloody remains
        carousels, kindergartens, and schools."

In my darkest dreams I see
                    my prehistoric ancestor:
he collected skulls like trophies
                    in the somber vaults of his cave,
and with the bloodied point of a stone spearhead
he marked out the first-ever border
                    on the face of the earth.
That was a hill of skulls.
                    Now it has grown into an Everest.
The earth was transformed
                    and became a giant burial place.
While borders still stand
                    we are all in prehistory.
Real history will start
                    when all borders are gone.
The earth is still scarred,
                    mutilated with the scars of wars.
Now killing has become an art,
                    when once it was merely a trade.
From all those thousands of borders
                    we have lost the only human one—
the border between good and evil.
But while we still have invisible threads
joining each self
                    with millions of selves,
there are no real superpower states.
Any fragile soul on this earth
                    is the real superpower.
My government
                    is the whole family of man, all at once.
Every beggar is my marshal,
                    giving me orders.
I am a racist,
                    I recognize only one race—
the race of all races.
How foreign is the word *foreigner!*
I have four and a half billion leaders.
And I dance my Russian,
                    my death-defying dance
on the invisible threads
                    that connect the hearts of people.

—*Yevgeny Yevtushenko*

Contents

Acknowledgments

The process of creating this book spanned three years, ten trips to the Soviet Union, and a total of seven months of living in that country. I am grateful to dozens of people in both the United States and the Soviet Union for their sustained help, encouragement, and insights. Many of them are mentioned in the text, but among those Americans deserving special thanks are Bob Alei, James Baumgaertner, Amy Donahue, Rick Donahue, Catherine Fitzpatrick, David Gershon, Diane Gilman, Robert Gilman, Taya Portnova, Sima Ressin, Diana Glasgow, Joe Kinczel, Joanne Landy, Ted Levin, Bob McGlynn, Stephanie Nichols, Danaan Parry, Sarah Peyton, Bill Shaw, Michael Shuman, Gail Straub, and Sharon Tennison.

In the Soviet Union, Joseph Goldin and Andrei Orlov helped initially convince me to, as the Russian saying goes, "*Vperyod! bez strakha i somneniya!* (Go forward! without fear or doubt!)" Igor Ovchinnikov, Kairat Umarov, and Yuri Dzhibladze assisted me as interpreters, advisors, and kitchen-table analysts. The Moscow staff of the Soviet Committee of Physicians for the Prevention of Nuclear War, in particular Vladimir Popov and Alexander Makotinsky, helped several times with visas. Zhenya Alekseeva, her husband Volodya, and her children Dasha and Vera have unselfishly opened their home and their lives to me; this book owes much to their steady love, laughter, and music.

My husband and partner David Kreger edited the book and kept me honest, laughing, and well-fed. Without him, and without the emotional and financial support of my parents, Louise and Jack Warner, I would never have completed this book.

Finally, I am grateful to Yevgeny Yevtushenko, whose poem "Fuku" inspired the title, and to Carl Sagan, who helped suggest the idea by writing in the foreword to my previous book *Citizen Diplomats:* "It will be a hopeful day when their [Soviet citizen diplomats'] memoirs are as freely published."

Introduction

This book is a journey into the lives of people whose voices have seldom been heard in the West, and who have much to teach us about living with integrity and without fear in today's world.

In a previous book, *Citizen Diplomats*, I told the stories of several Americans who had barged energetically into the quagmire of Soviet-American relations, with the aim of thawing the Cold War and unhooking the nuclear hairtrigger. At first they were ridiculed. But these citizen diplomats had, with surprising success, defied expert opinion and created a fertile network of non-governmental relationships between private citizens, cultural groups, and businesses of the two supposedly "enemy" nations, long before *perestroika* made their work easier.

It was while listening to their tales that I heard hints of other stories, as yet untold. Many made reference to their behind-the-scenes Soviet partners, individuals who were unobtrusively moving forward projects that might bring the countries closer together. These Soviets were translating and distributing anti-nuclear books, matching children with American pen pals, inviting Westerners into their homes, and coordinating exchanges. They were building lively personal networks across previously silent borders. They were trying to be agents of social transformation for their country and the planet. Although they were "ordinary people" in the sense that they held regular jobs, lived in normal apartments, and were not part of the Soviet *nomenklatura* (elite), they were, of course, exceptional, with a far-from-typical determination to carve out a path for independent action in a nation with few traditions of individualism.

The thought that even a few such people had survived the harsh political conditions of the Soviet Union intrigued me greatly. I was not sure that under similar circumstances, facing similar harassments and dangers, I would act with similar courage. Somehow, living in a culture of pervasive personal disempowerment, they had found the power to act; in a country thoroughly innoculated against optimism, they had found reason for hope. How did they do it? How might their stories illuminate our own choices?

When I began this project, I told others that I was writing a book on the independent Soviet peace movement. But the word "peace" always stuck in my throat. It is a word that makes people nervous. It smacks of naiveté and impractical idealism. And since no one is quite sure what it means, its usefulness as a modifier is limited. Many people are trying to revitalize this long-suffering word with new definitions, so that it will someday connote a colorful, dynamic world of interrelationship and creative tension. Certainly the wishi-washiness of the word "peace" underscores that we have not, as a species, given this concept sufficient attention. But at present, it still tends to produce either embarrassed coughs or cloudy thinking, or both.

The Russian word *mir,* which translates into English both as "peace" and "world," is even more problematic. For many Soviets, *mir* has been flensed of all meaning by its overuse in official government propaganda. The Soviet government has always insisted that it is leading *borba za mir,* "the fight for peace." After enduring decades of self-righteous official peace rallies and empty slogans such as *Miru mir,* "Peace to the world," and *Nam nuzhen mir,* "We need peace," it is no wonder that many Soviet citizens react to the word *mir* with rueful, if sometimes affectionate, skepticism. This is not to belittle the genuine yearnings of a people that has suffered more than its share of warfare, or claim that the average Russian *babushka* is not utterly sincere when she says that she wants peace. But the crudely one-sided, we're-the-good-guys, the-Americans-are-the-bad-guys flavor of traditional Soviet peace propaganda makes the word *mir* stick in Soviet throats, as well.

Many of the people in this book are thus repelled by the term "peace activist." Some call themselves "citizen diplomats," but this phrase, too, has been partially co-opted, and it now spills from the lips of well-paid bureaucrats at the Soviet Peace Committee with ease. Some call themselves "social inventors," but this concept is inconveniently broad. Perhaps the best title for them is *mirotvortsi,* a Russian word usually translated as "peacemakers" but that could be more accurately rendered as "peace-creators" or "world-creators." Here the conflation of the English words "peace" and "world" is useful, for the *mirotvortsi* are trying not only to prevent and eliminate war, and thus achieve peace in the traditional sense, but also to create something new in the world to take war's place.

In discussions with these Soviets about their work, the word that surfaces more frequently than "peace" is "global." In one way or other, these individuals and groups are attempting to prod their communities and nation into behavior based on the understanding that we all belong to a diverse global family living on a small and vulnerable planet. Such a movement is not unique to the Soviet Union, of course, but it has special meaning in a country that historically has been cut off from communicating with the rest of the world and that is still suffering today from a legacy of xenophobia, kneejerk militarism, and bitter nationalistic disputes.

Since I began this book in 1987, the Soviet Union and Eastern Europe have been unrecognizably altered by a dizzying series of social and political transformations. Much of today's reality in the Soviet Union—competitive elections, greatly increased freedoms of speech and press, the emergence of private businesses, open challenges to Communist Party control, and the development of thousands of independent civic and social organizations—was the stuff of yesterday's dreams. Several years ago, the main thrust of the work of independent *mirotvortsi* was organizing more contacts between Soviets and Westerners to counteract the widespread "image of the enemy" the peoples of both nations held of one another. Arranging an unsanctioned peace demonstration of any kind could, and often did, lead to arrests, and it took courage even to suggest that the Soviet government was not already doing everything possible for peace.

The world has changed; national leaders and the news media proclaim the Cold War over, and unprecedented numbers of Westerners and Soviets are now stampeding over the rubble of the Iron Curtain to participate in exchange programs, tourism, and business ventures. Soviet President Mikhail Gorbachev has pulled forces out of Afghanistan, reduced troops in Europe, retired many military officers, cut back on defense spending, and allowed "velvet revolution" to sweep through Eastern Europe. Independent street demonstrations of all kinds have become commonplace, and *Moscow News* now publishes lively debates on the question of a 95 percent cut in Soviet nuclear weaponry.

Yet far from being out of a job, Soviet *mirotvortsi* are busier than ever. They understand that the hard work of co-creating a livable future for their country and the planet is just beginning. Many are launching new cooperative projects with Westerners, ranging from environmental clean-up campaigns to aid for victims of Chernobyl, from new publishing enterprises to joint exhibitions on energy efficiency. Many are now turning their attention to peace within the country, and are using the skills they learned in citizen diplomacy with the West to facilitate nonviolent social change within and among their fractious republics. And many continue to point out that despite plentiful rhetoric about the end of the Cold War, billions are still wasted on building new generations of sophisticated weaponry, and existing arsenals of nuclear missiles still threaten us with the possibility of unintentional nuclear war.

Certainly no one, including the *mirotvortsi* themselves, would deny the enormous role Gorbachev has played in single-handedly warming East-West relations. But clearly he has had help. For years, the informal Soviet peace movement was a channel for new information and ideas pouring in from the West. Although it is hard to quantify the impact of years of patient grassroots work— pen-pal matchings, hand-typed translations, newspaper articles portraying Westerners as real human beings, hundreds of quiet exchanges, thousands of face-to-face meetings—all of this activity has helped create a groundswell of popular momentum for the Soviet government's more flexible and open relationship with the rest of the world.

As the powerful and unpredictable forces unleashed by *perestroika* continue to shake Soviet society in the years ahead, this support may prove more and more crucial. New challenges and dangers are arising as restive Soviet republics strain to leave the old empire and right-wing Russian nationalistic groups known for their strident anti-Westernism grow in size and influence. Only a strong grassroots movement for global thinking, for the peaceful resolution of conflicts, and for cross-cultural understanding and tolerance can protect the Soviet Union from the danger of slipping back into its militaristic and xenophobic past. For this reason, it is more important than ever that Westerners reach beyond their borders and begin to work in partnership with Soviets who share their commitment to building a humane and sustainable world.

The stories in this book are from a land unknown and unfathomable to most Americans, and yet they are also strangely familiar. For they are part of a story that is taking place all over the world. Today many people in many countries are denying themselves the unaffordable luxury of despair. They are spinning what the poet Yevtushenko calls "the invisible threads that connect the hearts of people." They are inventing plans to lead their communities out of poverty and hunger, planting gardens in urban wastelands, seeking common ground with old enemies, standing up for their human rights, and showing in hundreds of other ways that we can discover and wield an inner power that is rooted in our passion to love, to nurture, and to survive.

The nature of change is subtle. What may seem at the time to be sweeping change may be temporary; what may seem to be so much headbeating against a wall may in fact be creating change in ways no one will ever be able to trace. As Gandhi put it, what each of us does may seem insignificant at the time, but it is terribly important that we do it. This belief sustains the people in this book. It has sustained me in the writing of it.

We still have a chance to draw upon this power, this choice. We still have time to listen to stories.

And to tell our own.

Gale Warner
December 1990

1 | The White Crow

According to history, Vladimir Shestakov should not exist. At first he seems a rare and delicate exception, a lone flower that has somehow escaped the lawnmower of the Soviet system. But he is, in fact, rather tough and fibrous, someone who has been sliced to the roots many times but keeps springing back to toss seeds on the cracked asphalt around him.

Shestakov once described himself in a letter to an American as a "citizen of the Soviet Union, biologist by education, bureaucrat by job, peace activist (freelance) and conservationist by vocation." He should not exist because gutsy, active, free-thinking people who were not locked up or stamped down were not supposed to exist in the pre-Gorbachev Soviet Union. But Shestakov existed, and was active, long before the halcyon days of *perestroika*. He would continue to be active if *perestroika* were to collapse; he knows how to live through winter.

Shestakov lives, with his wife, Olya, their three daughters, and his father, in a two-room apartment near the center of Leningrad that has been in his family for four generations. His great-grandparents, grandparents and parents, together with a few neighbors, kept themselves alive here during the seige of Leningrad by huddling around a single stove. The apartment is frumpy and high-ceilinged, stuffed with the particulars of six people's lives. A baby's toilet seat, a pair of skis, a pile of newspapers, and an antique vase on a gilded pedestal are heaped in a corner. Photographs of sailboats and mountain landscapes wallpaper the hall from floor to ceiling, licking the moldings of a pre-revolutionary parlor. The wardrobe and closet doors are plastered with gentle but firm imperatives on American bumperstickers: "WORK FOR PEACE," says one. "THINK GLOBALLY, ACT LOCALLY."

Beneath the outward clutter are certain themes. There is, in the photos of seascapes and sunlit mountain scenes, a theme about the beauty of the earth. There are exhortations everywhere about what must be done to keep it beautiful. Even the water closet has a determined decor. Posted for easy reading are instructions for walking the "Twelve Pathways To Unconditional Love And Happiness." Under a spectacular photograph of an Alpine meadow is lettered the word, "THINK!"

"We need wisdom today more than at any other time, because of the damage we have already inflicted on the Earth's ecosystem, because of the powers we have at our disposal," Shestakov says. "What nuclear war can do in a matter of minutes, pollution can do in a matter of decades. We need new consciousness and we need to spread that knowledge. Real responsibility comes with education, and understanding that our individual actions can influence larger systems. We are not idle spectators. Time impels us to make a choice, and the battleground is in our souls."

Shestakov's perfect English and snazzy Californian T-shirts are, at first, disorienting. He seems to have been air-dropped into this apartment, into his citizenry, by mistake. At least that is the first impression of many of his American visitors, because of our tendency to label "American-like" those who fit our notion of ourselves as independent, creative, authority-be-damned individualists. Shestakov is, however, Russian, and his roots live in the rich stubborn sod of Russian culture. Often while walking city streets he will hum, in his soft baritone, a verse of a Russian folk song. In winters he rents a *dacha* (cottage) in a nearby village and skis through the forest, absorbing the air and the scent of the trees, singing at full voice an ancient chant against frost.

He is tall and slender, balding, fortyish, with rather small, very bright brown eyes. In winters he does not shave, in summers he does—a compromise to keep the peace among his daughters, who love his beard, and his wife, who hates it. His pale glasses and threadbare jackets give an appearance that is bookish but not quite professorial. He does not look well-paid enough to be a professor. He has the look, rather, of a graduate student who never gets quite enough to eat. This is certainly not the fault of his wife Olya, who does her best to keep him and her family fed. It instead stems from a perpetual restlessness, a constant energetic motion, that seems to burn off calories as quickly as Olya can put them·on his plate.

Shestakov is, by his own description, "a social mutation." He is an optimist in a culture conditioned to protect itself from hope. But he intensely dislikes the label "optimist." He knows that when others call him an optimist they are cordoning themselves off from his world, isolating and categorizing him as some special breed of human capable of such activities. "I am not an optimist!" he once exclaimed after a friend gently called him one, after he had spent the better part of an evening unsuccessfully coaxing a scientist to join one of his projects. "I am a *pragmatist*. Let's not just talk forever about whether what we can do will work or not work. Let's *try*. Let's see what we *can* do, that is practical."

His business cards, printed by an American colleague, list his occupations as "peace activist, translator, informal networker." The words "peace activist," however, have been crossed out in blue pen. An American woman meeting Shestakov for the first time asked why. "Because I realized this title is too often used by people who are for peace only when that means a free fancy dinner or a free trip to America," he answered. "I do not want to be confused with them."

"But you are letting them take the word 'peace' away from you!" the woman announced.

"I think it is not that I am letting them do it," Shestakov replied with a small pained smile. "I think it is already done."

How Shestakov became a peace activist, in deed if not in name, is told in a brief article he wrote for the Winter 1987 issue of the American magazine *In Context*:

> Prior to November 1982, I existed on the individual level of consciousness, believing that politics is made by big bosses . . . and lay people like me cannot influence it. Like many of the people in this country, I was sure that our government was doing its best to safeguard peace, and that it was their duty, not mine.
>
> In November, I met a charming mother of three children at a meeting of the House of Friendship. She gave me a [bestselling anti-nuclear] book entitled *The Hundredth Monkey* by Ken Keyes. There were tears in her eyes when she spoke about the future of our children. She insisted that I read the book at once, which I promised her I would. At that time, I had several books to be finished first, and I was going to put it away and read it later. But on the way back in the metro, I opened the book at a random place, began to read...and missed my stop.
>
> That very night, I finished it and couldn't fall asleep, feeling that something radical should be done that transcends individual limitations. I was sorry for my numerous friends who knew no English and couldn't read the book, so I decided to translate it for them. For some time, it circulated in this form, and more

and more copies appeared like mushrooms after rain. And yet, there weren't enough of them to satisfy the ever-growing interest and demand. . . .

His fingers sore from typing, Shestakov brought a copy of the translation to a well-known Leningrad poet who was also the president of the local branch of the Soviet Peace Committee. "At first his reaction was calm, solid, moderate," Shestakov recalls. "He put it on his desk and said he would read it sometime later. But that evening he telephoned me to say he had read it, and he was agitated, and he said he had been thinking of some of the very same ideas, and to prove it he read some of his verses to me over the phone." The poet recommended that he send the translation to the editors of *Twentieth Century and Peace,* the monthly magazine of the Soviet Peace Committee. An abridged version of the book appeared in the December 1983 issue.

Shestakov was thrilled: "It was my first experience of how good books can open the hearts of honest people." But he was dissatisfied with how the magazine's editors had cut the book. "They did not mention [Australian physician and anti-nuclear activist] Helen Caldicott, which I thought was a drastic mistake. Because Helen Caldicott has done more than anyone else in the world in informing people of the dangers. To me she is the undisputed leader. She shows what a single individual can do." Shestakov continued to distribute his own hand-typed, unabridged translations through a small network of interested friends and to send copies to prominent Soviet writers. "I realized that I could not live like I had lived before. I had the desire to reach out to every human being on the Earth and grasp him by the throat and say, 'How can we keep living like this? We are so close to the nuclear precipice, and who knows, our life may finish tomorrow, with all the mistakes and false alarms in the computers.' And I realized that I must try to educate people about the realities of our days, and to raise consciousness, so that we will begin to live as members of a global community."

Word of Shestakov's work eventually reached Ken Keyes, the author of *The Hundredth Monkey,* who wrote him an encouraging letter. Two of Keyes' colleagues dropped by to see him while visiting Leningrad in 1984. Shestakov's phone number and address began circulating among a small community of Americans interested in trying to establish "citizen diplomacy" with Soviets. These new visitors, in turn, brought more books. In the next few years, Shestakov produced translations of Carl Sagan's *Nuclear Winter,* Helen Caldicott's *Nuclear Madness* and *Missile Envy,* and excerpts from Jonathan Schell's *Fate of the Earth* and E.F. Shumacher's *Small is Beautiful.* His friends patiently retyped the translations and passed them on.

The network spread. Soon Shestakov was receiving calls from Soviets volunteering to type more copies, asking for American pen pals, and offering their homes as gathering places for the American groups that were now regularly descending on Shestakov's apartment. The network grew the way mushrooms grow: tiny strands weaving through soil, finding one another, suddenly reaching a critical mass and swelling forth into fruiting bodies that scatter still more spores. Shestakov became the center of something less structured than an organization, more closely knit than a phone list, something organic and fecund and invisible to those not looking down at the grassroots.

These were the grim, fear-ridden days before *glasnost* and *perestroika,* and American citizen diplomats passing through Leningrad found visiting Shestakov and his lively network a delightful contrast to their meetings with official peacemakers at the House of Friendship. They flocked to Shestakov's apartment for evening discussions with Soviet cab drivers, engineers, ecologists, artists, and teachers. They gratefully distributed their peace buttons and bumperstickers, drank tea at his round table, and wore with pride his strings of *sushki* (small dry Russian bagels) reserved for special guests. When asked whether the *sushki* necklaces are a Russian custom, Shestakov replies that he is trying to start a new tradition. "We need to evolve new rituals of goodwill," he says. "Circles have very special meaning. I think that a person whose values are well-organized and who is at peace with himself can be represented by a circle. So each *sushka* represents a self-actualized personality. And the necklace represents a circle of friends, a network of self-actualized personalities. When you wear it you are symbolically incorporated into this network."

His American visitors also brought dozens of ideas for peace projects, many of them involving children. Shestakov began regularly taking Americans to visit schools and persuading Soviet teachers to start pen pal projects in their classes. He recruited his thirteen-year-old daughter, Natasha, to stay after school and teach younger children how to fold Japanese paper peace cranes. (Natasha herself made more than 700 cranes, all from yellow paper—the only color she could obtain in such quantity.) He convinced a journalist acquaintance to write an article in a Leningrad children's newspaper about Birthday Friends for Peace, a project aimed at linking Soviet and American kids who have the same birthdays; a few months after the article appeared, more than 2,000 Leningrad children had sent in their names, addresses, and birthdays.

"The goal of these projects is to help us to overcome our limited identity, because we live in a time when global identity is vital," Shestakov says. "Once, when I was invited to speak to my daughter's class about the citizen diplomacy movement, I explained global consciousness in the following way. You are one class. Down the hall is another class. You are B, they are A. It doesn't mean that one is better than the other—you are only separated for the convenience of teachers. But you perceive the other form, the A form, as different, as not Us, but Them.

"Now imagine that your school is playing volleyball against another school. You now perceive those in the A form, which is part of your team, as Us, and the other school as Them. If Leningrad plays against Moscow, then you perceive that school in Leningrad as Us, and Moscow as Them. Now let's go further. If the Soviet Union plays against the United States, you perceive the Soviet team as Us, and the American team as Them. If a team from Mars comes to Earth, and Earth plays volleyball against Mars, then you perceive that the Americans are Us, and those from Mars are Them.

"But we are all living creatures! It's just by chance that you were born in this country, in this city, that you go to this school, and study in this form. Life is universal. It's a matter of how you perceive, and what stage your consciousness is in. That's what the new thinking is about, what *perestroika* is about—the growth of consciousness. Wars begin in human minds, and we can work on destroying the image of the enemy and spreading the truth about each other as human beings. Then there will be no pretext for spending billions more dollars on military programs."

Among Shestakov's projects is the International Peace Lantern Exchange Project, which since 1985 has been coordinated by physician James Baumgaertner and his artist wife Peggy Baumgaertner from a spare bedroom of their home in La Crosse,

Wisconsin. Impressed by the Japanese tradition of floating paper lanterns on the Ota River on each anniversary of the Hiroshima atomic bombing, the Baumgaertners hoped to draw attention to what happened in Hiroshima and help prevent it from happening again by spreading this custom around the world and involving thousands of children in making lanterns. In August 1986, the Baumgaertners organized the first "international peace lantern float" on the Mississippi River near their home. A few months later, James Baumgaertner hauled thirty pounds of lanterns to the Soviet Union and presented the project to officials at the Moscow headquarters of the Soviet Peace Committee, who were less than enthusiastic. "They started yelling at me, 'Who are you to come to the Soviet Union and tell us how to do peace?'" recalls Baumgaertner. "They had no interest in it at all."

Not long after this, an American friend of the Baumgaertners met Shestakov in Leningrad and gave him a small stack of lanterns. Shestakov was immediately taken with these earnest swaths of paper. Each was decorated with a child's vision of peace: orderly houses, shining suns, green trees, flowers, butterflies, dogs and cats, families holding hands. One section bore the maker's name, age, address, photograph, and hobbies, so that the lanterns also doubled as pen-pal invitations. Most of the lanternmakers were children in elementary or junior high school, but a few toddlers had left their handprints, and a few grandmothers had pasted on photographs of grandchildren. Most were from America, but a few came from Japan, Europe, and elsewhere.

Shestakov wrote to Baumgaertner requesting several hundred more lanterns. "He was the first Soviet to *ask* to become involved," says Baumgaertner. "I don't think anything would have happened there without him." Soon a steady stream of lanterns, hand-carried over the border by American travelers, were flowing into Shestakov's home and flowing out again into the hands of teachers and children. Soviet children began making their own lanterns and their teachers brought them to Shestakov for delivery abroad. Several boxes of lanterns, going and coming, were perpetually stacked in the corner of his kitchen.

Shestakov planned carefully for the first lantern float in Leningrad in August 1988. The local branch of the Soviet Peace Committee refused to sanction the event, but help drifted in from elsewhere. A Leningrad doctor got the local chapter of the Soviet

Committee of Physicians for the Prevention of Nuclear War to sign
a letter of support. A journalist friend promised to write an article.
A composer agreed to stage a performance with her amateur
children's ensemble. Some other friends donated enough money
for a sound truck, and an informal group called Peace Vigil se-
cured permission from city authorities for a small gathering in
Mikhailovsky Gardens.

On a golden August evening, forty Leningrad children sang,
read poetry, placed lighted candles within their lanterns, and one
by one set them adrift on a canal. A few Japanese tourists in the
crowd wiped away tears and a few invited staff members of the
unsupportive local Peace Committee listened and watched. Shestakov wandered in the background, happy to take photographs
and let others take the limelight. He had been nervous; it was the
first time that one of his projects had gone public. But the simple
ritual had meaning, he believes, because "no authority had organized a pre-set stage. People had authentic feelings. In the
informal movement we are all equal players, and we explore together; nobody is leader. The future is guaranteed for official
peace organizations, but the informal movement only exists as
long as there is inner feeling in all the participants."

Some of the Americans visiting Shestakov also brought with
them ingrained suspicions. Shestakov seemed too good to be true.
He did not fit into the usual American classifications of Soviets. He
was not a sharp-tongued dissident, nor an apolitical sheep in the
flock, nor a lackey of the ruling elite. The effort of creating a new
classification that could allow for Shestakov's existence proved too
much for a few of his visitors. They left, never to return, believing
that he was either a clever Peace Committee front guy or a fool.
Why else would he be welcoming a parade of Americans through
his front door during a time when most Soviets were nervous even
about speaking with foreigners on the street? Why else would he
be openly corresponding with dozens of people abroad? Why else
would he appear to have no fear?

"You see, each person decides for himself whether to allow
himself this degree of freedom or not," says Shestakov. "Whether
to keep his documents clean, or not. Well, I am not career-
oriented. I believe that marginal people like me, who are between
the two cultures, are necessary because they bridge the gap. Yes, I
do have fears. I understand that it's risky to behave like this. But at

the same time, the spiritual nourishment that I absorb from books and people is like an anaesthetic—it kills the pain and the fear. You forget to think about your personal destiny. You realize that if we all just live like ordinary people the world will inevitably die."

Still, not everyone was convinced. According to the rules of the litmus test that many Americans unconsciously applied to Soviets they met, some evidence of repression was the surest ticket to trust. Does the person criticize the government openly? Has he or she suffered under the regime? Then okay—he or she is not one of *them.* But with the exception of a string of refusals by Soviet authorities to allow him a visa to travel abroad (five in all), Shestakov did not have many repression credentials. He was never detained or arrested, because his activism was in kitchens and classrooms, not on the streets. He has no ill-feelings toward those who *do* take to the streets, but he considers himself part of a different game. "They discuss, they blame, they say good words, but they don't do any *practical* things," he says. "We are between two rocks—one is to become official, and the other is to become over-critical, nihilistic, cynical. I try to avoid both extremes. I try to listen to my inner voice, and not to imitate what people around me are doing. That's how I formed this network, this community. I tried to attune to something inside me that brought me into contact with all these wonderful people. And what prepared me to meet these people were books."

Shestakov grew up in a bookish family. His mother, a linguist, saw to it that he learned English at a young age, and managed to enroll him in an elite English-language school "which had a few ordinary children from the working class just to prove that it was not elite, and a few children like me with determined parents." Shestakov was expelled, however, when he was twelve. To this day he does not know why. "Perhaps my independence made them uncomfortable. I was not one of them and everyone knew it." At Leningrad State University he studied biology and animal behavior and did research on the genetics of aggression. After graduation he worked for a time in an agricultural research institute, but quit when he realized that the theories of the reactionary evolutionist Lysenko still prevailed there. He took a job in a soil reclamation agency and stayed there fourteen years. "It was dull, boring, and meaningless," he says, "but it was not far from my home, so I could dedicate much time to my family, and to reading, and to thinking. That was the Brezhnev time, and there was a lot of hypocrisy and double standards, where people openly expressed one idea at work, and different ideas at home. People who were career-oriented deliberately lied to each other, and lies, like rust, penetrated deep and destroyed their personalities. I felt that I intensely disliked to make a career, to be competitive, to climb on the hierarchical ladder. Organically I felt repulsion."

Instead, Shestakov read books. He read every American book he could find, especially books on ecology, philosophy, and global affairs. Rachel Carson's *Silent Spring*, Henry David Thoreau's *Walden*, and Alan Watts' *The Way of Zen* were among his early influences. He borrowed books from friends and practiced his English by working as an assistant Intourist guide for a couple of summers. He found out about the International Pen Friend Club and became a pen pal aficionado, eventually accumulating nearly 100 correspondents in most of the English-speaking countries of the world. He also became an "invited member" of the youth section of the local USA-USSR Friendship Society. This did not mean that the Society invited him to meet with visiting Americans—only that he would not be thrown out the door if he happened to discover on his own that such a meeting was taking place.

"The House of Friendship was the one place where it was possible during the Brezhnev years to meet Americans, practice English, have friendly conversations, and not have a policeman come up to you and ask, 'What are you doing?' But it was also limiting. The people in charge there were rather bossy." Shestakov tried to become a member of the Leningrad Peace Committee, but gave up once he learned that recommendations from his workplace and the district Party committee were required. "I realized that it is a bureaucratized organization, and that I can contribute more as an individual. I like to cooperate with people and I don't cut myself off from the Peace Committee. But unfortunately my relations with them are not very happy. You see, these people are members of *organizations*. As soon as I come to any official organization, the first question asked to me is: 'Who are you? What organization do you represent?' Because people are used to thinking in terms of organizations. They don't understand what a free individual can do."

Jealous officials in the Peace Committee and Friendship Society quickly made it clear that they considered Shestakov and his network to be crabgrass in their turf. Shestakov has a natural reluctance to dwell on the negative and thus is vague about the details of his past battles with them. When he speaks of them it is more with sadness than with anger. "They work for, as one American friend of mine put it, the Ministry of Love. They are good people, but it is like a factory. They meet so many people and they say the same words. It is difficult for them. They are trying to represent the whole country. I only represent myself, and just a small community of like-minded people. Psychologically I understand them. But at the same time I feel there is no room for me there."

Bureaucratic revenge took the form of preventing him from traveling abroad. Time and again, Shestakov's name appeared on American invitation lists for delegations to the United States; time and again, the Peace Committee crossed him off. He points to a thick file of denied requests for exit permission, and a rare shadow of bitterness darkens his mild features. "The bureaucrats fight back. I don't like to play their phony games. They would like to play with me, and say, 'Well, we'll send you, if you behave, and if you do this and that...' No. I will behave as I like, or I'm not going. I decided that I won't lose *myself* in order to go abroad. That's the most vital thing. Some people are ready to pretend anything, just to cross the boundary. I prefer to remain here, and to be integrated."

As *perestroika* warmed the Cold War, the stream of Americans bringing groups and projects to Shestakov's door became a flood. Despite the arrival from the United States of a donated Apple Macintosh computer, he began to fall behind in his translations. "Networking is really a very painstaking occupation. People call early in the morning, and late at night, and the phone is constantly ringing." Shestakov began to have to set priorities, to become well-organized, and to say no—three tasks that went against the grain of his warm, spontaneous, creatively chaotic nature. A typical mail pile contained a report on an Alcoholics Anonymous workshop in Leningrad, a proposal for an East-West development assistance project in the Third World, an article specifying the technical requirements for computer networks in the Soviet Union, and a prospectus for a "Soviet-American Dream Bridge" by a Californian who wanted "to incubate dreams on lasting peace." A Seattle cook wrote that she wanted to bring Americans to the Soviet Union "to make cinnamon rolls, not war." One document asserted that Shestakov was the Soviet contact for the "provisional Soviet branch of the World Flying Disc Federation."

As idea after idea flowed into his apartment, many of them requiring some degree of cooperation with existing Soviet institutions, Shestakov became more frustrated by the doors slammed in his face and more bold in circumventing them. Worried about his safety, both American and Soviet members of the network racked their brains trying to devise some official organizational "shelter" that would allow him to do this work without compromising his integrity. In spring 1988, a Soviet friend who ran an audio equipment cooperative offered Shestakov a job as "international liaison." This helped—at last he could legally quit the soil agency and spend all his time on translations and networking. But his clashes with indignant local bureaucrats only worsened. Those close to him knew it was only a matter of time before something blew.

Something finally did, in April 1988. "Dear Friend of Volodya [Vladimir] Shestakov," began the letter to fifty members of his American network from Sharon Tennison, the director of the Center for US-USSR Initiatives in San Francisco and one of Shestakov's closest allies. "Enclosed is a letter from Volodya that explains in his typical kind-hearted way the difficult situation that exists for him in Leningrad. Basically, he has become too well known for his informal citizen diplomacy work." Tennison wrote that Shestakov had arranged an unsanctioned visit for one of her groups to a Leningrad children's art school, which had led to several phone calls to the school insulting the teachers and complaining that Shestakov was a dissident, and "a very unpleasant call to Volodya himself." Shestakov's letter made no reference to the art school incident, but admitted that "here in Leningrad we grassroots workers have come to a point that creates an immediate need. After exerting many hours of energy that only ends in futility and after much thought about the dilemma, it appears to us that our only hope is to seek official sponsorship at some level. Time is of the essence." He requested that his American friends send letters documenting how he and his Leningrad network had been helpful to their work.

Several months later, as we are drinking tea at the round table, Shestakov shuffles through one of his desk piles and pulls out a binder containing forty letters from the leaders of many of the major citizen diplomacy groups in the United States—from Helen Caldicott, Ken Keyes, Sharon Tennison, and the directors of Physicians for Social Responsibility, Ploughshares, the Earthstewards Network, Beyond War, the Context Institute, the Rocky Mountain Institute, the Center for Soviet-American Dialogue, and others. All detail Shestakov's essential role in their work, past and present, and suggest that he be allowed to create an office for citizen diplomacy in Leningrad.

What had really happened at the art school? "The director at this school was upset that I kept bringing so many American groups. The teachers there are wonderful, very innovative, and they and their children are a treasure. There was a group from Beyond War that was coming to town and they had their TV cameras. The director told me that if I continued to bring these groups she would call the police. A person in the Peace Committee supported her because of the very bad relations between us. I was afraid she would ruin the whole thing. So I said, 'Please do that, and we will see how it will look when in front of all the TV cameras they haul me off to jail.' And she squealed to the KGB."

Pause.

"And what did the KGB say?"

"You see I am not supposed to tell all of it to you," he says, a little embarrassed. "I received a call from a very nice, pleasant, polite person, who immediately understood that it was a false signal. He told me that he had nothing against my activity, but to please try to make it so that no more false signals came his way." Shestakov pauses, takes one of the *sushki* necklaces off a hook on the wall, and places it around my neck. "Tomorrow we will go to the art school. And they will tell you the rest."

In their small office within Pioneer Palace #7, art teachers Natalya Gulyaeva and Slava Gerval serve us tea in colorful mugs hand-crafted by their students. Outside in the classroom, a few children are working on their oil canvasses; impressive paintings, sculptures, and ceramics line the walls. "We do not teach our children in the usual ways," says Gulyaeva, listing with pride the competitions their school's artwork has won. "But we are not on the approved list of Pioneer Palaces. Not because our art is not good. But because our building is rather old, and there are cracks in the ceiling paint. The authorities think that they cannot take Westerners to visit a place that has cracks in the ceiling."

Just across Fontanka Canal, less than a half-mile away, is the Leningrad House of Friendship, a former palace of a pre-revolutionary count that houses the offices of the Friendship Society, the Peace Committee, and several similar groups. Shestakov suggests that we visit; "I want you to feel the atmosphere." We walk quickly past the doorguards, who eye us darkly but appear to conclude I am a foreigner and thus ask no questions. Inside, gold drips from the ceilings, and huge stairways wind around grand white columns. Only now do I realize the full irony of locating a "house of friendship between peoples" in a building that has elitism and privilege embedded in its very walls.

Shestakov tries to make a phone call from the front desk to the Friendship Society office. "Who are you?" demands the woman behind the desk. "What organization do you represent?" Shestakov's body tightens and his words fly. The woman eventually points us down a corridor and returns to her magazine. We arrive at a shabby one-room office and find three women talking and smoking cigarettes. They stare at us with thinly veiled suspicion and ask us what we want. Just then, an official in the Leningrad branch of the Friendship Society walks in the door. From the displeased look on his face, it is evident that he and Shestakov are acquainted. Shestakov rapidly explains who I am, shows him a copy of my book *Citizen Diplomats,* and asks whether he can chat with us. The official says he is too busy now, but we make an appointment for two days hence. As we walk out, Shestakov whispers, "Did you feel the atmosphere? Something very unpleasant. Did you see the way he was smiling at us? It was a half-smile. Half-a-smile for you, and half-a-snarl for me."

Shestakov does not come with me to the appointment with the Friendship Society official. He gives me only one piece of advice: "Don't bring a copy of your book. If you have it, he will pressure you into giving it to him. But he wants it only for an ornament. You have only a few copies, and there are many other people who deserve it more." When I arrive, the women are gone and the official is sitting behind his desk. I explain that I am a journalist writing a book and that I would like to ask him some questions about the Friendship Society. He swallows hard at the sight of the tape recorder, but consents to talk. His whole manner, however, is guarded, even confrontational. "Do you agree with me?" he keeps saying, as if acquiescence is required for him to go on. "Do you agree?" As my questions become more specific, his answers become more vague and evasive. We are not getting anywhere, and after twenty-five minutes I decide to end this mutual ordeal, bringing the interview to a conclusion and thanking him for his time. "No problem—it was a pleasure for me," he says coldly. "It will be more of a pleasure when you tell me the *real* purpose of this interview. You see, we meet now for the first time, and we do not know each other." He gestures meaningfully toward the tape recorder, and I sense that he is resisting an impulse to smash it against the wall. "I ask that if you are going to publish my words that we correspond about them first."

The interview had been clearly on-the-record and my initial explanations thorough. "I can try, but that may not be possible," I hedge, wanting very much to get out of there.

"Can you leave a copy of your book for our society?" he asks as I head toward the door. I apologize and say I have none left to give. "You will not give our society one of your books?" he repeats in an offended tone, following me down the stairs. Inwardly I marvel at Shestakov's prescience.

"Where is Volodya?" he asks abruptly, as if I have spoken his name aloud. I tell him I don't know. "Are you in touch with him?" Well—yes. Suddenly he is full of questions for me. "How long have you been here? What hotel are you staying at?" But the main doors of the House of Friendship are near, and after a hasty good-bye I escape into fresh air.

"And just imagine," Shestakov says later, with both bitterness and triumph in his voice, "you are completely free, completely independent, and still you feel this. Just imagine how an ordinary Soviet person would feel in that situation." He is silent for a few moments. "I am very glad that the time is past when these bureaucrats were omnipotent. Now they do not really have any power over me. They know that. And they know that I know that."

In April 1989, Shestakov was at last allowed to travel to the United States; his exit permission arrived only a few hours before his flight. A second trip in June 1989 was cancelled when his visa was once again denied, but he received a visa for a December 1989 visit to California to plot strategy with his partner Sharon Tennison at the Center for US-USSR Initiatives. As a result of that visit, Shestakov helped coordinate grassroots Soviet participation in Earth Day 1990; his current projects include arranging meetings between Soviet and American environmentalists and establishing a "Green Library" in Leningrad. Although he is now able to travel to America nearly as frequently as his American friends come to the Soviet Union, he remains aware that his real work is in Leningrad, and he continues to puzzle over how to fit his odd-shaped vocation into the rapidly evolving but still often rigid framework of his own society.

Tracking Shestakov's movements on a typical day in Leningrad is not easy. After a brisk jog through Pushkin Park, followed by a cold shower and breakfast, Shestakov is in the kitchen helping decipher an American dental catalogue for a dentist friend who wants to import equipment to the Soviet Union. For hours they hack away at thickets of technical language (fortunately, the catalogue is illustrated). Then we are off to a cardiology institute on the outskirts of town to meet with Boris Bondarenko, the physician who had helped with the peace lantern float. Shestakov and Bondarenko confer for twenty minutes on strategies to get more schools involved in the lantern and birthday pen pal projects; Bondarenko then hands Shestakov a bundle of lanterns made by New York children that he had collected on a visit to the United States with his organization, the Soviet Committee of Physicians for the Prevention of Nuclear War (SCPPNW). Later, when I ask Shestakov whether he thinks SCPPNW could be doing more in Leningrad, he looks perplexed. He has never thought about it. As a matter of principle, he has no interest in organizations. "I think of Boris as a person, not as a representative of a group," he says with a shrug. "Organizations limit people's potential. Limited loyalties appear that separate people. I believe that the most powerful force in the world is the cooperation of free individuals. So I am independent even from independent groups."

"I get the feeling," I say, "that for you 'organization' is a dirty word."

"Yes," he replies with a grin. "'Organization' is a dirty word. And 'network' is a clean word."

Next we drop by the apartment of an unofficial artist to confirm that he will host six Americans for dinner that night. We have tea with an American friend of the artist, a Californian scriptwriter who proposes starting a joint venture to make contraceptives in the Soviet Union. A Leningrad medical student who is modelling for the artist agrees to give Bondarenko's peace lanterns to her younger sister. None of the Americans coming that evening speaks Russian, and the artist's English is minimal; Shestakov says he will try to make it, but the artist waves him off with a smile. Non-verbal communication sometimes works best anyway, he says. He encourages us to drop by an unofficial art exhibition that he has helped arrange, and we race there for an hour between appointments. A painting of a white bird standing in a crowd of black crows particularly catches Shestakov's eye. "It is the white crow, *belaya vorona!*" he almost shouts. "This symbol is very, very important for us! The white crow is the one who is not afraid to stand out from the crowd, who has the courage to fly where others will not go."

Back at Shestakov's apartment, a newly recruited teacher, surrounded by the photos of mountain scenery and the gentle exhortations, is sipping tea and waiting to be instructed in the ways of the lantern and birthday pen pal projects. After she goes home, Shestakov steals an hour to work on his latest translation, an article on energy efficiency by the American expert Amory Lovins. Then several other members of the network drop by, and the conversation turns to the need to move Shestakov's work out of the apartment and into a fully equipped office. "It would be a center for citizen diplomacy here, a sort of lighthouse for creative independent individuals, to bring the social mutations together and let them know and help each other," says Shestakov. "But it must be one hundred percent unofficial. It must have nothing to do with the Peace Committee or the Friendship Society. I don't know how to do it, but it must be arranged in a way that won't allow the state to dictate its conditions. I want only to be the switchboard, the place where the connections are hooked together, where the active independent individuals can meet.

"Before *glasnost,* I didn't realize to what extent a political mafia ruled our country. When Gorbachev and the mass media exposed this, I should have felt better, because the situation has changed and is changing. But at the same time I felt that I had been fooled, and that so many years of my life had been stolen. I lost so many opportunities. And now it is impossible to return all those stolen years. So I cannot fully enjoy that, and I feel very embittered about those in the political mafia who are still entrenched in the echelons of power.

"Still, my approach is to turn lemons into lemonade, to turn stumbling blocks into stepping stones, to work patiently with the bureaucrats to change them. Because they are members of this society, as we are. It is only that they have limited identity. They belong to organizations that have narrower interests. But they are members of the global community at the same time, and it's possible to change their paradigm and bring them into the movement."

The next morning, we rush to a foreigners-only hotel to drop something off for a visiting teacher from New Hampshire. Shestakov's pace never slackens as we walk past the doorguards unmolested. Safely inside the elevator, he answers my unspoken question. "The trick is to look straight ahead, to walk with purpose, to show no hesitation and no fear. If I allow them to wonder even for a moment whether or not I have permission, they will stop me." We knock on the door of a thirteenth-floor room, and the teacher sticks out his head and apologizes that he has no time to chat; inside, a dozen Leningrad teenagers are ranged on the bed and floor. Shestakov gives the teacher some letters in a manila envelope. "Thanks for your help with the home visits last night," the teacher calls out as we turn to leave.

Downstairs, a half-dozen Americans are waiting to be taken to the site of a former Buddhist temple by another member of Shestakov's Leningrad network, a portly man with thick glasses named Kostya whose homemade business cards are decorated with glitter and rainbows. "We are acquainted, but I cannot quite call him my friend," Shestakov whispers. "He believes that in a past life he was a high priest in Atlantis." Whatever their opinions of Kostya's religious affiliations, the Americans are looking forward to their personalized tour of the "spiritual sights" of Leningrad. "We had such a *wonderful* time in an artist's home last night!" an older woman from New York tells me. "We didn't speak the same language, but we understood each other perfectly."

Our next meeting is with filmmaker Konstantin Lopushansky, who is known in the West for his 1986 anti-nuclear film "Letters from a Dead Man." Now he is shooting a futuristic movie about ecological catastrophe, and we find him and his cast and crew amid acres of rotting metal in the biggest industrial junkyard in Leningrad. As we are leaving, one of the cameramen presents us with a tape of Leningrad jazz bands and a handwritten letter to the mayor of New Orleans proposing a jazz musician exchange.

Shestakov's face lights up; "This sounds like something I would like to support!" He eagerly takes down the man's name and address and presents his own card. Noticing that "peace activist" has yet to be crossed out, he asks for it back and does so.

As the day goes on, it becomes clear that Shestakov is a loose cannon in the cautious world of "who do you know," a mad cook tossing all his varied contacts into one huge networking stew, recklessly inviting them to each other's homes without consulting with them first or giving a thought to whether they come from compatible strata of society. Influential journalists and avant-garde psychologists are thus thrown together on a whim of scheduling. Mountaineers and art teachers, concert managers and soccer coaches suddenly find themselves sharing ideas over tea. He is constantly jiggling the layers, causing minor social earthquakes, but few seem to complain about the results.

"Initially, all the networking was through me, but I don't want it to always be this way. The more independently operating net-working centers we have, the better the context for all of us. That's why I'm always giving away my contacts. I regularly introduce all my friends to one another. I know that by doing this I am not losing friends but gaining them. I want to keep looking for and assembling all the wonderful people all over the place, and create something wonderful, something very loose and working."

It is late; we are riding the metro back to the apartment. Shestakov takes off his pale glasses and rubs his eyes. "Tomorrow I will feed the Lovins translation into the Mac," he says, and promptly falls asleep. Fortunately, I know the stop. The teeth of an autumn wind nip us as we step from the station. "Do you know what it is, *tao?*" he says. "It is impossible to hold it in. It is only possible to be in its flow." A swirl of dead leaves scatters before us on the sidewalk. The silver tracks of trolleycars split asphalt that is cracked and pulsing under our feet.

2 | In the Steppes of Central Asia

It is noontime on the sun-drenched steppes of Kazakhstan. A bus full of passengers has left the city of Semipalatinsk and is moving south on a narrow, seldom-traveled highway. Most of the passengers are dozing; the rest stare out the windows in silence at parched and desolate plains that stretch for a thousand kilometers before wrinkling into mountains. There is something terrifying about these sere wastes, and something familiar, as if we have seen them before in forgotten nightmares. It is almost believable that the bombs have already gone off, and the bus is moving through the aftermath, the emptiness of a post-nuclear landscape.

"You could film 'The Day After' here," I hear someone behind me remark quietly.

Thirty medical students from several cities of the Soviet Union are on the bus. They have flown to Kazakhstan, a Central Asian republic that borders China, to join a weekend of public protests in September 1989 against continued Soviet nuclear testing. About 120 kilometers west of Semipalatinsk is the Soviet Union's major nuclear test site, known here as "the polygon." The protests, organized by the Semipalatinsk student chapter of the Soviet Committee of Physicians for the Prevention of Nuclear War (SCPPNW), are part of a growing grassroots anti-nuclear movement centered in Kazakhstan. At present we are enroute to Karaul, a town downwind of the test site, where local physicians say the health effects on the population of radiation released from the tests have been particularly acute.

Our procession through the steppes is absurdly officious. In the lead are two police cars with wailing sirens, followed by three cars and a bus carrying officials, journalists, and other locals, followed by our bus, followed by yet another police car with flashing lights. For whose benefit the sirens wail, it is impossible to tell. There are no cars on this road, no villages, no signs of life beyond an occasional dusty swarm of sheep and a few long-legged hawks perched on telephone poles.

The closer we get to the test site, the more hawks I see, and I point this out to Yuri Dzhibladze, a Moscow cardiology resident and SCPPNW student organizer from Moscow, who is dozing next to me.

"More hawks?" he says sleepily. "Well, that's rather symbolic."

For me, sleep is out of the question. My presence on this bus is technically illegal and these steppes are touched with the lure of the forbidden. Despite efforts by Yuri and the Moscow staff of SCPPNW to arrange a visa extension, I have not received permission to visit Semipalatinsk, which is a closed city to foreigners from "capitalist countries." After numerous bureaucratic sorties we were told, two days before the scheduled protest, that such permission could only be granted by the Council of Ministers of the USSR. An application process existed, but at least three months were required. Without the word "Semipalatinsk" on my visa I would not be allowed to board the plane leaving Moscow.

Informed of this difficulty by phone, the Semipalatinsk students assured us that I should just come anyway—the city Party Committee knew about my coming and had arranged permission from the local KGB and other authorities. But comforting as this was to hear, it would not help me get on the plane. At midnight, exhausted by our fruitless battles with officialdom, Yuri and I agreed on a last-ditch plan: I would come with the Moscow students to the airport early the next morning, *sans* Semipalatinsk visa, and hope for the best. If we were caught and I was barred from the plane, I would wish them well and take a bus back to the city.

The events the next morning were either divinely arranged or borrowed from a Zoshchenko satire on bureaucratic ineptitude. Because our taxi was late, registration for the flight had closed by the time we rushed into the airport. The woman at the Aeroflot counter looked pained, but without bothering to check our documents she told us to run to the end of the terminal. There, a second woman in a blue uniform took our tickets and passports with a scowl, and promptly noticed that my visa made no reference to Semipalatinsk. Yuri and Vladimir Popov, the secretary of SCPPNW, unleashed a flood of complex and mostly untrue explanations for why my visa lacked a stamp for Semipalatinsk even though everything was actually in order. I stood behind them and tried to look harmless. Finally the woman rolled her eyes and pointed upstairs. "There is another checkpoint," she said. "Go."

Yuri's expression was somber as we climbed the stairs. "I don't think it will work," he whispered.

But the third woman, sitting at her desk in her tidy uniform, opened and closed my passport and stacked it with the others without comment. Perhaps she was sleepy. Perhaps she was lulled by the knowledge that we must have passed through two checkpoints to reach her. Perhaps she simply could not imagine that an American would have the audacity to fly to a closed city without permission.

Yuri scooped up the passports and we fled through the gate, holding our laughter until we were seated on the plane. Even then, I did not dare relax until we were in the air, and I felt certain that more trials would await us once we landed. I was right; on the runway stood the Semipalatinsk chief of police, who insisted that all foreigners on board come with him to a small room where their passports and visas would be thoroughly checked. Yuri, Vladimir, and I exchanged glances. "I think there could be some problems," Yuri whispered to me in English. "Be a Soviet citizen for the next ten minutes."

Now genuinely terrified, I stepped around the chief of police and followed my Soviet companions through a small exit gate, unable to rid myself of visions of men in dark glasses seizing me by the arms, putting me on the next plane to Moscow and deporting me within forty-eight hours. But nothing happened. A call was put in to someone at the city Party Committee, who promised help if any unpleasantness occurred. None did. However much fluster my arrival may have caused within the local KGB, a decision was made somewhere not to make a fuss. Hours passed and I remained at liberty. The next morning, no one objected when I boarded the bus for Karaul.

As I gazed through the bus window, I thought I could see a latent beauty in this land, hidden under the overt barrenness, the tragedies of overgrazing and famine, the cruel history of the round-ups and massacres of nomadic Kazakhs during Stalin's time—massacres that by some estimates had halved the population of Kazakhs from six million to three million in less than a generation. I tried to imagine this area as it had been described by Abai, one of the Kazakh epic poets: a fertile and unbounded prairie with waist-high grasses, sweet springs and flowing rivers, a land filled with flowers under a wide sweep of sky and dotted by the colorful yurts and flocks of its native people.

The first Soviet atomic bomb was exploded on these steppes on September 24, 1949. Between 1949 and 1963, 179 atmospheric nuclear explosions were conducted at the test site near Semi-palatinsk. After 1963 and the signing of the Partial Test Ban Treaty by the United States, Great Britain, and the Soviet Union, which forbade atmospheric tests, the Soviet nuclear testing program, like its American counterpart, went underground. The Soviets con-ducted an average of 18 underground tests every year until August 1985, when Gorbachev announced a unilateral moratorium on nuclear testing and challenged the United States to follow suit. After the Reagan administration repeatedly stated that it would not stop nuclear testing or begin new negotiations for a compre-hensive test ban treaty, Soviet nuclear testing resumed in February 1987.

For nearly forty years, the Soviet government preserved an impenetrable silence about possible health or environmental con-sequences of the testing. Before 1963, no effort was made to warn local people about fallout from atmospheric tests; after 1963, no data was published about leaks of radioactive gases from under-ground tests. Books, newspapers, magazines, television, films, and official documents seldom mentioned the tests and never implied that surrounding villagers had any reason for concern. Furniture toppled and water pipes broke in Semipalatinsk homes during the earth-heaves caused by large-yield tests, but no one dared to com-plain. True, there were whispered rumors about the "white death" of radiation, about high rates of cancer and birth defects in the region, about children dying of leukemia in oddly large numbers. But the taboo remained inviolate.

As *glasnost* spread from Moscow to the non-Russian Soviet republics, some suspected that eventually that taboo would end. But few could have predicted the dramatic circumstances under which the silence was broken—or that it would be due, literally, to a shift in the wind.

On February 17, 1989, an underground Soviet nuclear test vented radioactive gases into the atmosphere. This in itself was not unusual. But on that day the prevailing winds changed direction, and alarmed military personnel monitoring the test noticed that the radioactivity was heading directly for them. Emergency plans lurched into action and hasty phone calls were made to Moscow. Somehow, information about the leak made its way from Moscow to a small circle of intelligentsia in Kazakhstan. One of them was Olzhas Suleimenov, a well-known Kazakh poet and literary critic, the president of the Kazakh Writer's Union and a deputy to the Supreme Soviet.

As a candidate in the upcoming elections for the Congress of People's Deputies, Suleimenov was scheduled to appear live on Kazakhstan television the following Saturday afternoon. Instead of giving his expected campaign speech, however, Suleimenov shocked his listeners by devoting all of his time to a description of nuclear testing, the radioactive leaks, and the suspected health consequences. "We demand the stopping of the production and testing of nuclear weapons," he said. "No defense reasons can justify a silent nuclear war of the government against its own people." Then he invited all those who shared his concerns to gather at the headquarters of the Writer's Union in Alma-Ata at three o'clock on Tuesday afternoon, February 28, 1989.

Five thousand people came, overflowing the auditorium and spilling into the streets, to listen to passionate testimonials by people who claimed to have suffered illnesses caused by radiation. "Before we were silent because it was forbidden to speak," said one man who had lost both parents and seventeen relatives to cancer. Another woman said: "We cannot be saved, and we have already infected our children, but let the grandchildren—let them be alive and healthy."

In a statement greeted by loud cheers and a standing ovation, Suleimenov declared that on this day the people of Kazakhstan should form a movement for the end of Soviet nuclear testing, and that it should be known as the Nevada Movement to indicate their solidarity with Americans demanding an end to nuclear testing in Nevada. Suleimenov claimed that the average lifespan in Kazakhstan had shortened by four years in the past decade, and that every future test had the potential to become "a catastrophe more dreadful than that in Chernobyl." He also called for the closure of all nuclear production facilities in Kazakhstan, open inspection of radioactive waste burial sites, and the quarantining of contaminated agricultural areas.

"We have said that we have lived for more than forty years in peace, but it is not so. There has been war—but an invisible war," proclaimed Suleimenov. "We cannot wait for the doomsday without murmuring. A public movement against nuclear tests and against the production of nuclear armaments on the territory of the USSR has now appeared in our country for the first time. Our task is to change the whole political climate. We're accustomed to fighting for peace in the world. Now we understand that everyone must fight for peace on his own land."

Apparently caught off-guard by this outburst, political authorities in Kazakhstan did not know how to react. Should they condemn, support, or ignore this new movement? Condemnation ran the risk of inflaming passions still further; support ran the risk of openly contradicting Moscow. Ignoring it seemed the safest path. No news reports appeared about Suleimenov's television speech or the gathering at the Writer's Union, but word nevertheless spread rapidly through unofficial grapevines. Suleimenov and other members of the intelligentsia in Alma-Ata began firing off letters and appeals to the Ministry of Health, the Academy of Sciences, and the Supreme Soviet.

Everyone waited tensely for Moscow's reaction. By calling for the immediate closure of the test site, regardless of whether the United States continued testing, the Nevada Movement was placing itself in opposition to current Soviet policy. When the response came, it was subtle but clear. Suleimenov was suddenly invited to join the retinue of journalists accompanying Gorbachev on his March 1989 trip to Cuba and Great Britain. In London, Suleimenov was able to hold his own press conference about the Nevada Movement for Western media. Gorbachev avoided explicitly praising or endorsing the movement, but Kazakhstan authorities now decided it was safe to admit its existence. Following Suleimenov's return, articles about the Nevada Movement began appearing in the Kazakhstan press, and a forty-minute film about the Writer's Union gathering was twice shown on Kazakhstan television.

Bolstered by this new publicity, the movement grew rapidly, especially in regions near the test site. Donations and offers of help flooded the office of the Writer's Union. Many people wrote letters describing birth defects and cancer deaths in their families. Several parents reported that although their children had died of leukemia, hospital authorities had refused to write this on their death certificates—possibly in order to throw future epidemiologists off trail.

On August 6, 1989, the forty-fourth anniversary of the atomic bombing of Hiroshima, several thousand people gathered for a Nevada Movement demonstration about 100 kilometers from the test site near the small town of Karaul. Most were Kazakhs, but a sprinkling of other nationalities was also present. The protesters reached into their past for rituals, bringing stones and building a traditional cairn on the steppes to commemorate the event. They wrote their hopes for the future on strips of white cloth and tied them to a desert tree. And they walked in a procession between two bonfires in a re-creation of an ancient ceremony of purification called the *alastau*. For generations, nomadic Kazakhs had ritually passed between two fires on the eve of spring, just before leaving their winter homes with their flocks for the open steppes, to rid themselves of evil influences and strengthen themselves for the journey ahead.

"For forty years our land has suffered the equivalent of thousands and thousands of Hiroshimas," read the text of the appeal affirmed at Karaul. "Fear of the future has poisoned our consciousness. We are afraid to drink water, to eat food, to give birth to children. Citizens of the earth! The nuclear defensive shield has turned into a deadly danger for all humanity. We call upon our government and the governments of other countries to come to an agreement for the full cessation of testing in all spheres."

The view from the bus remains bleak, but a local tour guide, a middle-aged, pale-blond Russian woman, is now informing us in a monotonous tone about Kazakh legends and literature. Suddenly a few students on the right side of the bus are pointing out the window and laughing. On a small hillside next to the road is a slogan formed by white stones that proclaims, in majestic isolation, "SLAVA KPSS" ("Glory to the Communist Party of the Soviet Union").

The guide, unnerved by the laughter, interrupts her litany with the remark: "Well—you see, er, not all of the evidence of the period of stagnation has yet been removed."

More laughter, and a look of horror flickers across the guide's face as she realizes the compromising nature of what she has just said.

"Don't worry, we agree with you," Yuri calls out. "It's time for those slogans to go."

Behind him, a student from the Third Moscow Medical Institute named Sasha softly quotes Ecclesiastes: "There's a time to gather stones, and a time to cast stones away."

For the medical students from Riga, Kaunas, Leningrad, and Moscow, coming to Kazakhstan is a disturbing journey into their country's recent past. The dingy propaganda slogans and murals that are disappearing from their cities still festoon Semipalatinsk and surrounding towns. And more subtle vestiges of the Brezhnev era linger, as well; an occasional hesitation in people's words, a hard-to-define uneasiness with unorthodoxy. But for the Semipalatinsk students, who formed their student chapter of SCPPNW during the early days of the Nevada Movement, this weekend is a sudden jolt into the future, a dazzling taste of *perestroika* reaching their isolated land.

We arrive at last in Karaul, the capital of the Abai region, a careworn little town with a population of 5,000. Laundry hangs from the balconies of shoddy three-story apartment houses. Cows and sheep sprawl in the vacant lots between buildings. Gray-suited militiamen wave our little motorcade through empty intersections until we are deposited at a small cafe, where tables of food are already set and waiting.

But there is something odd going on, a funny feeling in the air. Through the cafe windows we see several hundred women and children who are waiting for the demonstration to begin. It takes a few minutes to realize what is so odd about this: the people are not milling about, swapping gossip, and seeing old friends as they wait. Instead, they are standing in neat, motionless rows, patiently holding their anti-nuclear signs, while uniformed militiamen and military police pace in front of and behind them.

Yuri and Natasha Makeeva, a student from Kaunas, Lithuania, begin exchanging furious whispers.

"What's going on?" I ask Yuri. "Why are these people standing there?"

"I don't know," he says in a low voice, "but we are late, and they are being kept waiting while we finish eating. And we are all very angry, because it looks like it will be an old-fashioned stagnation-era peace demonstration, and we don't want to be part of it."

But what could we do? After gulping down lunch we leave the cafe and walk to the waiting stage. Next to us is a large statue of Lenin, and portraits of all thirteen Politburo members stare at our backs. "Let us be active today so that we will not be radioactive tomorrow," declares a large red banner on a nearby building. The police are preventing the crowd from coming closer than twenty meters from the front of the platform; it is not easy to look into the eyes and faces of our audience, and the distance between us adds to the awkward sense of formality.

The first secretary of the regional Communist Party Committee, a Kazakh man named Khafiz Mataev, welcomes us with a brief statement to the effect that local Party officials are fully behind the goals of the anti-testing movement. Then the speeches begin. An old man in a traditional Kazakh cap, a representative of the Nevada Movement, makes a passionate appeal for linking their movement with efforts against nuclear testing worldwide. A woman introduced as the chief physician for the region recites a list of health statistics showing suspiciously high incidences of cancer, birth defects, anemia in pregnant women, and psychiatric disorders in the Abai region.

Behind the stage, I ask Khafiz Mataev why he and the other inhabitants of Karaul did not speak out against nuclear testing prior to February.

"Frankly speaking, it was forbidden," the Party chief answers.

"Forbidden by whom?"

"It is impossible to find the name," he says, shrugging and pointing to the sky. "It was not one person. It was a whole system, the legacy of Stalinism."

"How can you and other local Party officials support closing the test site when this goes against national policy? Doesn't this make people in Moscow upset?"

He eyes me for a moment, as if wondering whether I will comprehend the significance of what he is about to say. "Thank God, thanks to Gorbachev and *glasnost,* we can now speak our minds freely," he replies. "The people are against testing, and we are against testing."

Khafiz Mataev admits with pride that he and his committee

have assisted in organizing the demonstration, which helps explain its rather municipal character. The speeches continue, each receiving polite but not sustained applause. Perhaps the slight lack of enthusiasm in the audience is only due to tired feet and the glaring sun, but my suspicions prickle. Then Marat Musataev, the leader of the Semipalatinsk medical students, rushes up and asks if I, too, will speak.

I look at Yuri, who nods assent. Why not, I think. Every KGB officer within three hundred kilometers must know that I'm here by now anyway.

I begin by describing the movement against nuclear testing in the United States. Thousands of people have been arrested for civil disobedience at the Nevada test site, I say, not because they want to break the law but because they see no other way to express effectively their opposition to the continued development of nuclear weapons. To help explain the intention behind the Nevada protests, I say a few words about the theory and practice of nonviolence.

While Yuri translates, I look into the mass of faces staring upward at me, and suddenly know that it's not working. I'm not getting through. The format is all wrong. The concepts that I'm trying to put into words are so unfamiliar that they mean nothing to these people. And the very process of listening and watching this young foreigner stand on a platform above them and utter strange phrases is itself disempowering. We should be sitting in small circles, brainstorming, sharing ideas. *I* should be listening to *them.*

The women and children with their signs, the police, and the speechmakers on the stage wait expectantly for me to go on. I collect myself and finish with something half-coherent about the bonfires that are lit in the desert before protest actions in Nevada, bonfires that burn with the same light as their bonfires had during the Hiroshima Day protest in Karaul. Soon the demonstration is over, and the women and children swarm around me, shaking my hand, asking me to pose with them for photographs. "Please go home and tell all Americans that we here in Karaul are fighting against nuclear testing, and that we are a peaceful people and do not want war," a woman holding a child by the hand tells me.

There is no doubting her sincerity. Yet the protest has left a strange taste in my mouth. Why were there only women and children in the crowd? Why so many police? Were local authorities trying to co-opt the genuine feelings of the people and channel them toward their own mysterious ends?

"A mixture," says Yuri as we walk to the bus. "A mixture of old and new."

On the bus, the blond Russian guide approaches us. "May I ask you a question?" she addresses Yuri. "I'm interested to know— what concrete results do you expect this protest action to have?"

Yuri blinks, then answers: "Just what we said in our talks. We believe that if enough people speak out, and protest, and lobby their governments, we can bring about an end to nuclear testing and to the arms race."

"Do you *really* think so?"

"Yes."

The guide shakes her head doubtfully.

"Why do you ask?" says Yuri. "You seem a little skeptical."

She laughs uncomfortably. "Oh, I don't know anything about it. I'm just a simple person. But I have a friend, a scientist, who works at the test site. And *he* says," she lowers her voice almost to a whisper, "that we have to keep building nuclear weapons, because they're the cheapest way to defend ourselves."

Yuri's eyes brighten: he loves to convince people, and this is an argument he knows he will win. "But you see, that's just not true. Nuclear weapons are really—"

The guide cuts him off. "I don't know anything about it," she repeats, and hurries to her place in the front of the bus. Yuri and I exchange glances, and he raises his eyebrows with a look that means: Let's talk about this later.

We are next scheduled to watch a performance of Kazakh folk dance and song at the local Palace of Culture, which has a comfortable auditorium, a well-appointed stage, and no restrooms. There are no restrooms, we soon learn, because the entire town has no running water. One of the Semipalatinsk medical students leads us to a filthy shed that functions as an outhouse. Afterwards I can see that Yuri is angry. "At least twenty million rubles spent on every nuclear test," he says, "and here a whole town without running water."

We walk until we find a street pump where we can wash our hands. The town seems deserted, abandoned. What do people *do* here? I wonder aloud. Is there a factory? How do they survive? Yuri says he will try to find out. Soon we see a young Kazakh woman coming toward us on the sidewalk. "Excuse me, but we are visitors, and we would like to know what the main work is here in Karaul," Yuri asks her politely.

The woman keeps her eyes down and murmurs, "I don't know."

"Don't you live here?" asks Yuri, surprised.

"No," she answers shortly, and hurries away.

We cannot find anyone else to ask; the only other people on the street are police. No less than seven militiamen are standing in front of the tiny Palace of Culture. It is as if I am back in the Soviet Union of the mid-1980s, living again with that queasy sensation of never quite knowing what is going on, what is surface and what is real, which of my own thoughts are insights and which only exaggerated suspicions. The difference is that now I am sharing these feelings with a similarly perplexed Moscow friend. "Of course, she lives here," Yuri muses, "but for some reason she was afraid."

In the lobby of the Palace of Culture several students are surrounding the woman physician who had recited health statistics at the demonstration. They ask her to repeat the numbers, scribbling them down in their notepads. Eighty-five percent of pregnant women in this area are anemic, and there have been eleven cases of severe birth defects among 521 births this year. These babies are the grandchildren of those exposed to fallout from atmospheric tests. It is difficult to give accurate statistics about cancer rates, she says, because until 1985 there was a special national oncology hospital near Semipalatinsk, which is now closed, and they can't get any information from the Ministry of Health about what went on there.

I am scribbling, too, and I ask her for her name. Too late, I see her stiffen. Wrong move. She spells it for me, but then becomes vague when a student asks her for exact statistics on the number of psychiatric disorders and suicides in the region.

"Ask for names *last*," Yuri chides me as we get on the bus.

On the long ride back to Semipalatinsk, the Soviet students discuss the day's events. Most are convinced that the local people genuinely want the test site closed. But some suspect that people here are caught up in "radiophobia," the indiscriminate blaming of all problems beyond their ken on exposure to radiation. Some find the lack of precise medical data disturbing; one points out that the woman physician had been unable to give an exact definition of what she meant by "anemia." Some are bothered by the things that had smacked of *pokazukha,* of an old-fashioned orchestrated attempt to impress out-of-towners.

A soft golden moon rises over the steppes as the debates go on. The guide has put away her microphone and listens in, wide-eyed. Someone points out that the people's radiophobia, if that is what it is, is understandable given the years of silence and lies. How can they be expected to trust official reassurances now? Only a study conducted by an international team of medical experts would have any chance of being believed.

As we step off the bus, I notice that the guide has pulled Yuri aside for a few last words. A minute later he runs up to me with a pleased grin. "You'll never guess," he says. "She says that the day has changed her a little bit. She says she thinks maybe we can make a difference, and she wishes us luck." He squeezes me around the shoulders as we walk into the hotel.

The next day our group is scheduled to go near the border of the test site. We know that the Semipalatinsk students and physicians have been trying for months to arrange permission to visit Kurchatov, a "secret city" of about 30,000 military and support personnel that lies within the test site's borders and that appeared on no map until May 1989. But all we hear as we board the bus that morning is that we have permission to conduct a demonstration at a recreational area by the Irtysh River, some twenty kilometers from the test site. Accompanying us are about forty young people from a Danish youth organization called Next Stop Soviet, which had chosen, in an apparent coincidence, this same weekend to send a delegation to Semipalatinsk to protest Soviet testing. It had taken the Danes nearly two years to arrange their visas, and they are rather startled to see me.

For two hours the buses speed west through the steppes, once again sandwiched between siren-wailing police cars. Then the whole procession pulls over for a few minutes and the journalists and officials who have been riding in private cars climb aboard the buses. I ask Marat Musataev, the Semipalatinsk student organizer, why.

"They say only the buses can go through the fence into the test site," he says.

"We are going into the test site?"

He mirrors my surprise with a shrug. "They say plans have changed, and the test site personnel have invited us to come to Kurchatov for a press conference before the demonstration."

News that we are, in fact, going through "the fence" spreads quickly, and a wave of excitement ripples through the bus. The students sit up straighter, pull out their cameras, and stare through the windows at the empty plains with renewed interest.

Then we see it—a nondescript barbed wire fence, a small guard station, a few parked cars and some uniformed military officers. I am half-expecting to be ordered off the bus at any minute, but my presence seems to be thoroughly unimportant to the several non-uniformed men who get on our bus. One of them, a large, bland-faced man in a gray suit, blocks the doors by positioning himself in the bus stairwell.

"Looks like KGB," I nudge Yuri.

"*Is* KGB," he replies with a grin.

I want to take pictures of the fence, but I am inhibited by the gaze of the man in the stairwell. Vladimir Popov sees my hesitation and matter-of-factly asks the man if photographs are permitted. The man nods yes. Astonished, I lean from the windows and snap away.

We are inside. The city of Kurchatov rises dimly on the horizon, a low clump of white buildings amid scorched and blackened fields. Four plump white jets and a hangar are visible; as we come closer we see construction cranes and trees among the apartment buildings. Soon we are speeding through the city, past grayish buildings surrounded with barbed-wire and catclaw, grocery stores with windows full of vegetables, and a playground with a huge sign that reads: "OUR COURSE IS THE COURSE OF PEACE." The buses let us out in the center of the city. Large, administrative-looking buildings face each other across a wide square, each draped with a red slogan. "LET US HAIL COMMUNISM—THE BRIGHT FUTURE OF ALL MANKIND" blares one. "GLORY TO THE SOVIET ARMED FORCES," says another. But we are soon distracted from the slogans by the presence of about forty military officers, including a one-star general who waves his arm toward the buildings with a brief explanation and then motions us down a street. As we start walking, a tall, non-uniformed man falls into step next to Natasha Makeeva.

"Why are you here?" he says in a quiet tone.

"We are medical students and doctors, and we are here to talk to people about their health, and to protest against continued testing," Natasha replies evenly, her guard up.

"Why are you here and not in Nevada? I am not trying to be provocative," he says with an unpleasant smile, "I really want to know."

"We are an international group. Our American colleagues go to Nevada. As you know, it is rather expensive for us to go to Nevada."

"It seems to me that members of a group like yours would be better off going to Nevada."

"We think there is also a reason to come here."

I do not hear the rest, because several of the Moscow students are tugging me on the arm, saying something about a two-star general, the chief of the test site, who will receive us in person at the press conference.

As we walk through the doors of a pink imitation pre-revolutionary building, an officer hands each of us two small mementos of our visit: a pin featuring Kurchatov, the "father of the Soviet A-bomb," after whom the city is named, and a medal commemorating the fortieth anniversary of the test site. Soon one of the Danes approaches me, his face tight. "We are asking people to give us these medals so that we can ceremoniously return them," he says. "It was really quite a provocation, to present us something that glorifies the test site when we are here to close the test site down."

The hall where the press conference will take place is decorated with quaint, gory paintings of nineteenth century battlefield scenes, filled with cavalry charges, swordfights, and soldiers in hand-to-hand combat. Hung on the curtain behind the stage is the proclamation: "HAIL TO THE VALIANT ARMED FORCES OF THE USSR—THE TRUSTWORTHY GUARDS OF THE ACHIEVEMENTS OF SOCIALISM!" Below this is a large round poster of a mushroom cloud with a red X through it that announces, with no apparent irony, "FOR A WORLD WITHOUT NUCLEAR WEAPONS."

Six representatives of the test site take seats at a long table, but it is soon evident that only one will speak. Lieutenant-General Arkady Ilyenko, the chief of the test site, a compact, square-jawed man with steely eyes, gold teeth, and silver hair, is a man clearly accustomed to center stage. With little preamble the general informs us that since we are here as guests of the test site, we would do well to abide by the instructions of our hosts and not stray into places that are not safe for us to go. "We have about thirty or forty minutes for your questions," he says, eyeing the roomful of medical students, young Danes, and local inhabitants with an air of *noblesse oblige.*

But a rumpus is already brewing over the problem of translation. The nervous-looking woman sitting at the general's elbow cannot interpret half of his words, and the Danes begin shouting that someone better must be found. I look at Yuri. "No, I don't want to," he says hastily. "I don't want to associate myself with these people." But as a few more minutes pass and the Danes become more angry, Yuri yields to the inevitable and offers to interpret. Neither he nor the general look comfortable next to one another, and they are a study in contrasts: the aristocratic old military man in full uniform, the young bearded doctor in a pale-blue American "Physicians for Social Responsibility" sweatshirt.

"It's all very well that you are so concerned about our safety here in Kurchatov," begins a correspondent from the Soviet weekly *Medical Gazette,* "but I wonder if you are equally concerned about the safety of children living in this area who are being exposed to radioactive fallout."

"There are no official documents showing that there are dangers to the surrounding population during the present conducting of tests," the general replies frostily. "Such facts can only be found in the presentations of people who are incompetent in these questions, and in the press, including in *Medical Gazette.*"

There are murmurs and shufflings among the crowd. A young man from Alma-Ata representing the Nevada Movement goes to the microphone and quotes statistics about the high rate of birth defects and cancers in the Abai region, downwind of the test site. What explanation does the general have for these facts?

The general answers that such medical questions are outside of his competence. He points out that a special three-day medical conference in Semipalatinsk held in July 1989 had not been able to come to any definite conclusions, and that a special commission to investigate possible health consequences of the testing was being formed by the Ministry of Health.

"But I declare to you that at the present time, the tests are completely safe," he adds. "We would not live here on the test site with our families if it were not safe. My own daughter came here to have her baby, and my grandson has lived here for four years, and he is perfectly healthy. Obviously if I thought it was dangerous I would have sent them away."

The young man continues to recite statistics from the Abai region. The general raises his hand as if to interrupt him. "Aren't you interested in hearing these facts?" asks the young man.

"No, I am not," says the general. The crowd makes restless sounds. "The scientific approach is needed," he·continues. "Nobody knows what factors are leading to these pathologies. It could be drug abuse, or alcoholism, or many other things besides radiation. Only doctors can decide, and they will study this question for two years."

A woman goes to the microphone and demands to know why the workers of Kurchatov receive such high salaries if the test site is so safe? Applause breaks out in the audience.

"This question is illiterate and wrong," replies the general, his jaw tight. "The workers here receive slightly higher salaries only because they live in a closed military city. It has nothing to do with the polygon."

"But on the way here," insists the correspondent from *Medical Gazette*, "we could see that your stores sell vegetables and cigarettes that cannot be found in Semipalatinsk, or even in Moscow."

"The people of Kurchatov are normal people fulfilling their duty," says the general. "They often ask permission to go to Semipalatinsk and buy goods which they cannot obtain here. If you like I can show you our ordinary ration cards for sugar, tea, and soap." His voice is loud and emphatic; several of the Kurchatov residents applaud. "I do not like the hostile attitude of this correspondent," adds the general. "I suggest he sit down and let our other guests speak."

The debate continues, with the medical students grilling the general about the precise level of background radiation on the test site, the lack of dosimeters or other monitoring devices in surrounding villages, and the continuing leaks of radioactivity despite repeated assurances that changes in technology would preclude any further releases. Few find the general's answers satisfactory, and the tension in the room builds.

One of the Danes asks whether his group can collect some soil samples from the test site to take home for analysis. The general claims that a reciprocal agreement with the American government forbids the taking of any samples off the site. But he adds that the Danes are welcome to collect samples just outside the test site boundaries, if their local hosts, such as organizers in the physicians' peace group, will allow it.

"Will you allow it?" the Danish man promptly asks Yuri.

"Sure," says Yuri, jolted for a moment out of his role as an interpreter. The crowd laughs and the test site representatives look stern. "I don't understand why you want to take our soil," says the general. "Did you bring us a sample of Danish soil, for an exchange? I know you have no nuclear tests in Denmark, but maybe your soil is dirty in other ways."

The audience mutters at the insult. "I don't want to be rude," says the Danish man patiently, "but to be honest we don't believe you. You say the radiation level here is low. We want to take a sample home and verify this for ourselves."

A Kazakh man stands up and begins speaking in an agitated tone. The general asks us to believe him that the radiation levels here are normal, he says. But during a meeting with local people three months ago, this same general conveniently "forgot" about a nuclear test that took place in February 1989, claiming that test site personnel had conducted two nuclear tests in 1989 when in fact they had conducted three. How, therefore, can we believe what this general says?

There is applause. The general stiffens. "I repeat, I do not like the aggressive tone of this conversation. If the meeting goes on in this way, I will stop it." The way he frowns at the crowd makes it clear that he believes he could end the meeting if he wished, and that we would trundle out of the room if ordered to do so.

"Now about this meeting with the local people. I wish the man asking this question had been in my place. It was very difficult to defend myself against all the attacks from the local people. Some of the people of Kazakh nationality were rather hostile toward the Russian workers here. I was several times insulted by people who came up to me and said, 'You're a bureaucrat with no roots, and you've been sent here to do whatever you want.' And those people were of *your* nationality."

A soft gasp riffles through the audience. For the Kazakhs present, the general has just stepped over the bounds of polite discourse. Up to now, everyone has been carefully avoiding the fractious topic of ethnicity, the unspoken fact that the population of Kurchatov is almost entirely Russian and Ukrainian, while the population of the villages surrounding the test site is almost entirely Kazakh.

One of the Semipalatinsk medical students jumps to his feet and demands that the general apologize to the Kazakh people.

"I owe no apology," says the general.

"It is not appropriate to say that this problem is due to the aggressiveness of the Kazakh people."

"We are not here to talk about national problems."

"My people have lived here on this land for centuries. And they will live here in the future. I don't know where the daughter and grandson of the general will live, but I know that my children will live here."

"The Kazakh people are less than half of the population of Kazakhstan. If the nuclear explosions were to affect the population they would affect everyone—Russians, Ukrainians, Germans, Kazakhs—equally. This matter has nothing to do with nationality." The general gestures impatiently toward the next questioner.

I am waiting my turn at the microphone, and rehearsing my words. For all its heat, it seems to me that the discussion is avoiding a central issue. Whether current nuclear testing is damaging the health of local Kazakh villagers is debatable. A more fundamental question is whether continued nuclear testing threatens everyone because of its contribution to the upward technological spiral of the arms race. I am not sure the general knows I am here, but since he has permitted the Danes to come it seems unlikely that he will mind a stray American.

When I introduce myself, a murmur of surprise rustles through the crowd. I thank the general for the opportunity to be here and explain that I have also visited the Nevada test site and spoken with workers and officials there. "In Nevada, the local workers often resent the protesters, because they are afraid to lose their jobs if the test site closes. Do people in Kurchatov feel any resentment toward the people in Kazakhstan who are opposed to the testing?"

If the general is surprised to see me, he hides it well. "All the people in Kurchatov, from the first party secretary to the most ordinary workers, are for the cessation of nuclear testing," he declares. Many in the audience sit up, startled, at this unexpected answer. "And we are not afraid to lose our jobs," he adds, in a tone underlining that the fear of losing one's job is a distinctly American problem.

"In the United States, we often hear the argument that we must continue nuclear testing because it is vital to our national security. I would like to ask the general: in his personal opinion, is continued nuclear testing vital to Soviet national security, and if so why?"

"I repeat that we, together with all Soviet people, are for the cessation of nuclear testing. You know, if the Americans had not dropped their bombs on Hiroshima and Nagasaki, maybe we would not have had an arms race. Maybe we wouldn't be having these explosions on this test site." The rest of the general's answer is a textbook sample of the old Soviet hard line: The United States has initiated every step of the arms race, the Soviet Union has only been trying to catch up, now the Americans are building the Strategic Defense Initiative, we can't allow them to achieve superiority, we stopped tests for eighteen months while the Americans kept testing, we'll be happy to stop testing again once the two governments agree to do it simultaneously. And so on.

Yuri looks embarrassed at having to translate this answer. He clears his throat and manages to say the words.

The crowd looks at me curiously to see how I will react, but I only nod my head and sit down. The general did, after all, answer my question.

"But don't you think the human rights of the people in this area are being violated, since they are so angry and upset about the testing, and yet the testing goes on? Is the government really listening to the people?" demands a Lithuanian student.

"I will not answer any questions about human rights. It is too long a discussion for the time we have," the general replies.

"Your *personal* opinion," insists the student.

The general ignores him. One of the other uniformed men sitting at the table angrily points to his watch; the meeting has already lasted two hours. Only one more questioner, a medical student from Semipalatinsk, is allowed to speak.

"If everyone here in Kurchatov truly is for the cessation of nuclear testing," says the student, "I have a suggestion for you. Why don't you form a new organization called, for example, 'Military Officers Against Nuclear Testing'?" The crowd laughs.

"We are part of the Ministry of Defense, an arm of the government. We cannot organize an anti-government society," the general says in some confusion. Then he hits his stride again. "But I can assure you that we, together with all people, are for the cessation of nuclear testing. And we are grateful to all the people, especially the young people, who are struggling toward this goal. Although I must say, there is no use in protesting against nuclear testing only at the Semipalatinsk polygon. Nuclear tests must be stopped all over the world."

And with these words he closes the meeting. We are shooed toward the waiting buses. Outside, one of the Danish young women politely returns a handful of the anniversary medals to the general, saying that they cannot in principle keep something that celebrates the existence of the test site. The general's reaction is unexpectedly calm. "You have that right," is all he says. A bemused colonel takes the medals and puts them in his pocket.

Soon we are speeding out of the city, through the blackened plains and back to the gate, where the KGB men disembark without a word. The buses careen through the steppes. "Notice how fast we are moving," observes Natasha, "so that the Danish people have no chance to gather their soil."

Yuri and I have the same idea. "Do you have a plastic bag?" he asks.

When the buses pull aside to allow the journalists and officials to get back in their private cars, Yuri and I dash off the bus, run into the ditch, and start scooping dirt, stones, and small plants into the bag. "GET BACK ON THE BUS!" we hear the megaphones on the police cars boom. "FASTER! FASTER! RETURN TO THE BUS!"

Our bag full, we sprint back, instinctively ducking as if any minute bullets might start whizzing over our heads. The megaphones continue screaming until the doors have closed behind us.

"That was good," says Natasha appreciatively. "Only next time, show me how to use your camera first, so that I can have a photo of you guys getting shot."

We are still panting when the buses arrive at a small park by the Irtysh River. Permission has been granted to hold a protest demonstration here. The problem is that only a few dozen inhabitants of Kurchatov have followed us out of the city. We hold our banners and make our speeches, but after the drama of confronting the general it is a bit of a letdown. The Semipalatinsk students read several appeals to Presidents Gorbachev and Bush. A young military officer announces that he cannot wait for the day when he can change his profession from the military to peaceful work. The Danes huddle under white sheets in a "die-in," a symbolic enactment of the consequences of nuclear war, and we observe one minute of silence. The Soviet medical students link arms with the Danes and sing "We Shall Overcome."

Then a small rock band strikes up a tune, and soon the young military officers are dancing with the Danish young women. But I do not see much of the dancing, because one of the Lithuanian students has grabbed me by the arm. "There's a man here who wants to talk to you," she says.

The man is an army doctor from Kurchatov, a trim and mustached Ukrainian in his late twenties. He has lived and worked on the test site with his wife and two small daughters for five years. When he was first sent here, he explains, he had no strong opinions about whether nuclear testing was good or bad. "I was all the time looking at both sides of this question, trying to find an answer," he says. "But now I have decided that the testing is definitely bad. Even though I work at the polygon, and I know I ought to be defending its interests, I am a human being first, and now I realize that the explosions are bad for all of humanity."

He is not alone in his opinions, he says; there are many physicians and others in Kurchatov who would like to join the anti-testing movement. But they have no idea how to begin. He asks me how they can join SCPPNW, and what useful, concrete contributions they could make. I suggest that they should be in close contact with SCPPNW physicians and students in Semipalatinsk, Moscow, and other cities, and that perhaps they could collect first-hand testimonials from Kurchatov residents about the testing. As I speak I find myself wondering what this man's fate will be if he actually tries to do these things. "Aren't you afraid that joining SCPPNW will get you in trouble?" I ask.

"Perhaps," he shrugs his shoulders, "but I have no examples before me of others who have done this, so I have no idea what might happen. Therefore all I can do is try and see." His manner is earnest and upbeat. Several medical students are listening to the young army doctor with silent respect. I ask him whether he is afraid that living on the test site will harm his family. "It's not like a constant horror, but sometimes I do wonder what the future will bring for my children," he replies. We exchange addresses; he seems to think that he will be permitted to write to me. I am initially puzzled when he writes "Semipalatinsk-21" in his address, until he explains that this is the code name for Kurchatov.

The sun is nearly down, and voices over the loudspeakers are urging us on the buses. As the army doctor and I shake hands and say good-bye, I wonder if we will meet again, if the official rules that separate us will ever again be breached. The steppes darken to blackness as the buses speed toward Semipalatinsk. The weekend of protests is over. Once again the students debate and argue the day, and another heavy golden moon rises in the east.

Two days later, I am at the Kazakh Writer's Union in Alma-Ata, listening to Murat Auezov, the vice-president of the Nevada Movement, tell me their strategy for the next several months. Auezov, a soft-spoken Kazakh man in his forties, is a writer and the chief editor in the translation department of the Kazakh Writer's Union. He comes from a famous literary family; his father, Mukhtar Auezov, the author of a beloved epic called *The Way of Abai*, is considered the greatest Kazakh writer of his generation. With his round bookish spectacles and gentle manner, Murat Auezov seems more suited to the study of classical literature than to the leadership of a burgeoning populist movement. But now that Olzhas Suleimenov, the founder and president of the Nevada Movement, is living in Moscow as an elected member of the Supreme Soviet, Auezov has been left in charge of their work in Kazakhstan.

The room is wallpapered with signed petitions calling for an end to nuclear testing in Kazakhstan. Although the Nevada Movement has always urged that governments work toward the cessation of nuclear testing all over the world, clearly its emotional focus is stopping testing locally. If the Soviet government moved its test operations to Novaya Zemlya, a remote island north of Siberia which already has a small nuclear test site, would the Nevada Movement declare victory and go home?

"Of course, we would regard it as a victory, and as a very important first step," Auezov says. "In fact this is what we are asking for in our discussions with the Ministry of Defense and the Supreme Soviet. We are asking why they cannot at least move all of the testing to Novaya Zemlya."

But what would then happen to the Nevada Movement—is it truly an anti-testing movement, or an anti-testing-in-Kazakhstan movement? "Yes, some of the enthusiasm would probably go away," Auezov replies. "But we are trying to broaden consciousness through our movement, to educate people with the idea that we are all interconnected, we are all living on one small planet. Then they will understand that testing in other parts of the world also affects us here in Kazakhstan. It is impossible to create enthusiasm artificially, but if we succeed in the broader humanistic goals of our movement, then the enthusiasm will maintain itself.

"That's why it is essential that now we have tighter relations and more joint actions with the American anti-nuclear movement, so that we can move away from just a regional understanding of our problems. During the action in Karaul on Hiroshima Day we knew that similar actions were simultaneously taking place in Nevada, in Hiroshima, in many other places. And this gave us a strong feeling of unanimity and support."

Auezov points out that in a republic long-fractured by tense ethnic relations, this is the first public movement to unite the different nationalities living in Kazakhstan. One-third of the members of their coordinating council are Russian; Germans, Koreans, Uighurs, and Jews are also represented. The Nevada Movement has already taken a stand on many other ecological and social issues, such as the destruction of the Aral Sea, and Auezov hopes that in time it will metamorphose "into a strong and genuine People's Front of Kazakhstan—a movement of people against bureaucracy, against the idiotism of past years, and for the solving of some of our very great environmental problems. We want to establish a moral basis for our movement, and to become an independent source of ideas and information."

For four months after the Nevada Movement arose in February 1989, the Soviet government conducted no nuclear tests. Many in Kazakhstan and in the West began to wonder if this new movement was responsible for the undeclared cease-fire. Some whispered that Moscow authorities were fearful of riots erupting in Alma-Ata, a city where some of the first violent ethnic clashes of the Gorbachev era took place in 1986. But then Semipalatinsk test site authorities invited twenty representatives of the Nevada Movement to witness a new nuclear test on July 8, 1989.

"They took us three-and-a-half kilometers from the center of the explosion. They were hoping to show us that the tests are harmless," recalls Auezov. "But when the explosion was made, the ground heaved and trembled in a terrible way. We who were born on this land, who have lived here for centuries, could hear this land crying out to us. And the people from the test site could hear nothing. I asked General Ilyenko how many *suslik*, one òf the small animals of the steppes, probably died because of this explosion. He looked at me and could not even comprehend my question. And it is not surprising that someone who does not think about the people living on these steppes would not be able to think about *suslik*."

I tell Auezov about General Ilyenko's assertion that he and everyone else in Kurchatov are opposed to nuclear testing. Could the general be believed? Auezov pauses before answering. "You know, there are different kinds of people at the polygon. For example, I am acquainted with one man there, a colonel, who writes poetry, who is an intellectual and honest man. But such a man as this General Ilyenko, I cannot believe him. These are people who live only by the order, the *prikaz*. These are people with a definite psychology. All their lives, from their youngest years, they have fulfilled someone else's orders. They don't have any ideas of their own. They can say one thing today, and quite a different thing tomorrow."

On September 2, 1989, less than a month after the Hiroshima Day demonstrations in Semipalatinsk and Karaul, a nuclear test was again conducted at the Semipalatinsk test site. This time no one was told in advance and no witnesses were invited. But residents of the nearby village of Kainar suspected the day before that a test was planned, because military helicopters arrived in their village with dosimeters to measure radioactive fallout. Ironically, September 1 is national Peace Day in the Soviet Union and the Kainar schoolchildren were studying their traditional "lesson of peace" when the helicopters appeared. The children ran out of the school, shouting and waving their arms, and tried to prevent the helicopters from landing.

The timing of the September 2 test was interpreted by the Nevada Movement as a deliberate slap in the face. "It showed us that we must become more effective and more strong in our efforts," says Auezov. "We received many calls and letters from people demanding that we organize strikes all over the republic. But we decided to try once more to resolve this problem on the diplomatic level. Olzhas Suleimenov is now arranging for a discussion between members of the Supreme Soviet and the Ministry of Defense on this question. We will make our demands at this discussion. If they are not met, we are ready to organize strikes. The Karaganda coal miners have a very powerful organization, and they are ready to support us."

I ask Auezov about a rumor I have heard in Moscow: the Semipalatinsk test site is nearing the end of its life because after forty years there are few "good" places left to conduct explosions. A secret decision has already been made to close down operations and move the tests to Novaya Zemlya. Therefore the Soviet government can afford to tolerate the Nevada Movement, and when someday they "give in" to its demands and close the Semipalatinsk test site, they will reap the public relations benefits of appearing to acquiesce to a people's movement.

Instead of scoffing, Auezov replies that he has heard this rumor in Kazakhstan, too. "Perhaps," he says. "But if that is the intention of the authorities, they are making a very great mistake. Because this movement is training us. It is a great school in the struggle for peace. Perhaps the government is only playing with us, like a cat with a mouse. But meanwhile we are learning, and our little mouse of a movement is growing into a big tiger. Our consciousness is changing. The people are growing up from day to day. We are learning how to organize ourselves, how to speak out, how to express ourselves. We will use this training to confront many of our other problems."

He hands me a small pennant with the symbol of the Nevada Movement: a Shoshone Indian, one of the original inhabitants of the Nevada test site, offering a peace pipe to a Kazakh elder. I tell him about the dirt and plants that Yuri and I had scooped up near the test site, and mention that the small fragrant plants remind me of sage, an herb burned by Native Americans in purification rituals. His eyes light up as he tells me that this plant, called *gusan,* is a traditional symbol of the Kazakh homeland.

I promise to send the *gusan* to Nevada; perhaps the Shoshone will use it in one of the ceremonies they often conduct before test site protests. And perhaps, he says with a smile, a small bundle of sage can come here.

Soviet officials admitted in early 1990 that public pressure generated by the Nevada Movement had compelled them to cancel eleven of eighteen scheduled nuclear tests in 1989. On March 10, 1990, *The Washington Post* reported that senior Soviet defense officials had announced their intention to phase out the Semipalatinsk testing program by 1993 and to shift all future testing to the Arctic island of Novaya Zemlya. Colonel General Vladimir Gerasimov told the Soviet legislature that tests were still necessary, however, because "warheads of a new quality are required and it is practically impossible to create new warheads without tests."

Legislators from the Novaya Zemlya region and government officials from nearby Norway and Sweden immediately declared they would oppose nuclear testing on Novaya Zemlya. While hailing the decision as a partial victory, leaders of the Nevada Movement vowed to continue to press for an immediate halt to testing at the Semipalatinsk site and elsewhere. In May 1990, the Nevada Movement, together with the group International Physicians for the Prevention of Nuclear War, co-sponsored a conference and series of demonstrations in Alma-Ata and Karaul that brought together hundreds of grassroots anti-testing activists from around the world. "After 45 years of the nuclear arms race, we cannot look to our governments to bring about an end to the deadly process. We, the people of the world, must instead look to and support each other," declared a joint statement issued by the Nevada Movement and American Peace Test, a group which coordinates protests at the Nevada test site. "Radiation knows no borders and crosses ethnic and racial lines. Our vision of peace and justice must also be global."

3 | Family Ties

Siberia. A land of fierce summers and legendary winters, of hardy natives who have clung to their customs and hardy newcomers who have clung to their ideals. History has not been kind to Siberia, and its name is often equated with terror and brutality. Yet there is a protected, almost innocent quality to life in Siberia as well; the tang of the wilderness is never far away, and the news of the world is softened by a vast buffer of trees, rivers, silence. The politics and pressures of Moscow are distant and dimly felt. Intellectual creativity and social experimentation have long been Siberian traditions; in its harshness and remoteness has also been a kind of freedom.

Americans who have met Olga Bazanova speak of her in awe-tinged tones. The impression created is one of immensity. The image that forms in the mind is of a large Siberian matron with flaxen braids and commanding organizational abilities. Children cling to her embroidered skirts while she expertly cooks traditional feasts for her American guests. The earth trembles a bit under her feet as she strides through the city of Novosibirsk and delegates responsibilities to the members of her group, which goes by the title "Association of Siberian Families for Interrelationship and Mutual Understanding Among the Peoples of the USSR and the USA."

At the Novosibirsk airport in October 1988, I am scanning the crowd for such a peasant peace queen when a petite, dark-haired, slightly Asian-looking woman in a white sweatshirt rushes toward me and her small daughter places a bouquet of orange wild berries in my hands. Pointing to the butterfly on her sweatshirt, which has an American flag for one wing and a Soviet flag for the other, Olga Bazanova announces with pride: "It is the uniform of our Association!" On the bus to Novosibirsk she loads me with presents and rapidly explains the events of the next few days. Apparently a large group of Hawaiian hula dancers is in town and the Association is in full mobilization. "I have proposal!" Olga Bazanova exclaims, clapping her hands together. "I have brilliant idea! You want to learn about our Association? Then live with me for next few days. Because my life *is* Association life."

Bazanova was born in Novosibirsk, as were her parents; on one side of her family she is descended from Polish revolutionaries, on the other from a line of Russian Orthodox priests. She graduated from Novosibirsk State University with a degree in biology and worked fifteen years in a laboratory before becoming a teacher. Her husband, Volodya, is a physicist. They live in a small apartment amid birch trees in Akademgorodok, the scientific suburb of Novosibirsk, with their fifteen-year-old son Misha, who loves computers, and six-year-old Anya, who loves her violin.

To say Bazanova has a positive outlook is to put it mildly. Her apartment is tiny, her family has no car, Misha must commute to Novosibirsk for school, and she must cope with the usual difficulties of maintaining a Soviet household. But Bazanova takes what is given without complaint. She and her husband joke with Anya that a car would be unhealthy because then they would not walk so much. Standing in lines, she says, gives her "time to think about life."

Bazanova is a career woman and a dedicated mother, a born leader who believes women should not be leaders, an atheist who nevertheless speaks matter-of-factly about her "dreams to God." She is a scientist with a rational bent of mind who reads Lenin for intellectual pleasure. Yet when it comes to Soviet-American relations, she is no theorist. She believes, deeply and without complication, that the secret to peace lies in shared laughter over home-cooked meals and high-spirited parties full of dance and song. Endowed with the penetrating voice of a camp counselor, a good memory for games, and a complete lack of self-consciousness, Bazanova has a kind of virtuosity for play. In gatherings she barks instructions for games or dances with the assurance of a field sergeant, hauling reluctant people by the hand into the circle and forcing them to have fun. Her creed is summed up in one of the Association's theme songs, which she sings whenever she has an audience: "The more we get together, the better friends we are!"

Since 1987, the Association of Siberian Families has hosted an American group every two months. "I will tell you funny story!" Bazanova says. "You know, Dennis Bowman is a big man in the American group Peace Table, which is one of our main partners. Not long ago someone in Intourist tells us that a group with

'Bowman' is coming from Alma-Ata. So we all go to the airport, we bring our Soviet and American flags, we wear our Association uniforms, and we are singing 'This Land is Your Land' as they step off the plane. And the Americans are *very* surprised! It was not Dennis Bowman, but Mary Bowman from somewhere else! They are very surprised, but they are *so happy!* When they left they said they had been to twelve cities in the USSR, but Novosibirsk was the *best.* It was wonderful!"

Few things fall between "wonderful" and "terrible" for Olga Bazanova. The Association's projects, ranging from sewing peace quilts to designing a children's museum in Novosibirsk, have thrived because she and other Siberian women and men have seized upon them with zeal. They raise money through bake sales and raffles. They stomp into classrooms and teach children how to make peace lanterns and write to American pen pals. They persuade grandmothers to embroider aprons to send to American grandmothers. And, everywhere, always, they sing. Loudly.

"We want you to be HA-PPY now, Happy in the hard world of change," Bazanova sings on the bus to Akademgorodok, bouncing in her seat and slapping her hands on her knees, while Anya and a woman friend who is a university instructor of Marxism join in with equal abandon. The other passengers smile or look away discreetly. "We are making a scene," Bazanova says with delight, and starts another song.

By the time we arrive at School #162 in Akademgorodok, one of the Association's parties is in full swing. Some fifty Hawaiian hula dancers, musicians, and assorted American tourists are "doing the hokey pokey" with some fifty Siberian school children. The Siberian children are dressed in colorful homemade folk costumes, the Hawaiians in jeans and sweatshirts. A ukelele player is providing the music, but shrieks of laughter drown him out as this unlikely crowd attempts to put its left side in and shake it all about. "They organize the most incredible things for people here," an American group leader murmurs as the Hawaiians and Siberians wind themselves into a huge spiral hug.

The Siberian girls sing several folk songs, their young voices blending in eerie, forceful harmonies as they sway in their full-length frocks. The Hawaiian women dancers reciprocate by taking off their tennis shoes and dancing the hula. The contrast in music and dance styles could hardly be greater, but the flow of cross-cultural appreciation in the room is wide and full. Motioning everyone to join in, a Siberian teacher brings out a rope for a spirited tug of war. The girls' ornate costumes are in some danger but no one seems to mind as a hundred people scream and dig in their heels. After this, Bazanova can no longer contain herself, and she leaps into the center to lead two circle dance-games.

"The main thing is *personal* relationships," Bazanova says later. "If your persons are friendly to our persons, it will be peace. Persons. Not abstract 'people.' Not 'people-to-people,' but person to person. Family to family. Because family is a global thing, a natural type of society. Our governments are made of simple persons who have families, too. And if we are active, and elect responsible men in our government who will not forget their humanity, then problems will be decided in a clever way, a kind way, a goodwill way. Yes?"

On a wall in Bazanova's apartment is a map of the United States with little red stick-on hearts over every city where she and her family have friends. The living room is jammed with books, including Lenin's complete collected works. Music for one of Anya's violin pieces lies open on an upright piano. "I am a simple Soviet teacher," says Bazanova as she stirs a bowl of cookie batter in her kitchen. "No. I don't know what I am." She pauses, her hands full of dough, and looks at the ceiling. "Ah! I am *mother!* That's what I am. My family comes first. I have the best husband in the world, and the best son, and the best daughter." As cookies take shape and dumplings boil, she explains how she first became mixed up with "wonderful Americans."

In 1986, her son Misha telephoned from school and told her that his principal had said he would travel in a few months to the United States. "Of course, I didn't believe," says Bazanova. "I began to laugh. What? United States? Ha Ha Ha. I said, 'Misha, your principal had a joke. Don't believe.'" But soon she learned that a Seattle-based American group called the Holyearth Foundation was arranging an exchange of computer whiz-kids from Novosibirsk and the United States. Although only a few years later such Soviet-American "kids-to-kids" swaps would become relatively commonplace, in 1986 it was a unique and difficult idea requiring months of hard work and negotiations on both sides. Fortunately,

Danaan Parry and Diana Glasgow, the directors of the Holyearth Foundation, found a willing and powerful partner in Academician Andrei Ershov, a respected computer scientist in Akademgorodok.

Ershov gathered a group of thirty high school students who had placed well in computer competitions and organized an after-school training program at the university. "There were thirty kids, and only twenty will go, so there was a very strong competition," says Bazanova. "For two months Misha studied English, he sang Russian songs and learned Russian customs, he studied political news. And every day there were competitions to go to America. Every day with them were psychologists, computer specialists, a person from Komsomol [the Young Communist League]. One night I come back from work and my son is lying on the floor. I ask my son, 'What are you doing?' He tells me he is dancing. I say, 'What dance?' He says, 'I dance break. I study break dance.'"

She laughs and slips the cookies in the oven. "You see, these were simple kids. They were not like Katya Lycheva [a Soviet child actress who went on a high-profile tour of America in 1985]. They cannot sing, they cannot dance, they cannot speak English brilliantly. Only one thing they can do—they can work on computers. That is why Ershov organized this training." Misha was selected and at age thirteen became the youngest member of the Soviet group. Only then did the reality of his trip begin to sink in. "It is like going to moon! It is not possible! I am not afraid because I don't believe!" recalls Bazanova. "But my mother, Oh! She was so afraid! She knew that America has much crime, and because of this she was afraid. And when his train left I cried very much, too. Suddenly I began to be afraid. I don't know why. And every night I wake up at three o'clock and wonder what he is doing in America. Every night all month. Usually I sleep very strongly. But my heart was with him, of course. I am mother, first of all."

A few days after Misha returned in December 1986, Danaan Parry and Diana Glasgow of the Holyearth Foundation brought a group of Americans to Novosibirsk. Bazanova met Americans for the first time at a dinner party in her mother's apartment. "We were so frightened, to have Americans as guests in our flat. My God, we were afraid! We felt so responsible! OH! THEY ARE AMERICANS! They are not simple people! And my English was more terrible than it is now.

"Then I met the Americans at the door, and they were afraid

too! We are all afraid, because all the TV cameras are in our flat. The central TV program *Vremya.* Our regional TV programs. Our radio program. The correspondents from TASS. Only my Misha was not afraid. It doesn't matter! he said. Why are you afraid? He had just returned from USA, he is accustomed to TV, he is accustomed to correspondents, he is accustomed to Americans of course too. He said, my dear Granny, please be silent. Don't pay attention to correspondents. But she kept saying, please give me some pills for my heart, to keep calm. So finally we all sit at the big table, and all of us are afraid. And we start to pour wine, and the correspondents say, No wine. No wine. We are too afraid to ask why! We put away the crystal wine glasses and we drink only Pepsi-Cola! It was our first experience with anti-alcoholic campaign!"

She pours two glasses of sweet homemade berry wine as we laugh. "The only person at the big table to eat was my son. He was very comfortable and poised, he sang songs, he played the guitar. At last our correspondents left us. THANK YOU. We drank wine, and we began to speak with American people. It was very nice. And I saw that they are normal people, that it doesn't matter that he is black, that she is a student, that he is older, that she is younger than I am. They are normal people.

"Before, I had stereotype. I had the impression that every American would like to have *much* money, that this was the main purpose of his life. But now I think that we have those type of Soviet people, too. And I think that there are American people who are the same type as I am. All people are equal. All. It does not depend on his eyes, his color of skin, his riches, his position. There are all types of people, in every nation."

At a large farewell party for the Holyearth group, Bazanova organized the dances and the games. "It was a brilliant party," she remembers, "because Danaan Parry, with his big cleverness and big heart, asked all the parents of the children who had visited the United States to stand. And we stood, and he said: 'I would like to say thank you, for giving your children to us. Let's be together always, let's keep playing together and working together.' It was amazing! It was a message from heart to heart! And we sang many, many songs. And one of the American boys got down on his knees and said, 'Forgive me, because I thought Russians were terrible people. And now my heart is in Russia! I love you!' And that was amazing too!"

The Americans went home, promising to bring next time to Novosibirsk the American families who had hosted the Siberian teenagers during their U.S. trip. Two months before their visit in September 1987, the Siberian families began meeting to make plans. "We thought about all things. About our greeting at the airport. About planting of garden of peace. About our travel on ship. About our farewell party too!" How did Bazanova become the leader of the Siberian families? "Whenever I am among people more than three, I am leader!" she says, laughing. "It's my possibility! I begin to organize, to comment: 'You must know this, you must do that,' and I try to stop myself. But I am leader always. My boss says I am not so much *active* as I am *intense*. I am very *intensive*."

Bazanova took a week off from her laboratory, Anya took a week off from kindergarten, and they spent their time with the visiting Americans, going with them on excursions and masterminding their placement in homes during evenings. At the farewell party, the Americans gave Bazanova a beautiful handmade peace quilt. "They say they want to give it to me because I am *so active*. And they say many good words about me, and I am pleased! I feel good! And at the airport, when they left us, Oh! How we cried! Anya cried very much. And all American girls cried. And all American boys cried. And we all cried. It was terrible! But it was also amazing!"

She takes the cookies out of the oven. "A few days later I have good idea. To organize *our* Association of Families. The purpose: to invite Americans and to meet with them. We have so many common things to speak about, so many common songs. It's wonderful! I met with other families and we decided to organize this club."

But was it difficult to form an independent group back in 1987? "OOHH," groans Bazanova, "it was *very* difficult. *Perestroika* only begin. Bureaucratic relationships, old formula, still very strong." Just then her watch alarm beeps and a look of horror crosses her face. "We will be late to folk festival!" she says, tearing off her apron. "I tell you about difficulties later! Let's go!"

Down the street, the Hawaiian dancers are the feature attraction at a large evening concert of folk performers. Most of the singers and dancers are Siberian, but there are groups from the Urals and Latvia as well. Bazanova cannot sit long in her seat, however; she keeps running into the foyer to consult with other women in the Association about plans for the Halloween party the next day. None of them, it turns out, has the slightest idea what Halloween means; all they know is that it is a big American holiday and therefore something to be treated with respect. Bazanova asks the Americans she bumps into whether they are "having good time;" they assure her they are.

On the walk home, as Anya skips ahead humming a Siberian melody, Bazanova says cheerfully, "I have many problems. It's terrible. I must organize home visits for Americans for tomorrow evening." Although it is nearly midnight, she begins to make calls, jotting notes in a ledger book that lists the phone numbers of Association members. She asks whether they are free, whether they can manage in English, how many they can handle for dinner. At last, twenty calls and an hour later, all the Americans have been safely placed. She has also found volunteers to bring a bucket, towels, pumpkins, and apples to tomorrow's Halloween party. "I don't know," Bazanova says with a sigh, looking up from the phone with a rare hint of tiredness, "why I always feel so *responsible.*"

The instructor of Marxism calls; she is in a bar with several Americans and they are having a hot discussion about whether it is possible to achieve the ideals of Communism in a practical society. "What did you tell them?" Bazanova teases her. "Is it possible or impossible?" There is a pause. Bazanova laughs and reports, nodding her head with mock seriousness, "She says, yes, *of course* it is possible."

Bazanova gives the ledger book one last look before putting it away. "There are eighty families in our Association, but only about twenty are really active. The others do not appear until Americans appear. Then they say, 'Oh yes, Americans, I want to invite them to my home and have discussions with them.' But after the Americans go home, if we ask them to make peace lanterns, or to make calls, or to organize something, then they say, 'Oh, I have no time, I am too *busy.*'" She suddenly claps her hands and sits up very straight. "I have idea! Would you like to see photograph albums?"

Bazanova's albums are filled with baby pictures, family vacations, portraits of her parents and grandparents (her ninety-three-year-old grandfather, she says proudly, "still sings beautifully"), and snapshots of visiting friends from all over the Soviet Union. Many of them she terms "friends from Artek." As the daughter of two Communist Party members and an active Young Pioneer,

Bazanova was able to spend two summers as a teenager at Camp Artek, the elite international children's camp on the Black Sea that Maine schoolgirl Samantha Smith visited in 1983. Bazanova's Artek friends are still among her closest and she considers her summers there the happiest of her life. In a way, the Association is her attempt to re-create Artek in adulthood. Through her songs and games, she is trying to awaken in others the enthusiasm for international harmony that she first experienced as a child.

The next morning, a dozen of the Hawaiians follow Bazanova and two dozen Association women and children across the street from their hotel to, of all places, the Communist Party headquarters of Novosibirsk. It is a Saturday, and the empty meeting rooms were the best Bazanova could find. She is gleeful about this invasion of fun into the very fortress of seriousness. "It is our historical first Halloween Party!" she announces, and begins organizing get-acquainted games. Soon Americans and Soviets are bobbing for apples in a bucket filled with cold water and untangling themselves from games of "knots." There are not many costume materials to go around, but the Siberian women become very inventive with a few scarves and beads, decking out several Americans as gypsies and peasants. Bazanova's daughter Anya rolls up her pants, untucks her flannel shirt, puts on huge black hair ribbons and declares that she is a "hooligan."

During a lull in the games, Bazanova seizes an opportunity to make a speech. "Two years ago our children visited USA, and one year ago the families who hosted our children visited us. And we had brilliant idea to found Association of Families. The purpose is to make interrelationships and mutual understanding among peoples of USA and USSR. And we think nothing is better for mutual understanding than families. Because all families on the earth have similar problems. Yes?

"Now about our projects. Our main project is the international peace lantern exchange project. We exchange these lanterns with people in Japan, in USA, in many other countries. In August we had a wonderful lantern floating ceremony on the Ob River. We had 200 lanterns made by American, Soviet, Bulgarian, German, Japanese, and Czechoslovakian children, and we floated them together. It was a big sea of lights! On violin we played 'We Shall Overcome,' and it was wonderful! And now we have about 2,000 lanterns, because we organized the making of peace lanterns in all our schools on September 1, Peace Day.

"Next we have Peace Table. Very interesting people with Peace Table organization in Seattle came and we exchanged recipes of our national dishes. And they left for us dried mushrooms, and we cooked pies with these mushrooms and sold them and sent the money to the Samantha Smith Fund. What else? We also have our own projects, not just Soviet-American projects. We organize help to our old lonely ladies, and also to orphanage children. What else? We have *many* projects. Maybe you have questions?"

No one does, and the party resumes. A famous poet-singer from Leningrad, Alexander Dolsky, has heard about the party from a friend and drops in unannounced to treat the group to an impromptu concert. After he leaves, things become disorganized. American 1950s rock screeches on an old record player and a few people are dancing. A Hawaiian real estate agent and the instructor of Marxism are trying to do the hula. Other people are carving Jack-o-lanterns. The Siberian children are wearing Mickey Mouse hats and happily accepting bubble gum from the Hawaiians. Misha and one of the Americans are deep in conversation about computer hardware. "Why you go?!" shrieks Bazanova when she sees two of the Hawaiian women putting on their coats.

"We thought it was over," they reply.

"But we still have not had contest for the best costume and the best pumpkin! There will be prize!" Bazanova's distress is genuine. The Hawaiians exchange looks, and start unwrapping their scarves.

After the party ends, the Americans scatter to shops, museums, and theaters. Bazanova spends the rest of the afternoon tending to small urgent needs. One of the Americans has lost her camera and a search must be organized. Another American wants a record of Siberian folk music, but all the proper shops are closed. Bazanova must also find lunch for herself and her two children (she will not be allowed to eat in the restaurant at the Americans' hotel) and take Anya to her violin lesson. The weather has suddenly turned wintry, the sidewalks are frozen and treacherous, and she is horrified at the thought that American feet and hands might be getting cold. "Take my gloves!" she keeps saying, and when her offers are refused she declares: "It's terrible!"

During a taxi ride I remind her to speak about the difficulties of setting up the Association. "It was only one year ago. But it was big difference from now. In those times we have only a few informal societies in our city, maybe one or two. And they said, 'Don't be in a hurry. For what purpose would you like to have such an organization? When Americans come next time, we'll call you. You'll go to the airport and meet them. So why do you need an organization? Who are you?' But fortunately we have good helpers. Viktor Yukechev, who is a correspondent with the Novosti Press Agency, and Academician Ershov helped us very much. They are really clever men. And Academician Ershov became our president. Not our real president, of course, he doesn't know what we do! But he is our shelter. He signs all important papers. And then they say, 'Oh, you are from Academician Ershov?' and everything is okay."

The Association has survived financially on bake sales and a one-ruble-per-family membership fee. It was recently "registered" under the umbrella of the Soviet Friendship Societies, and a number of cooperatives and official organizations (such as Komsomol) have said they would like to fund its activities. Bazanova, as executive director, is weighing options carefully. "Now our Association is very popular, and has respect of high-level people. We would like to have Komsomol become one of our sponsors, because they are a respectable organization, a state organization. But we must have an agreement, where we write out our rules and their rules, our responsibilities and their responsibilities." Her Association has so far had little to do with the local Peace Committee. "But I know it is a bureaucratic organization, because one of my American friends sent an invitation for my family to go on peace cruise with Peace Committee, and they lost the invitation. They lost it, and I am angry!" She laughs. "Of course, I am sure they did not lose it. They used it for their friends or relatives, probably."

She then claims that she would like to abdicate her leadership as soon as a good man comes along to replace her. "I know it will be better when a man, not a woman, will be head. Because men, from a physiological point of view, are stronger and have more possibilities to think and to organize." Really? "Yes, really!" she insists. "In the home, with my children, I am irreplaceable. But it is difficult for my mind to embrace all these things." I point out that as far as I can tell, her entire Association, with few exceptions, is led by women. "Ah," she says, thinking it over. "Maybe. Well, maybe for family association you are right, it is okay with women."

Bazanova sees no contradiction between her activism and her loyalty to her country. Although she has never joined the Party, she calls herself "a Communist in my heart," and she has never thought to question Soviet foreign or military policies. She believes that the arms race is caused by the drive for profit within the capitalist military-industrial complex. Period. "We have no such rich military people here," she says simply, with none of the self-righteousness that can make similar statements by Soviet officials irritating. "We have military bureaucracy, of course, but we have no millionaires with war plants, no persons interested in developing the military because of greed. It is difference between our countries. So maybe if you can stop your rich military men, everything will be all right.

"Of course, we have many foolish men too. And it is our big task, the main task of *perestroika*, to stop our foolish men. In our country we made a big mistake. We did not pay enough attention to the teaching of children. And so we make by our own hands foolish men. It's terrible in our schools. We have no real method of teaching. We do not value teachers' work. Only ten percent are clever teachers. The rest are those who could not enter university, or enter medicine, and so became teachers. It is a terrible problem, and I don't know how to solve it."

In 1988, Bazanova left the laboratory for the classroom, becoming a chemistry and biology teacher and the vice-principal of a school in Novosibirsk. As a first step, she attempted to organize an informal parent-teacher association. But the principal, jealous of Bazanova's popularity with the children and their parents, soon quashed it. "She said, 'It is not your job to have ideas. It is your job to organize the cleaning of our halls.'" Bazanova now teaches at a school in Akademgorodok with a principal who supports her work. Even so, she has not found the transition from the laboratory to the classroom easy, and she admits she misses her "very interesting" research. "But I will not go back to science, because I see that it is my duty as a citizen and as a patriot of my country to teach in school," she says. "And there are three things I love most of all in life: to sing, to dance, and to be with children."

Just before dinnertime, she is in the lobby of the Americans' hotel, checking to make sure each person has an invitation to a home that night. Two of the American women thank her but say they would prefer to go to the circus. Bazanova's eyes widen in disbelief. For decades, Americans have complained that they have had few opportunities to see real Soviet life because official tour guides book their evenings solid with "cultural events." And now Bazanova and her friends, working day and night to arrange home visits, have been upstaged by the circus! "It's terrible," she says, with a bewildered smile. But she does not try to dissuade the women, even though a family of Siberians who have been preparing food all day will now be disappointed.

As we walk toward a friend's apartment she turns reflective. "Before Misha went to USA, I said in my dreams to God: 'Dear God. Please say to Americans, say to rich military men in America, that there will not be war. Only this one request I have for you. Please, give health to my children and my husband, and please say to Americans that there will not be war.' And now I say in my letters to God, 'Please, only make it so that there will not be war anywhere.' I am only afraid of one kind of person, those who are fanatics, who are interested in making profits through war. It doesn't matter what country they are in. I am afraid of them.

"But since I began working with Americans, I am not so much afraid. I believe in kindness. I believe in cleverness. I believe that kindness will have victory over foolishness, over anger, over violence. I told you before that I am Communist in my heart because I believe in the ideal of a society of brothers and sisters. The ideal that all people will have equal rights. The ideal that all will be kind to each other. It is my ideology. I believe in this future.

"But we must explain to children how terrible is nuclear war, and how to prevent it. We must teach them to live without conflicts and be friends. Not only with Americans, but among ourselves, too. We must explain to our children these simple things. To be kind. To see in everybody brother and sister."

That evening, two Association women put on a feast for Bazanova's family and three American guests. Multiple courses of salads, meat, and vegetables appear, the wine flows, and soon songs are flowing as well. When everyone is too stuffed to consider another mouthful, the hostesses proudly produce a huge cake and start pouring tea. A family friend, the assistant concertmaster of the Novosibirsk Symphony, drops by after his evening concert and gives a passionate private recital. Little Anya's eyes shine with adoration as Paganini and Tchaikovsky fill the room. Outside, the first snow of the year drifts to the ground, and the city grows quiet.

We are sleepy and content when suddenly Bazanova announces, "I have idea! Let us visit office of our Association!" Misha takes Anya home to their grandmother's place while we head to another friend's apartment to collect more Americans for our excursion. The fact that it is past midnight and snowing hard does not seem to daunt Bazanova in the least. Through sheer enthusiasm she persuades twenty people to follow her on a half-mile walk across town to the modest room in a youth club (procured because the director is an active Association member) that houses their peace quilts, lanterns, and posters.

Once there, she makes a speech describing all of their current and future projects. Everyone laughs when she holds up a long cloth ribbon of children's footprints that was presented to her by an American group called Mothers Embracing Nuclear Disarmament. The Association expects to become very active in sister city activities, she says, since Novosibirsk has recently been paired with Minneapolis/St. Paul. They hope to send a group of Siberian folk singers and dancers to the 1990 Goodwill Games in Seattle. They plan to launch a major campaign against children's war toys and expect to organize several Soviet-American "peace voyages" on the Ob River.

"And we also sing," Bazanova says brightly. "Let's sing a song, yes?" But both Americans and Soviets are, by this time, exhausted. She suggests several of their usual songs, which are voted down with groans. Finally everyone consents to sing "If You're Happy and You Know It, Clap Your Hands." By the time the song reaches the stamping-feet part, people are laughing again and the energy in the room has quickened. Bazanova's face shines with triumph. It is nearly two in the morning when the group leaves for home, walking arm in arm and singing "My Bonnie Lies Over the Ocean" with gusto. The apartments lining the streets are silent and dark. Despite the cold, people linger on the corners where they must part, not wanting to say good-bye.

4 | The Trust Group

Ekaterina Podoltseva sounded surprised that a Western journalist had called her on this bleak wintry day. "Come to my apartment at five," she said. "We won't discuss the place for the demonstration on the phone."

It was February 23, 1988, the day of a relatively obscure Soviet holiday called Red Army Day. No one gets off work, and there are no ostentatious public displays of military equipment such as those on May Day and the anniversary of the October Revolution. To the average Soviet citizen, Red Army Day means only a brief flowering of fresh propaganda posters. But to members of the Group to Establish Trust Between East and West, the Soviet Union's oldest and most well-known independent peace group, Red Army Day is an affront, a reminder of the pervasive militarization of their society, a day for protest and action.

Podoltseva, a tall, leonine woman with waist-length blond hair and thick bangs, motioned me into her apartment with a quick nod. She led me to her kitchen, pointed to an empty chair, and poured tea. The conversation began awkwardly. Neither she nor Vladimir Yaremenko, a young artist also involved in the Trust Group, spoke any English. I explained myself in Russian as well as I could.

Soon Podoltseva drew a map of where the demonstration would take place. Pointing to the street name, she asked, "Can you read it?"

"Bolshoi Prospekt," I said.

She and Yaremenko burst into nervous laughter and shook their heads. "Don't read it aloud, just read it," Podoltseva said, pointing to the cross-street.

But again I missed hearing the crucial word, *vslukh*—"aloud." I assumed their laughter had been directed at my poor pronunciation. "Kolpinskaya," I said, doing my best to speak clearly.

At this, Yaremenko put his head down on the table to muffle a guffaw. Podoltseva resisted an impulse to clap her hand over my mouth and, still chuckling, pointed meaningfully to the radio on the table. Finally I understood. So much for trying to keep the location a secret from KGB eavesdroppers.

However serious my gaffe may have been, they took it in good humor. It was clear that Podoltseva's laughter was a shield to ward off nervousness. She chain-smoked cigarette after cigarette hungrily, as if trying to stoke her body with enough nicotine to last two weeks. "Volodya will explain to you more about our Trust Group here in Leningrad after the demonstration," she said.

"Where will you be then?" I asked.

She crossed her index fingers and raised them in front of her eyes.

"You expect to be arrested?"

"Yes," she said. Again that nervous chuckle. "I expect to be arrested."

I watched another cigarette perish in her saucer. "For how many days?"

She shrugged. "Maybe overnight. Maybe fifteen days and a fine. Maybe. . . ." She shrugged again.

Their plan was simple. She and four or five fellow Trust Group members would hold up their banners at eight o'clock that night in front of a public monument. If their efforts to hide the location were successful, they might stand there for ten or fifteen minutes. If not, they might last a minute or two. The most likely consequence was a fifteen-day jail spell for "hooliganism." Then again, one team of players in this elaborate game could change the rules at any time.

I was reminded of the atmosphere surrounding anti-nuclear civil disobedience protests in the West, and I told them so. Seeing their curiosity, I described a recent demonstration at the U.S. nuclear test site in Nevada. Podoltseva grimaced when she heard that 200 people had been arrested. "You won't find 200 people with us tonight," she said with a deprecating wave at the city outside her window.

Gradually the facts of her life emerged. She had been trained at a good institute as a mathematician, but she lost her job when she became active in the Trust Group, a little more than two years ago. She has a teenaged daughter, who at one point in our conversation slipped into the kitchen to pour herself some tea. No husband was apparent. I asked her what she now did for a living.

"Trust," she replied, laughing again in that half self-mocking way. She admitted that living without a job in the Soviet Union is "very complicated," but did not volunteer any insights into how she managed it.

Then she showed me her hate mail, letters with no return addresses crudely scrawled to her home address. "Stop your disgusting activities," read one. "You and I have a date in the future."

I asked her about the goals of the Leningrad Trust Group. "Are you familiar with our declaration?" she asked, referring to the group's statement of principles adopted in April 1987. When I said yes, she seemed to feel that this should be enough of an answer. But I prodded a bit more, and finally a few things came out.

"It's a complicated process, not one that could have taken place ten or fifteen years ago. When a person takes part in one of the actions of our group, and for example protests the war in Afghanistan, he begins to understand that it's our disgrace that we started this war. He begins to understand what activism means, and what the struggle for peace means. This realization is the goal of our group.

"For me, peace means creating trust in our country, trust between a government and its people, trust between nations. Peace and human rights are indivisible. For there to be peace, our government must be a legal government, not a police state or a totalitarian state. By working for human rights, we're working for absolutely necessary conditions for peace.

"The moral atmosphere in our country is very sad, because our government just doesn't trust its people. But I believe we have a chance to change this situation, to heal our society. Either we have to admit to ourselves that we're slaves, and that we're powerless, and that there's nothing we can do, and calm ourselves down with that, or else we have to solve this problem somehow. The chance has arisen to do something, although it may be very little.

"Some say that our radicalism only leads to more and more confrontation. I don't agree. If we don't stand up to the government when it tries to fool us, there will be more catastrophes. And as soon as you start agreeing with the government, it's all over. You're theirs. They have you against the wall, and you won't be able to talk.

"There is a dangerous tendency in our country to believe that we are a peaceful country, that we are fighting for peace. It's a kind of mass hypnotization. Soviet people are very passive—most of them want peace, but they trust the government. That's why it's so important that we know the full truth about Afghanistan. The country that does not know its own history is condemned to repeat it."

The conversation dwindled. I saw her looking at the plastic alarm clock on her table. She seemed more and more pre-occupied, as if she had already begun to remove herself from this warm shabby kitchen. I asked Yaremenko and his wife Anna questions while Podoltseva put the teacups in the sink, wrote a note to her daughter, and put a few things in a plastic bag. When I asked if I could photograph her holding her poster, she ducked out of the room to brush her long hair, laughing quietly at her own vanity. The poster was hand-lettered in Russian, in blue paint:

Immediately
Put An End To
The Occupation
Of Afghanistan

It was time to go. She put on a green coat with a fur collar and opened the bedroom door to give a small, awkward wave good-bye to her daughter. Vladimir and Anna Yaremenko clung to one another and tried to smile as the door closed. Podoltseva and I stepped into the elevator and the metal gate snapped shut with a bone-shivering clang.

Across the street, we turned to wave at the two figures sil-houetted in the small square of warm yellow light. Once we had walked out of sight of her one safe refuge, Podoltseva seemed to withdraw into silence. I was silent as well, anxious to avoid another gaffe. I wanted only to observe, and I half-hoped to be given instructions, or at least a few hints as to what would be acceptable behavior at the demonstration. But Podoltseva was too enmeshed in her own inner struggle to think about me.

As we rode in a taxi through the darkening city, I thought of the image that some Westerners have of Trust Group members: romantically inclined martyrs who rather enjoy the drama and publicity of their arrests. There was nothing romantic or glamor-ous about this for Podoltseva. She was scared beyond words. As for publicity, it was clear that I would be the only Westerner present.

The taxi let us off near the square, and we walked up and down the street for a few minutes while Podoltseva furtively peered over the edge of her fur collar, looking to see if the others had shown. As we began walking toward the monument, I wanted to say to her, "Good luck." But before the words were out, we had drifted apart as if borne by two separate currents. She strolled behind the statue with a colleague and I took my place on a nearby bench. Soon four people were huddled discreetly in the dim light. The square seemed empty and peaceful save for a few passersby hurrying to catch their trolleybuses.

I was not prepared for the speed with which it happened. The four of them—Podoltseva, two men and a teenaged girl—slowly walked in front of the statue. One of the men helped the girl put on a cloth sandwich board that read, "Fewer missiles—more prosperity to the people." Podoltseva held up her poster and the other man unfurled a paper banner: "We don't need five million soldiers."

Suddenly, the scene was engraved on my mind: the four of them, their simple statements, the statue behind them, the trolleybuses of commuters, the violet sky. I had not intended to draw attention to myself with flash pictures, but I couldn't help reaching for my camera. When I looked up, two seconds later, the photo was gone, unless a photo of the backs of two dozen men in long coats is one worth risking a roll of film.

I couldn't believe how quickly they were arrested. They had been surrounded by both plainclothes and uniformed police and KGB men within three seconds of unfurling their statements. About a dozen passersby gathered around them as well. I watched the four of them be led away, each lightly held by the arm by two plainclothes men. There was no struggle, no shouting, no resistance of any kind. It was all ridiculously polite and calm. I couldn't see Podoltseva's face, but her walk was smooth, her head unbowed. She is probably glad to have that part over with, I thought.

Immediately I wondered if I should have taken a photograph, if I should have identified myself more clearly. If I'd pulled out my camera, would they have felt more constrained in making arrests, knowing a Western journalist was there? Or would they have merely seized it and ripped out my film, and begun to question *me*? Faced with uncertainty, I had hung back and made the split-second decision not to draw attention to myself. I had my reasons, of course: the other pictures on that roll, my exit customs, my next

Soviet visa. Perhaps the decision was the right one. But I also realized, sitting stunned on that freezing dark bench, that I had faced the same terrible choice that constantly faces Soviet citizens: do you risk singling yourself out in the eyes of the authorities if you have something to lose? In this case, I had acted the way most Soviet people do most of the time, and decided: no.

After they were led away, I cautiously approached the remaining cluster of people. A man was trying to persuade a plainclothes officer to let him read one of the banners. He got nowhere. Gradually the crowd dispersed. Both uniformed and plainclothes officers hung around the square to see if others would come. Less than ten minutes had elapsed since our taxi had arrived; clearly, they had been lying in wait. Were my slips to blame? But on the other hand, it had been too easy simply to follow us here.

I stood alone in the dark, unnoticed as far as I could tell, and felt a chill welling within me. There was no point in staying. I walked away from the square, stepping around the body of a drunk draped over a curb; the drunk seemed a fitting final detail. Disoriented, my toes numb, I wandered from wrong bus to wrong bus, unanswered questions coursing through me. What was the point of showing banners for three seconds, then getting fifteen-day jail terms? What was the point of arresting these people with such routine and methodical speed? It had been a lackluster performance by all parties, of a hackneyed choreography. I rode the buses and wanted only to be warm.

Back in my hotel room, I crawled under extra blankets, turned on the television and caught the end of a news segment about Red Army Day. Artillery guns swivelled smartly on their pedestals. Tall young soldiers in uniform, of whom any mother would be proud, told reporters about the latest advances in military preparedness. "No one will catch us unaware," one said. I turned off the television and thought of Podoltseva, her fingers aching for cigarettes, rolling over on a cold prison cot. We slept that night in the beds we had chosen.

Nearly six years earlier, on June 4, 1982, the eleven founders of the "Group to Establish Trust Between the USSR and the USA" had invited Western reporters to a Moscow apartment for a press conference announcing their existence. "The USSR and the USA possess the means to kill on a scale capable of putting an end to the history of human society," said the text of their founding appeal, signed by about thirty people. "A balance of terror cannot be a reliable guarantee of security in the world. Only trust between nations can create a firm assurance of the future. . . . This problem demands immediate action."

The Trust Group's appeal called for the creation of a "four-sided dialogue" where "average Soviet and American citizens are included on an equal footing with political figures." This was necessary because "it is entirely evident that politicians on both sides are incapable of coming to an agreement in the near future concerning any appreciable arms limitations, much less about substantive disarmament. Politicians are impeded in maintaining objectivity in questions of disarmament by their political interests and obligations." The appeal also called for abolition of nuclear weapons, limits on conventional weapons, and establishment of citizen, cultural, and scientific exchanges to create "conditions for an open exchange of opinions and the informing of the public of both countries on issues relating to the process of disarmament."

Although the Trust Group's appeal did not mention the Soviet Peace Committee, the Western press found comparisons irresistable. According to a *New York Times* article appearing the next day, Sergei Batovrin, a twenty-five-year-old artist and spokesman for the group, "made it plain that the impetus for the group's establishment flowered from their perception of the Soviet Committee for the Defense of Peace as an instrument of Soviet foreign policy, incapable of advancing disarmament proposals not previously sanctioned by the Kremlin."

Yet the founders insisted that they were not a dissident group, and that "any action taken against us would only be a result of a misunderstanding," as one of them put it. "If [the Soviet authorities] understand us correctly, they will not apply repressive measures to us," said Batovrin. "Our press always says that everyone should take part in the peace movement, and we see no contradiction between that and what we are doing."

Official Soviet reaction to the group, however, was swift and unequivocal. Within ten days several of the group's founders had been placed under house arrest; two who had previously applied to emigrate and been refused were suddenly given exit visas; and Batovrin and others were called in for "chats" with local KGB agents who warned them that their activities were "provocative and anti-social."

Westerners who had read the Trust Group's initial appeal were perplexed. To the Western eye, the Trust Group's positions seemed innocuous, carefully phrased in symmetrical language to avoid criticizing specific nuclear policies or blaming one side more than the other. "It is agreed by all who have read it that this appeal is not the least bit anti-Soviet and corresponds with official governmental views in many ways," wrote two British peace activists who visited the group in 1983. A 1982 Helsinki Watch report asserted that "the peace group's position had stuck close to the official Soviet line."

Few in the West understood that the Trust Group appeal was in fact a direct challenge to Soviet authorities. It called into question the enshrined assumption that the Soviet government and the Communist Party were already doing everything possible to create peace in the world. It rejected the hallowed tenet that the desire for peace among ordinary Soviets was already perfectly represented by official Soviet peace leaders. Its symmetrical wording implied that the Soviet and American governments were equally responsible for the arms race, which ran directly counter to the prevailing Soviet line.

The appeal did not lay out plans to take part in the official Soviet peace movement, but instead stated the necessity of creating an alternative to it, a network of "independent citizens' peace groups." By claiming that "due to their political interests and circumstances, politicians find it difficult to be objective on disarmament issues," the appeal cast doubt on the Soviet government's ability to keep the peace. By maintaining that "the time has come for the public . . . to participate in the decision-making process with the politicians," the appeal implied that the Soviet public did not at present participate in this process—another piece of heresy. And by calling for "conditions for an open exchange of opinions," the appeal made it clear that such conditions did not exist.

As Catherine Fitzpatrick, research director at the American human rights group Helsinki Watch, who was among the first Americans to visit the Trust Group and who soon became their main advocate and chronicler in the West, later put it in her book *From Below:* "The authorities understood what was 'anti-Soviet' about [the appeal]."

Unfortunately, most Westerners did not know enough about the Soviet Union to be able to look past the Trust Group's avoidance of criticizing specific Soviet arms policies and see how profoundly it was criticizing Soviet *processes* of peacemaking. The ensuing controversies over the Soviet government's treatment of the Trust Group were thus plagued by misunderstandings from the start. Because the Soviets appeared to be squashing a group for amplifying the official line on peace and disarmament, many Westerners—some with reluctance, some with glee—concluded that this official line must be insincere. The existence, and harassment, of the Trust Group was soon being trumpeted by conservative forces in the West as proof that official Soviet arms control policies were riddled with duplicity and hypocrisy.

But in fact, the Soviet government was not worried about the possibility of growing Soviet public support for a nuclear freeze, test ban, or no-first-use policy. It was not mainly worried about the spread of pacifism, nor was its almost panicky response to the Trust Group primarily rooted in a kneejerk reaction to independent initiative *per se*. The Soviet government was worried because it knew that the Trust Group had hit upon an uncomfortably powerful—and potentially popular—combination of ideas that, if unchecked, might have far-reaching effects on Soviet society.

The key term was "trust," and the idea that the arms race is perpetuated by "mistrust between the USA and the USSR." In a November 1982 interview, Batovrin spoke of "trust" as "a complex matter which is mainly about free exchange of information and unimpeded contact between people of different nations." Trust Group member Yuri Medvedkov, an internationally respected geographer and former Soviet secretary of the World Health Organization, said in 1982 that "trust is exchange, getting to know one another, trading opinions, going to each other's countries to understand each other's cultures."

In other words, the Trust Group was connecting long-smoldering resentments about free expression, free travel, and the right to organize independent groups to the emotionally powerful issue of peace. The group's ideology thus had the potential to have broad appeal both in the West and among Soviet citizens. With its linkage of human rights and peace, and its heretical assertions that the Soviet government's approach to peace might be failing, the Trust Group represented a fundamental threat to established Soviet ideas.

The founders of the Trust Group themselves probably were not aware of the immensity of the powder keg to which they had put a match. "In some ways the group members reminded me of the 'flower children' of the 1960s," Fitzpatrick of Helsinki Watch wrote after visiting them in September 1982. "They have the same childlike sincerity and simplicity and innocent, idealistic suggestions."

At the same time, the Trust Group had stumbled onto a brilliant strategy. From the beginning, its members were interested in a far broader range of issues than merely promoting exchanges and improving East-West relations. But traditional dissident human rights groups had at that time been thoroughly squashed, and it was not hard to predict what would happen to a new group that tried the old approach. Defining themselves as "peace activists" was a stunning tactical move that won them widespread press coverage, created an instant bevy of sympathizers in the West, and threw Soviet officials completely off guard.

"We were concerned about a lot of different issues, but we knew that if we started talking about human rights or Afghanistan in the beginning, we just wouldn't survive at all," says former Trust Group leader Olga Medvedkova. "So we had to keep to this very narrow agenda, the establishing of the human right to struggle for peace, and wait until we got bigger and more influential before we could broaden our agenda."

Trust Group members had expected trouble, but they initially hoped their emphasis on peace would protect them from the full wrath of the government. Mikhail Ostrovsky, a Trust Group founder who emigrated a month after its initial press conference, said in fall 1982 that "we had supposed that there would be some kind of hostile reaction on the part of the authorities. But we never anticipated that it would be on such a large scale, so extreme, and last for such a long time." Olga Medvedkova recalls that "we could never have imagined what would happen to us for supporting such a simple and harmless program as establishing contacts between rank-and-file citizens of East and West. But of course we were a challenge to the state, because it had a monopoly on everything, including peacemaking. We were a competing power for the part of the establishment represented by the Soviet Peace Committee.

We interfered with this committee's monopoly on relations with foreign peace groups, and so they couldn't stand us."

In July 1982, two members of the Trust Group—geographer Yuri Medvedkov and physicist Yuri Khronopolo—were arrested while they were on their way to a press conference to announce plans to meet a group of 200 Scandinavians who would soon arrive in Moscow on a Peace-Committee-sponsored "march for peace." The two men were jailed for fifteen days under charges of "hooliganism." Two other Trust Group members were temporarily sent out of town, and others were placed under house arrest.

Outraged Western peace activists sent long telegrams of protest to Yuri Zhukov, then president of the Soviet Peace Committee, who responded with even longer telegrams of his own. "You have been misled by false reports of Western mass media," wrote Zhukov. "Not a single person representing peace movement in the Soviet Union is being repressed and of course no one of them has ever been arrested. As for tiny group of eleven people pictured by Western press as independent peace movement. . . I was informed that two of these people . . . had beaten a woman in a bus and were sentenced to fifteen days on charges of hooliganism. You qualify their behavior as example of independent struggle for peace. I would call it flagrant breach of peace. But of course I cannot insist that your view of what is good and what is evil coincides with mine."

On August 5, the Trust Group attempted to hold a Hiroshima Day exhibition of Batovrin's anti-war paintings in an apartment. Foreign reporters were blocked from entering the apartment, police arrived and confiscated 88 of Batovrin's paintings, and the next day Batovrin himself was bundled off to a psychiatric hospital where, he later reported, "they told me only the government can work for peace." During August, members of American peace groups such as the Fellowship of Reconciliation and the War Resisters League waved protest signs calling for Batovrin's release in front of the Soviet Mission to the United Nations.

"Right now it's hard for me to speak because they're giving me strong drugs," said Batovrin in a taped message that was smuggled to the U.S. "I'm going to fight for peace no matter what . . . even in these conditions." On September 5, the *New York Times* reported that twenty leaders of the American anti-nuclear movement had signed a letter protesting "the double standard by which the Soviet government abides—applauding widespread public debate in the West, while crushing the most benign form of free expression at home." Two days later, Batovrin was released.

But Soviet authorities continued to try to bully the Trust Group into silence with interrogations, house arrests, phone cut-offs, threats of job loss, and even sabotage of one member's car. "The KGB was putting enormous pressure on all members of the group," Olga Medvedkova later recalled, "using arguments like: If you don't terminate your activities, we'll put you behind bars anyway. We won't charge you with fighting for peace, that's not illegal. . . . [Instead] they said, 'The Criminal Code is big, and we'll find some criminal article with which we can put you behind bars.'"

Only one person was explicitly arrested, tried, and sentenced for spreading the Trust Group's message: Alexander Shatravka, who already had spent ten years in and out of mental hospitals and who in 1974 had attempted to flee the country. (Finnish border guards had caught and returned him.) Shatravka was not a member of the Trust Group, but he had signed its initial appeal in June 1982 and then circulated it among fellow workers at a logging camp in Siberia. A month later he was arrested and sentenced to three years of labor camp for "having the intention of disseminating deliberately false ideas that denigrate the Soviet political and social system." A commission of legal experts who had studied the Trust Group's appeal testified at Shatravka's trial that the appeal was "slanderous" because it promoted "the well-known thesis of Western propaganda concerning the equal responsibility of imperialist and socialist countries." The commission further warned that the appeal "could give rise to incorrect ideas, especially among that part of the population which is not well-prepared politically."

Buoyed by Western support of their cause, Trust Group members continued to circulate their appeal, gathering a total of 900 signatures. Affiliated groups soon formed in Leningrad, Odessa, and Novosibirsk. In October 1982, the group issued a proposal for an international ten minutes of silence for peace on January 1, 1983. The main author of this proposal, a twenty-four-year-old teacher named Oleg Radzinsky, was soon arrested and charged with "anti-Soviet agitation and propaganda" under the supposedly unrelated charge of teaching banned Soviet authors in his literature classes.

"Although we do not criticize in any way the peace initiatives of the government, we are nevertheless persecuted by the authorities," complained Batovrin in November 1982. By this time, group members knew what it was about their ideas that irritated Soviet officials, but they continued to express innocence and bewilderment when they spoke to the Western press. In a January 1983 statement, the Group insisted that their "activities do not contradict the government's policy" and called the measures taken against them "inexplicable." The apparent paradox in the official reaction to the group continued to win them wide sympathy and press coverage in the West.

Having failed to suppress the group, Soviet authorities shifted tactics and launched a campaign to discredit it. They looked for an Achilles heel, and found one: ten of the group's fifteen members were Jewish refuseniks whose applications to emigrate from the Soviet Union had been turned down. Soon Soviet authorities were proclaiming that the Trust Group was merely a bunch of malcontents who were trying to provoke the authorities into letting them leave the country under the cleverly protective rubric of peace.

On November 26, 1982, the Soviet news agency TASS denounced members of the group as "anti-Sovieteers, renegades, and criminals," "moral degenerates," and "a bunch of swindlers, trying to infiltrate the peace movement as a Trojan horse." TASS claimed the group's formation was "an act of provocation of Western secret services" and said there was evidence that the group was trying to "taint the true Soviet movement for peace" and "disrupt contacts of peace supporters in the USSR and the West." At the same time, the authorities continued their harassment of Group members, knowing that if they succeeded in radicalizing them, turning them into outcasts and pushing them to the edge of society, then the danger inherent in their ideas would be defused.

Catherine Fitzpatrick reported in 1982 that the group itself was aware that "becoming lopsided with Jewish refuseniks left them open to criticism." She and others pointed out that refuseniks were in general well-educated, already skeptical of official propaganda, and unafraid of tangling with Soviet authorities; it should thus not be surprising that they would play a leading role in an unsanctioned group.

Nevertheless, the impression lingered that Trust Group members were not fully "ordinary" members of Soviet society, and it may have been true that at least a few members initially hoped their activities would encourage the authorities to expel them. In a 1982 interview, one of the Trust Group's refusenik members, Mark Reitman, admitted that some refuseniks who joined the group were at first more interested in getting out of the country than in working for peace. "But . . . if before [joining the group], many had put an exit visa as a first priority, and peace as a second priority," he said, "then afterwards, peace became the main goal."

The Trust Group faced a choice: to back down, realize they had miscalculated the severity of official resistance to their ideas, and find a less confrontational way to spread their ideas within their society; or to continue a public crusade, depending on Western reporters and visitors for protection. In January 1983, five of the Trust Group's fifteen members, including most of its non-refuseniks, decided to pursue the former course. They announced that they were withdrawing from the group and forming a new association called Friendship and Dialogue which would engage in "educational and research-oriented activity" in contrast to the "demonstrational activity" of the Trust Group.

The remaining members continued to meet openly with Westerners, organize public events, and express bewilderment at the repressions aimed against them. They attempted to hold an exhibition of anti-war photographs in a private apartment in February 1983; the exhibition was broken up by the KGB, one group member was attacked and beaten by six men, and another was arrested and jailed for fifteen days. Batovrin and another group member, Sergei Rosenoer, protested with a hunger strike that lasted 32 days. "Our worry over the nuclear question, which has made our lives a trial since we began to put it into words, has involuntarily taken the form of an anti-nuclear fast," wrote Batovrin in a statement printed by the European Nuclear Disarmament (END) *Journal.* "While megatons accumulate life looks as fragile as a paper landscape. . . . The threat originates not in launching pads or in rocket barrels but in the failure to find common ground."

Batovrin's uncompromising, charismatic style did much to set the tone for the Trust Group's early days. The son of a high-ranking Soviet diplomat, Batovrin had as a child watched picketers in New York City protesting the 1968 invasion of Czechoslovakia from the windows of the Soviet Mission to the United Nations. Returning to the Soviet Union as a teenager, Batovrin rejected the establishment values of his father and became a hippie and an artist. In his early twenties he was briefly put in a psychiatric hospital after attempting to organize an independent art exhibition. He and his wife applied to emigrate, but his father refused to give the necessary parental permission; by 1981, when his father relented, the gates for Jewish emigration open in the late 1970s had been closed.

Batovrin claims that twice the KGB offered him an exit visa if he would stop his activities in the Trust Group, and that both times he refused. In May 1983, however, the authorities gave Batovrin an explicit choice: prison, psychiatric hospital, or immediate emigration. Batovrin chose emigration, and soon arrived in New York with his wife and mother, where he began organizing U.S. support for the Trust Group. Before leaving, he and his colleagues stuffed several thousand Moscow mailboxes with leaflets listing the addresses of American peace groups and suggesting that ordinary Soviets write them to obtain pen pals.

During the next year, the Trust Group continued to issue appeals, hold seminars with Western activists, and circulate proposals for citizen exchanges, ranging from television spacebridges to the creation of a "Soviet-American marriage bureau." In May 1983, two women British peace activists brought Trust Group member Olga Medvedkova with them to a meeting at the Soviet Peace Committee. A Peace Committee official, Oleg Kharkhardin, became incensed and refused to continue the meeting in Medvedkova's presence. "The only reason why the Western press won't listen to your official peace movement is because you persecute the independent one," the British women told him.

On Hiroshima Day in 1983, the Trust Group successfully held a small poetry reading and exhibited peace placards, buttons, and literature. But matters worsened again in December 1983, when several Trust Group members were rounded up and Medvedkova, a petite woman who was pregnant at the time, was accused of assaulting a police officer. Before her trial in March 1984, Medvedkova told Western supporters in a taped message that "the hawks" were trying to crush the group and that "facts and publicity are my only rescue." Medvedkova was found guilty and given a two-and-a-half year prison term which was, however, suspended due to her pregnancy and to the storm of protest building in the West on her behalf.

In spring 1984, the Trust Group began taking more direct

action. Using flower seeds sent to them by the Fellowship of Reconciliation, Trust Group members sowed a small "peace garden" in front of a Moscow police station and held signs that read "Flowers Instead of Bombs." The garden was bulldozed two weeks later after the plants sprouted forming the words "Ban the Bomb" in both English and Russian. The Group began issuing a small *samizdat* (self-published) journal called *Trust* and holding weekly seminars on topics such as the economic conversion of military factories. In May 1984, they took to the streets with a petition calling for the resumption of arms control negotiations. Five members were arrested after collecting 350 signatures in a few minutes, and one was jailed for fifteen days. An attempt to hold a Hiroshima Day "peace march" with rallies and lectures on nuclear disarmament failed when the KGB put the march's organizers under house arrest.

Nevertheless, the group stayed alive. For the next two years they organized regular events and seminars, met steadily with Western visitors, replaced members who emigrated with new ones, and clung to their message. Catherine Fitzpatrick describes the Trust Group during these years as a coalition of scientists interested in arms control, artists and intellectuals interested in free expression and communication with the West, and members of the youth counterculture interested in street protests on pacifist issues such as conscientious objection and the war in Afghanistan. These very different subgroups "were essentially held together by the repression against them," Fitzpatrick says.

With few exceptions, Western press coverage of the group dwindled to brief news items about one member or another being arrested, detained, or jailed. This raised a dilemma for the group: how to remain active and visible without allowing their activities, and the resulting crackdowns, to be used as ammunition by Western conservatives to sustain the very Cold War they wished to dismantle. As Joanne Landy and Thomas Harrison, leaders of a group called Campaign for Peace and Democracy East and West which supports independent peace movements in Eastern Europe, wrote in 1987: "The problem, of course, is that sympathy for the victims of Communist oppression tends to get translated into support for the American government's conservative and militaristic brand of anti-Communism."

Trust Group members had long been aware of this dynamic. In

January 1983, Sergei Batovrin had observed that Western journalists "prefer to report on the KGB's activity in suppressing the group rather than on the activity of the group itself." Two Americans visiting the group in August 1983 reported that group members had said: "We regret that the Western press has focused on harassments rather than our programmatic proposals. Too often, the Western press has used our activities to encourage anti-Communism." When President Reagan brought up Oleg Radzinsky's case on a Radio Liberty broadcast as an example of Soviet human rights abuse, Radzinsky wrote to him and told him to stop taking political advantage of his case.

But Trust Group members were not always able to guard against unwanted conservative backing of their cause, and at times they appeared to invite it. In September 1984, the exiled Batovrin began publishing his own magazine, called *Return Address Moscow,* which emphasized horrific stories about Trust Group members being held as political prisoners. Members of the group still living in Moscow were disturbed by the magazine's many inaccuracies and sensational tone, and the fact that Batovrin, although working entirely on his own, had published it in the Trust Group's name. "We have our losses, and it is inhuman to forget them, and so I can understand that Sergei is very much preoccupied with this," Yuri Medvedkov said in an interview that appeared in the magazine *Christianity and Crisis* in August 1985. "But the main thing is not to overlook the positive aspects. We have achieved a positive response to some of our proposals."

Soviet officials seized upon the magazine as further evidence that the Trust Group was merely an oppositional human rights group in disguise. After reading Batovrin's brilliant but bitter diatribes against the repressive machinery of the Soviet state, many Westerners also found themselves wondering whether the Trust Group was truly as peace-oriented and non-partisan as they had once believed.

Batovrin had arrived in New York with many painful stories to pour out to those he considered his colleagues, but most leaders of mainstream Western peace groups did not give him the kind of interest and attention that he felt he and the Trust Group deserved. The nuclear freeze movement was in full swing, American peace movement leaders believed they were on the verge of creating a new public consensus on nuclear weapons policy, and while many were sympathetic to the Trust Group members' plight, they had little time and energy to spare from their campaigns. Besides, Moscow was far away; no one could be exactly sure what the Trust Group stood for; and Batovrin's own writings and speeches seemed more calculated to reinforce kneejerk anti-Sovietism than to nurture a climate conducive for arms control.

Frustrated and disillusioned, Batovrin began to lambast Western peace groups, particularly those that had contacts with the Soviet Peace Committee. "Do exchanges and cooperative projects involving Western peace organizations and the official Soviet Peace Council [sic] serve the cause of improving mutual understanding between East and West?" Batovrin asked rhetorically in an interview with himself published in *Return Address Moscow*. "Unfortunately they do not. Exchanges and joint activities in which the Soviet side is filled with Soviet officials only create the illusion that something is happening. Western participants in exchanges often do not realize this, being insufficiently familiar with the nature of Soviet society."

In fall 1985, Batovrin and the Trust Group were suddenly catapulted to fame during the controversy over the awarding of the 1985 Nobel Peace Prize to International Physicians for the Prevention of Nuclear War (IPPNW). The furor began when it was revealed that Evgeny Chazov, the Soviet co-president of the group, had in 1974 joined other prominent Soviet academicians in signing a letter condemning physicist and human rights campaigner Andrei Sakharov. In a *New York Times* op-ed, Batovrin called the Soviet affiliate of IPPNW "a front for a non-existent mass movement" and claimed that "it has not distributed a single book or published a single leaflet . . . or held a single public lecture."

While Batovrin's indignation was real, the *New York Times* took liberties in editing his article to increase its damage to IPPNW's reputation. Without Batovrin's knowledge, an editor spiced up the first two paragraphs with new sentences calling Chazov "a stooge of the Kremlin with little real concern for either peace or human rights" and IPPNW "a Government-run propaganda arm that justifies competition, not co-existence, with the West." The *New York Times* also added the provocative headline, "Dissidents Deserve Dr. Chazov's Nobel," implying that Batovrin believed the prize should have gone to his own group, and it twice used the word "dissident" to describe the Trust Group, a label Batovrin had carefully avoided.

Both Batovrin's op-ed and a *Wall Street Journal* editorial that similarly contrasted IPPNW with "the Soviet Union's real peace activists" were widely reprinted in U.S. newspapers and magazines. Batovrin was playing the latest variation of an old theme: Western peace activists are naive dupes, the official Soviet peace movement is only propaganda to throw the West off guard, you can't trust the Russians. American activists were deeply split. Some sympathized with Batovrin, because his overall point that the Soviet affiliate of IPPNW had not done all it could to promote nuclear education within the Soviet Union was generally true. Others criticized him for his factual errors, his vitriolic tone, and his willingness to stab leaders of his own cause in the back. The perception that the Trust Group was a radical, dissident group more interested in gaining Western publicity for its troubles than in improving East-West relations gained strength.

Predictably, more moderate views about official and quasi-official Soviet peace groups put forward by other Trust Group members gained far less attention. Yuri Medvedkov insisted in 1984 that the Trust Group "always recommends that Western peace groups maintain contact with the Soviet Peace Committee. We provide some competition for the Soviet Peace Committee, but we are not against it." Vladimir and Maria Fleishgakker, Trust Group members who emigrated in 1984, said in 1985 that "we don't sling mud" at the Peace Committee and added that the Soviet affiliate of IPPNW had "done something useful, a positive action, with the doctors' talk show on television [about nuclear war]. . . . Even dependent groups have some positive sides."

Some vocal Trust Group supporters claimed that other Americans were cold-shouldering the group because of a fear that this would endanger their cozy contacts with the Soviet Peace Committee. Perhaps this was true for some of the less self-confident groups. The Fellowship of Reconciliation, however, demonstrated that such caution was unnecessary by openly meeting with the Trust Group while at the same time organizing a number of successful exchanges with the Soviet Peace Committee and the Russian Orthodox Church.

The dampening of enthusiasm for the Trust Group on the part

of some Western peace activists had more subtle roots, as well. Many Americans who visited Trust Group members simply had little desire to return. Those interested in developing practical exchanges—a pen pal project, an art exchange, a school-to-school or sister-city program—found that Trust Group members, already ostracized and alienated from their society, had neither the contacts nor the inclination to work within Soviet schools and other institutions to make such exchanges a reality.

Whether or not this had been their original goal, many Trust Group members were indeed handed exit visas; by 1987, a total of twenty-two core members of the Trust Group had emigrated. This continuing exodus made it difficult for Westerners to sustain contact with the group, and given the jealousy and suspicion with which Jewish refuseniks were generally regarded by other Soviets, it also helped guarantee that the Trust Group's domestic constituency remained limited to those already on the margins of Soviet society. "Most Soviets see right through the Trust Group's game," a Western correspondent based in Moscow remarked in 1988. "They consider them either eccentrics or opportunists, and they won't have anything to do with them."

Still, by early 1986 the Trust Group had chapters in eight Soviet cities, about 2,000 supporters, and growing attendance at its weekly seminars despite periodic crackdowns. In February 1986, sixteen Trust Group members were detained on their way to a seminar; most were released, but others were beaten, given fifteen-day jail terms, or put into psychiatric hospitals. After the Chernobyl meltdown, Trust Group members took to the streets with posters declaring "Atoms Can Never Be Peaceful." Most of those arrested were soon released, but one was sentenced to nine months of labor camp. In early August 1986, two Americans flew to Moscow to hand out leaflets describing health precautions against radiation exposure in a joint action coordinated by the Trust Group; the Americans were nabbed in about fifteen minutes, held for an hour's questioning, then let go. Two weeks later, two British activists repeated the action, and this time KGB plainclothesmen only watched and did not interfere.

By mid-1986, Mikhail Gorbachev's more relaxed attitude toward informal political expression was beginning to reveal itself, and most of the Trust Group's major political prisoners were soon released. Alexander Shatravka was freed from labor camp in July

1986 and allowed to emigrate to New York. Vladimir Brodsky, a physician, refusenik, and long-time Trust Group activist who had been sentenced to three years of labor camp in August 1985 on fabricated charges of assaulting a police officer, was released in September 1986 and permitted to emigrate to Israel with his wife. That same month, Olga and Yuri Medvedkov were also handed exit visas.

With the departure of the Brodskys and the Medvedkovs, the Trust Group was compelled to re-group. Those remaining had joined in 1984 or later, were not as good with foreign languages, and did not have as many international contacts. Of the fragile coalition of scientists, artists, and counterculture youth, only the youth were left in appreciable numbers. Most expected to spend their lives in the Soviet Union and were committed to internal political reform. They felt little sense of continuity with the original founders, who in turn felt little connection to them. (In 1987, a battle-weary Batovrin, still frustrated with the American peace movement but glad that his friends had been released from prison, dropped his efforts on behalf of the Trust Group and began concentrating on his art.).

By early 1987, repressions against the group had more or less come to a halt. Members were allowed to carry out their seminars and publish their magazine without harrassment, although their street demonstrations still often ended with arrests, detentions, and jail sentences. For five years the Trust Group had fought simply for the right to exist, for "the opportunity to defend peace," as their original appeal had put it. Now that they were being left largely unmolested, they needed a new *raison d'etre*. As the unifying pressure of repression was lifted, the group began to splinter. One faction announced to the Western press in December 1986 that the group had disbanded. Another, larger faction quickly denied this, and began to work on a new "declaration of principles" made public in April 1987.

The new declaration reflected the Trust Group's shift of interests away from disarmament and international exchange and toward domestic Soviet issues of militarism and human rights. Although the declaration still called for East-West "trust-building" measures such as joint cultural centers, television shows, and children's exchanges, most of this language was recycled verbatim from earlier appeals. More significantly, the declaration condemned "military-patriotic education," the war in Afghanistan, and the absence of an alternative to military service for young men. It called human rights and peace "inseparably linked" and presented a human rights wishlist for the Soviet Union that included the right of free travel and emigration, free circulation of information, "irreproachable adherence to the constitutional rights and freedoms of citizens," and an amnesty for all political prisoners. The Trust Group also included environmental degradation and nuclear power among their concerns and pointed out that "by cutting military expenditures, many internal problems could be dealt with in the USSR."

In May 1987, thanks to pressure from several Western peace groups, a Trust Group representative, Irina Krivova, was allowed to speak for ten minutes at an international "peace meeting-dialogue" sponsored by the Soviet Peace Committee. For a short time it appeared as though a reconciliation might be possible between the Trust Group and the Peace Committee, but such hopes (cherished more by Westerners than by either the Trust Group or the Peace Committee) soon dissolved. The Trust Group rejected the Peace Committee's offer to include one member of the Trust Group on the Soviet delegation to the 1987 European Nuclear Disarmament convention in Coventry, England, when it became clear that this offer was conditional upon the Trust Group bringing its platform into alignment with that of the Peace Committee. The Peace Committee responded by sending a woman to Coventry who had belonged to the faction of the Trust Group that had declared itself defunct in December 1986, and then loudly announcing to the Western press that the Trust Group would be fully represented at the conference. Although the sham was soon exposed, it did little to build trust between the Peace Committee and the Trust Group.

Also in spring 1987, the Trust Group changed its full name to the "Group to Establish Trust Between the East and West" instead of the "USA and USSR" to reflect its growing ties with like-minded groups in Western and Eastern Europe, such as the Green Party in West Germany, the Radical Party in Italy, Freedom and Peace in Poland, and Charter 77 in Czechoslovakia. A separate but closely linked human rights group called Democracy and Humanism arose alongside the Trust Group, aimed at attempting "to restore the historical truth about the country's past and present" and "to strive to bring about the establishment of democracy in the USSR."

In June 1987, seven Trust Group members were prevented from joining a Soviet-American "peace walk" from Leningrad to Moscow sponsored by the Peace Committee. Nevertheless, near the end of the walk more than a dozen Trust Group members managed to address several hundred of the walkers in a campground outside of Moscow. A shouting match soon erupted between the Trust Group members and several infuriated Soviet walkers, with a young Peace Committee translator attempting to interpret the mêlée for the astonished Americans.

Some of the American walkers later visited Trust Group members in their apartments, but many came away with mixed feelings about the group. "It seemed as though their agenda was rapidly becoming marginalized, that they were having trouble adapting themselves to the new changes," commented one walker. Others remarked upon the Trust Group's "negativity" and "emphasis on the dark side." British activist Kate Soper noted in the *END Journal* in 1987 that Trust Group members were pessimistic that the newly formed independent ecological groups would be able to accomplish anything. "We sometimes had the feeling that the Trust Group might be wrong," she wrote, "[and] that more was now permitted in the way of independent action than they were prepared to admit."

Beginning in summer 1987, the Trust Group, which had been the only surviving independent political entity in the Soviet Union for nearly five years, suddenly became just one of hundreds of informal democratic groups, "new left" clubs, and even informal peace groups in Moscow. With old dissident titans such as Andrei Sakharov and Lev Timofeyev back in Moscow and available for interviews, few Western reporters felt the need to seek out "the boys and girls in the Trust Group," as Timofeyev once termed them, and Western press coverage of their activities dropped to almost nothing, a fact which concerned the Trust Group a good deal.

Nikolai Khramov, an energetic twenty-five-year-old with a trim beard, thick glasses, and the self-confident bearing of a seasoned activist, is now one of the Trust Group's main spokespersons. Khramov lives in a one-room apartment in a quiet part of southeastern Moscow; an Amnesty International banner and several hundred Western peace buttons and stickers hang on his walls. He speaks fluent German but little English, and answers questions in swift Russian between pauses to stoke his pipe.

A son of the intelligentsia, Khramov has paid his dues for his convictions. He was kicked out of journalism school at Moscow State University and expelled from Komsomol when he became active in the Trust Group in 1984. Exiled Trust Group members recall that Khramov "always had a piece of chalk in his pocket and would write peace signs on walls and sidewalks." Khramov also distributed his own handmade peace buttons and organized several "anti-war" concerts at the university. When the Trust Group planted its peace garden in spring 1984, Khramov was the one who found the trowels. In summer 1984, he was arrested three times for collecting signatures on the streets for Trust Group petitions, each time spending fifteen days in jail and protesting with a hunger strike.

Why did he join the Trust Group? "I wasn't a hippie, and I didn't really take part in the youth movement, or know people in any of the human rights groups," says Khramov. "But in December 1983 I met some members of the Trust Group, and I started going to their seminars. And I understood that I wanted to be free, to freely talk about these ideas, and to join in this group's activities. I understood that I would have to pay for this at the university, but my desire to be free turned out to be stronger."

Khramov's father, a poet and well-placed member of the Writer's Union, strongly disapproved of his son's activities; once, in December 1985, Khramov's father burst into a Trust Group seminar with four KGB plainclothesman in tow, shouting "Eighteen-year-olds shouldn't be allowed to discuss politics! Take them home to their parents!" Although his family is still not happy about his work in the Trust Group, Khramov says they are less afraid for him than they once were. And he credits his father with instilling in him a love for classical Russian literature, particularly the works of Tolstoy, that has influenced much of his thinking.

Khramov was the sort of Trust Group member—fearless, well-connected, and very bright—whom Soviet authorities most dreaded. Having failed to discourage him with three arrests, KGB officers were soon threatening to draft him into the Army, despite his medical exemption for poor eyesight. Khramov refused to leave the Trust Group, and in October 1984 was served a draft notice. He returned it with a long written explanation of why he could not in conscience serve in the military. On the day that he was supposed to report to the draft office, two men met him on the street near his home and took him to a police station; from there he was hauled off to the airport to join other conscripts on a flight to the Amur region in the Far East. The KGB telephoned his parents and told them to bring warm clothes to the airport. "My parents tried to convince me to accept things the way they were, and to take the path of least resistance," he recalls. "But I told them I was not going to accept this."

On the long flight east, Khramov sat between two sergeants, thinking about his parents, his girlfriend, his home left behind. "But I also felt a certain joy," he says. "I felt an inner freedom, because I knew that I had made my choice, and that I had said everything I wanted to say. I realized, of course, that there was uncertainty ahead, and maybe even prison or labor camp. But still I felt free. I knew how I was going to act."

When Khramov arrived at the military base, he was placed in a construction unit with other new recruits, whose attitude toward him, he recalls, "was mostly compassion mixed with curiosity. Most of them assumed I was a Baptist." At first the commanders of his unit did not know what to do with this calm young man who refused to obey orders. Perplexed, they isolated him from the other soldiers until instructions arrived from above: Make him conform. "They tried to make me do the things that every soldier is supposed to do. And when I refused, I was beaten up by some soldiers and an officer. So I went on a hunger strike, and I was immediately taken to the psychiatric department of the local military hospital."

After what he calls a "difficult" month in this department, a military officer came to Khramov and told him that a criminal case would be launched against him if he did not go back to the Army. When Khramov suggested that they arrest him for refusing to carry arms, he was transferred to the psychiatric department of a nearby civilian hospital, where he spent an uneventful five weeks. After civilian doctors declared him sane, he was transferred back to the military hospital, but this time to the ophthalmology department for eye tests. He spent another quiet two months here, and even got a job as hospital librarian. Finally, the doctors gave him an ultimatum: military service or prison. Khramov chose prison.

Three days later, he was suddenly released, officially for medical reasons, and flown back to Moscow, where he learned for the first time that an international protest campaign on his behalf had been under way for four months. Within weeks he was again an active leader in the Trust Group.

Khramov is now preoccupied with creating a civilian alternative to military service, and under his influence this has become the Trust Group's major issue. He keeps track of Soviet conscientious objectors, many of whom are forcibly drafted into the Army or placed in psychiatric hospitals, and publicizes their cases in the West. "Right now in the Soviet Union we have no legal right to refuse to serve, not even on religious grounds," says Khramov, "and the punishment for refusal is up to three years of prison." But he is hopeful that the Soviet Union will soon follow the example of Poland, which recently created a legal conscientious objector status.

Why has the Soviet military so adamantly refused to allow for conscientious objection? Khramov speculates that "it's because the Soviet Union, and also Russia, has traditionally been a militaristic state, with the military at the top of society. There's no real danger for them if 10,000 people are carrying out some civil service alternative. But they don't want to surrender, or to be slightly moved aside, even in such a small way. It's a question of ideology. Every day, every year, more and more young people all over the world are refusing military service. It means that the whole idea of the Army, and of militarism, is being undermined."

Another top concern for the current Trust Group is generally opposing what is known as "military-patriotic education" in Soviet society. Khramov believes there has been "a new wave of patriotism" created by the return of Afghanistan veterans and the proliferation of amateur military clubs for boys run by veterans "who teach the kids everything they've learned about killing." What disturbs him most about these clubs is that they are springing from a grassroots movement rather than a government-sponsored campaign. "Still, military-patriotic education begins much earlier than the time when these kids voluntarily go to these clubs," he says. "It begins the very first time a person falls into the hands of the government. Even in kindergarten, the boys are celebrated as future warriors. It starts with innocent activities like learning songs about spies and the Red Army. And then in the ninth and tenth grade, four hours a week are spent on 'military training.' They do drills, they learn songs, they play war games."

The Trust Group tries to counter this mentality through its seminars and articles on nonviolence and pacifism, but Khramov admits that the task is far too huge for them. "A lot of young people don't want to come to our meetings because they've heard rumors like, 'the Trust Group is trying to undermine the Soviet government.' And we try to tell them it's not true, that we're not trying to undermine our government or any government. We're just simply for peace. But we have to explain these simple things again and again. And meanwhile the press and the authorities accuse us of 'instigating the youth to shirk their sacred, holy obligations.'"

A third current focus for the Trust Group is human rights. "There are traditional human rights groups in the Soviet Union, like Lev Timofeyev's Press Club Glasnost, and we are distinct from them," Khramov explains, "but we work together. We consider ourselves at heart members of the same organization." The Trust Group also has a close relationship with the informal political party formed in May 1988 called the Democratic Union. Evgenia Debryanskaya, a leader in the Moscow Trust Group, was for several months also a leader in the Democratic Union (until an internal dispute forced her to quit in fall 1988). In October 1988, Leningrad Trust Group leader Ekaterina Podoltseva stated that in essence the Leningrad Trust Group and the Democratic Union had merged.

Khramov, however, denies that such a merger has taken place in Moscow, and says that the two groups work in "different dimensions." While the Democratic Union has a fixed membership and an explicit political platform, he calls the Trust Group a "fundamental movement" which unites "all people who partially or fully support our ideas." Although there is some competition between the groups for Western media attention, there is overlap rather than rivalry for members and attendence at events. "Our group was one of the first non-official groups, and it united people with a very, very wide spectrum of convictions," he says. "Now when there are many groups it is natural that people choose, and some have left the Trust Group. But from a certain point of view it is even better, because when someone in these times comes to us it means that he really shares our ideas."

Khramov, who calls himself "a left-wing liberal democrat," says the Trust Group "has a political character. We openly use the ideas of Gandhi, Martin Luther King, and the principles of nonviolent resistance. But we are not a political group in the sense that we strive to seize political power. We are closer to the philosophy of Petra Kelly of the German Greens, who said, 'Politics for us is not a means of getting into power, but a means of expressing our views and ideas.'

"Yesterday some Swedish friends from the Fellowship of Reconciliation asked us, 'Are you a human rights group or a peace group?' And we answered that we aren't a human rights group in the narrow sense. We aren't an ecological group in the narrow sense. We aren't a peace group in the narrow sense. We are a human rights, and an ecological, and a peace group. We consider these programs indivisible. Our group rose out of a simple, pure concern, that there should be more contacts between simple people. But since then we've grown, both in numbers and in goals. Now we're concerned with equality, human rights, peace, trust, disarmament, and ecology.

"For us, peace is not only the absence of war. It's completely indivisible from the word justice. We want people to truly live in peace, to be free of living under the violence and force of governmental power, and to be free of persecutions for their convictions." In cooperation with several other informal political groups, the Trust Group has staged several rallies against the Chinese government's violent suppression of China's pro-democracy student movement, and in spring 1990 it helped organize demonstrations in Moscow and Leningrad protesting the Soviet government's economic squeeze on Lithuania and demanding a nonviolent resolution to the conflict.

Khramov admits, regretfully, that the Trust Group spends little time on disarmament or ecological issues, and its citizen diplomacy efforts are limited to arranging for visiting Western activists to give occasional seminars. "Unfortunately, we are so few, and we don't have enough time to fulfill even the narrow tasks which we have set for ourselves," he says. "When the group began six years ago, it was a citizen diplomacy group rather than a pacifist group. But over the years the character of the group has changed as more people with pacifist views, especially young people, have joined.

And we think we must mostly be concerned with such issues as an alternative to military service, because no one else is likely to do that except us."

Alexander Rubchenko, another active Trust Group member, also admits that "we feel strongly about the peace movement and removing the nuclear threat, but it does not have primary importance in our activities now." Rubchenko, a soft-spoken young man with long brown hair and a slight limp, once worked as a stage decorator for a film studio, but was kicked out of his art institute when he joined the Trust Group in 1984. He is now unemployed and living on a disability pension of twenty-six rubles a month. Like Khramov, he has been frequently arrested and sometimes beaten, and in fall 1988 the KGB visited his parents and "tried to scare them by telling them I could be sent away from Moscow, and that I take part in anti-social activities and am a public enemy."

Rubchenko says plainly that "all our actions are aimed at protesting Soviet militarism and Soviet domination in different regions of the world." In February 1988, he outlined a much darker picture of current Soviet reality than Khramov, and a brief debate between them ensued. For Rubchenko, the glass of *perestroika* was mostly empty, and for Khramov it was, if not half-full, at least somewhat full. "A lot has been accomplished in international politics, the climate is much warmer," said Rubchenko, "but at the same time, though, there have been no changes in the USSR."

"You can't say there have been *no* changes," objected Khramov.

"The same problems exist," Rubchenko replied. "More than 150 political prisoners in psychiatric hospitals, for example. And people have not freed themselves from the fear of past centuries."

"Although it's not as bad," Khramov amended, "as it was two years ago—"

"In the provinces the changes are not felt," Rubchenko said firmly.

"In Moscow and Leningrad some changes are felt," insisted Khramov. "People are not so afraid. They are willing to join groups and get involved."

The Trust Group still holds several demonstrations a year, often in cooperation with other informal groups. But other days now loom larger on their calendars than Hiroshima Day: April 26, the anniversary of the Chernobyl meltdown; August 21, the anniversary of the 1968 invasion of Czechoslovakia; and October 30, an unofficial day of remembrance for Soviet political prisoners. In general, Khramov says the group is moving slightly away from street actions and toward concentrating on seminars and on producing its monthly magazine, *Day by Day*. They now print about 3,000 copies of each issue and sell them on the streets, as well as distributing them to Trust Group contacts in cities such as Baku, Kuibyshev, Odessa, Lvov, Riga, and Leningrad.

Khramov and other Trust Group members know how to laugh, but their gatherings tend to be rather somber affairs. During a Trust Group seminar that I attended in January 1989, ten young men and one woman gathered on wooden benches in Khramov's Moscow apartment to hear him read a long prepared lecture on the history of nonviolence in Russia and the Soviet Union. For more than an hour, Khramov turned pages in a composition book while his audience listened with respect and attention, clearly appreciating this opportunity to hear history previously unheard.

Later, Khramov read the texts of several appeals on behalf of conscientious objectors. The others nodded their heads soberly and said little. A visitor from an ecological group reported on a recent informal ecological conference in Moscow, and then I was invited to take the floor. Soon I was besieged with questions. What did American peace groups know about the Trust Group? Did any newspapers write stories about them anymore? What did Americans think of Gorbachev? Did I think their tactics were an effective way of reaching their goals? What concrete joint actions might be possible with Western groups? After tea, the young people drifted home, but Khramov and I kept interviewing one another until three in the morning.

It is the Trust Group's role to remain forever dissatisfied, forever astringent, forever demanding that things can be better than they are. Others may sing praises to the improvements *perestroika* has brought, but Trust Group members believe that someone has to keep pointing out what is still wrong and pushing back the edge of change. They will never trust those in power, and they will always find something to complain about. "We are by nature oppositionists," Alexander Rubchenko says, with a trace of a smile.

Such people can try one's patience. But it would be necessary to invent them if they did not exist. The Trust Group has stretched the spectrum of debate on peacemaking within the Soviet Union and opened up a middle ground that has been occupied by other, less confrontational Soviet peacemakers and citizen diplomats. They have also compelled many Westerners in the peace movement to think hard about uncomfortable Soviet realities. For all its "negativity," the Trust Group has made a difference.

Somewhere around two in the morning, I press Khramov to tell me what sort of *positive* vision he has for peace. I know very well what he is against—but what is he for? It is a new question for him, and he has trouble answering it. Finally he says: "I would be happy to feel that I live in a free democratic country which never threatens its citizens or its neighbors."

Of course, he says, they have more hope now that this vision might be realized than they did several years ago. "But even before, we were not pessimistic," he adds. "I can give you an example from your own country, from the time of the Vietnam War. A single demonstrator against the war was standing with a poster in front of a military base, alone, in heavy rain. And someone asked him, 'Why are you standing here? Surely you aren't thinking that you are going to change something, are you?' And he said, 'I'm not trying to change anything. I just want to make sure that no one changes me.' This is the idea that keeps us going."

5 | The One Who Didn't Shoot

On a breezy June day in 1971, the flower children came out in Moscow. Someone had hinted that it was spring, and they left their secret gathering places and came into the sunshine with their beads and their dyed shirts, their beards and their long hair. Someone had a guitar, and they were singing. They held posters proclaiming "Flower Power" and "Make Love Not War" in English and Russian, they waved their three-legged peace symbols aloft, and they came to Kalinin Prospect and Gorky Street, singing "Imagine" in Russian, singing "Let it Be."

They sang about children, for it was the official Soviet holiday known as the "Day to Defend Children." They sang about the Vietnam War, and the horrors there, but the authorities did not care that the flower children were only singing in the streets what the authorities were shouting in the newspapers. It was the singing that bothered them. The singing, the long hair, the gathering freedom, the wands of peace, the words about love: all this meant trouble. The young people were following Lennon, not Lenin. The young people were attracting a curious crowd. Some of the passersby smiled, and began to hum along. Then the police moved in.

The police began using their sticks, and the flower children crumpled before them, clutching their posters around their heads. Blood ran on the posters, on the ground. The guitar was smashed. The passersby fled. The flower children fled, holding each other, stumbling, some in tears, fleeing back underground, back to the safety of their hidden world. It had all been a cruel mistake. It was not spring.

One fourteen-year-old boy with long dark hair and luminous green-blue eyes watched from a few feet away. His eyes burned with what he saw. He saw the flower children's blood running, he saw the police beating on their innocence, he saw how they had made their dreams vulnerable. He watched it all, hovering on the edge, melting into the safety of the crowd.

And looking at the peace symbols and ripped posters scattered on the sidewalk, he knew what their mistakes had been. The flower children had sallied into the sunshine with their innocence, but without their cunning. To survive would take cunning. He might not be able to outrun or outfight the system, but he could outsmart it. And if he was not clever enough to beat the system, the system would beat him. These were the rules of the game. He never forgot them.

Eighteen years later, Andrei Orlov is still living by those rules. Beating the system has become a skill that preserves his integrity. He has learned to play upon the idiosyncrasies of his society like a musician on a complex instrument. Sometimes he will outfox the system for a reason, like forging his father's signature to get into a better high school, or faking a medical disability to avoid the draft, or bluffing editors to get certain stories into print. And sometimes it is pure diversion. More than once he has gotten into theaters or crowded churches on holidays by walking up to a policeman at the front of a line and saying in a conspiratorial whisper: "Okay, comrade, in ten minutes I'm going to come back, I'll try to get past you, we'll scuffle for a few moments, and then you'll let me in. Got it?" The astonished policemen nods his head yes. The little drama unfolds according to plan.

For six years, Orlov has parlayed his gift for beating the system into guidance that has helped many Americans wriggle their ideas for East-West exchanges through the maze of Soviet bureaucracy. "But if you write about me, don't call me a 'citizen diplomat,'" he cautions. "Both words are not right. Citizen means nationalism, means borders and separate nations. And diplomat means the state, means governments. What we are doing is contrary to both of those things."

Orlov works as a freelance writer, an unusual job in the Soviet Union and one that allows him unusual independence. He belongs to the Journalists' Union and can write for any newspaper or magazine he chooses. He worked his way into freelancing, and survived, because he was good. Editors were willing to overlook his independence in return for solid feature stories about music, sports, and the lives of young people. Even during the Brezhnev era, he wrote exactly what he chose, and got much of it published.

His bookshelves are heavy with old newspaper clippings. Pointing to them, he says, "People make excuses now, and say they didn't have any choice before *glasnost,* they had to write garbage. But there's nothing in those articles that I would change. It was always possible to write truth."

A loner, Orlov is distrustful of groups and wary of belonging to any cause, even one with which he sympathizes. He is not a joiner, by habit or by instinct. He proudly claims that he was the last kid in his class to join the Young Pioneers, and he quit Komsomol at nineteen. He swears no allegiance to any movement—not even to the counterculture, to citizen diplomacy, or to *perestroika.* Instead he circles on the outside of the pack, not quite belonging to it but not wholly unattached either, keeping vigil for the sake of the young ones, guarding them with the keenness of his observations.

"There's a song by Vladimir Vysotsky that's very important for anyone who wants to understand how to influence governments, or how to change the course of humanity," says Orlov. "It's called, 'The One Who Didn't Shoot.' It's about someone who was supposed to be executed by a firing squad during the war. There were regulations that said if someone survives the firing squad once, he can't be executed a second time. The whole firing squad had guns, but there was one who didn't shoot. There was one bullet missing from the body. And he sings, 'I was able to live my life, because of the one who didn't shoot.'

"When you're standing there as part of a firing squad, it's very easy to say: 'What difference does my bullet make?' But it's a question of personal responsibility. Each of us faces this several times in our lives. We can choose to do what everyone else around us is doing, or to do our own personal thing. You don't have to murder the sergeant or try to kill the firing squad or start a new war. You just take your gun one inch higher, and that's all that's needed.

"Someone who doesn't think that inner peace matters, who doesn't think that changing himself can do anything—those are the people who are afraid. They think: 'Whatever I do, the system is still going to work, the war machine is still going to work.' Then someone offers this person a military-related job. And he thinks: 'Well, if I don't take it, someone else will, and the machine will still work.'

"People who do things they don't believe in, who compromise

their beliefs every day, who lie or cover up their beliefs or feel-ings—they are the dangerous people." A half-smile crosses his face. "Because—well, they're the ones who shoot."

Orlov shares an apartment near the Moscow Zoo with his brother, his sister-in-law, and his niece; he shares his room with his niece's pet turtle, which crawls out from underneath the book-shelves about once a month. The room has a cozy, protected feel. On the walls are collections of frisbees and hockey pennants, maps of the United States and the Soviet Union, an American-made peace quilt, and some of his own art. Among his creations are a series of playful portraits of Gorbachev. Gorbachev with mustache and slanted eyebrows, masked as Lenin. Gorbachev with jaunty naval cap and striped shirt, masked as a sailor on the *Aurora*. Gorbachev with red-white-and-blue leotard and cape, masked as Superman. Next to his newpaper clippings, on the topmost shelf, are two military helmets from World War II, one Nazi and one Soviet. "Without them," he remarks cryptically, "I would not be who I am."

He keeps odd, Bohemian hours, and seldom looks wholly well. When we first meet, he is wearing a red headband, a gold earring, and a dolphin T-shirt that reads "Save the Humans." He sits cross-legged on his couch, chain-smoking cigarettes and holding a quartz crystal. Although he is young, there is something about him that seems unspeakably old. His eyes are the illuminated, uncom-promising eyes of a wolf, or a panther, or some other honest predator.

Orlov's expectations for *perestroika* are modest. In his living room hangs one of his recent works of art, a collage made up of hundreds of slivered strips of photographs of the current Polit-buro. Ties are glued next to other ties, necks next to other necks, eyes next to other eyes. From a few feet away, the collage bears a uncanny resemblance to a bust of Brezhnev. "So this is the face of *perestroika*—so far," he says, with a humorous gleam in his eyes. He then reaches into a drawer and pulls out a faded tie-dyed hippie shirt. "This is my other illustration of *perestroika*. You see all these swirls, all these very pretty colors, but there is no pattern to it. A lot of motion, but no pattern. And you see here is a bit of green, and there is a bit of green, but there is all this red in-between: and so how do the green bits get to one another?"

As a writer, language is important to him. He does not use the word *inostrantsi,* "foreigners," for example, believing that "the word itself creates borders between people." On his well-stocked bookshelf of Western paperbacks, which he terms "the lending library," is a copy of George Orwell's *1984* with pages worn to translucence. He estimates that perhaps 500 people read it before he managed to procure another copy and retire this one.

Orlov is fascinated by the semantic ambiguities of the word *mir,* which means both "peace" and "world." As a teenager, he and his friends amused themselves by painting graffiti on the numerous Soviet posters that proclaimed: *Nam nuzhen mir,* "We need peace." By inserting the word *ves,* "all," they transformed the phrase into "We need the world—all of it." Orlov collects, as a hobby, the cheap propaganda posters that are available at Soviet kiosks. He ponders their imagery and slogans for hidden meanings like an archaeologist trying to reconstruct the beliefs of a lost civilization from shreds of pottery.

Writing came easily to him, as a manifestation of his constant testing of the system. Although his real love was languages, his father persuaded him to go to a chemical engineering institute after high school, promising him that good technical training would increase his chances of being able to travel abroad. Orlov was more interested in hanging out with his hippie friends than studying inorganic chemistry, however. His hair reached his waist, his music collection grew, and he lived and thrived in the fertile hippie counterculture network of Beatles freaks, nonconformists, and pacifists that is known by the name of its antithesis—*sistyema,* "the system." A few times he was picked up by police, kept in jail for one night, and then released. His grades fell; his determination to live by his inner principles rose.

Then, in 1976, he read an article in the newspaper *Moskovski Komsomolets* that primly railed against high school and college students who frequented a certain popular bar. Among their crimes: speaking Westernized slang, wearing Western clothes, and avoiding the library. This bar was a favorite hang-out for Orlov and his friends, and the article enraged them. He and a buddy (now a reporter for *Moscow News*) wrote a long letter to the newspaper in reply, and cunningly began it with the line: "We know that letters like this don't get published." The newspaper printed the entire letter, and Orlov and his friend were briefly famous. In a later letter, a reader complained they were "too smart, and that's why they're dangerous." "Can you imagine," Orlov recalls with relish, "being eighteen years old and picking up a newspaper that says you're smart and dangerous?"

Orlov was hooked on journalism, and after his low grades eventually got him kicked out of the chemical engineering institute, he started writing part-time for *Moskovski Komsomolets*. To practice his English, he also worked as an assistant tour guide for Sputnik, the Soviet youth travel agency, taking groups of American and Canadian tourists around the Soviet Union. But slowly he began drifting beyond the system's edge. He spent several months hitchhiking around most of European Russia in the cabs of Soviet trucks. He was looking for an escape from his parents, from his girlfriend, from the necessity of going back to school. So in 1979 he decided to join the Red Army. For an avowed pacifist, it was the equivalent of deciding to go on a two-year exploratory mission behind enemy lines.

It wasn't easy; "I was the first person in my region of Moscow to volunteer in several years," he says mischievously. "No one knew what to do." His faked medical exemption almost prevented the whole idea, but he fought his way into the Army with the same cool single-mindedness with which he had fought to keep himself out.

Once there, he immediately began testing the limits of this new system. His Army base needed to replace a propaganda "artist-decorator," and because he said he could draw he was given the position. One of his first assignments was to design a giant outdoor mural of four clean-cut Soviet soldiers striding valorously in formation. He dutifully executed the mural, but with a twist: he gave each of the four soldiers the face of one of the Beatles. "It was just like your Mt. Rushmore," he recalls with satisfaction. "There they were, the Fabulous Four, promising to protect our motherland." The other soldiers on the base kept the secret, and the commanding officers did not suspect the invasion.

But finally a young officer blew his cover. Orlov had to report to an ideological panel, which informed him that they had heard that the soldiers in his mural resembled the Rolling Stones. Orlov managed to procure some photographs of Mick Jagger and the officers had to admit that there was little resemblance. But why, they asked, did one of his soldiers have glasses? Because members of the Soviet intelligentsia also belong to the Red Army, Orlov replied with a straight face. The ideological panel dismissed the case, but ordered Orlov to remove the glasses from the mural. "It was," he remarks with a wry grin, "the biggest compromise of my military career." Lennon and company were still defending the motherland when he left the base two years later.

Somehow, despite his constant pranks, he was never court-martialed. He was questioned once for possessing a relatively recent (a few months old) copy of an American newspaper, and once he was detained as a suspected French spy. "I wanted to learn French in my spare time, and some friends in Moscow sent me some tapes. But the only tape recorder I could find was in the base communications center. It was my first lesson in French, and I was supposed to repeat the words four times. So I went in one night, and there I was, with headphones on, with a microphone, sitting in the middle of this multi-megawatt radio station, saying '*Je suis Francois, Je suis Francois,*' when an officer walked in. That was my last lesson in French."

Orlov is still grateful for what the Red Army taught him about learning to see beyond uniforms and labels and about the colorful diversity of human nature. "It was the best, most interesting two years of my life," he says. "It was going abroad to Russia. I lived with people who were on all levels of consciousness. People who were like me, and people who said they wanted to go to Afghanistan to find out what machine guns could do. People of all different nationalities. I never could have met them, or learned to communicate with them, any other way." He was also lucky; thanks to his skills as a propaganda artist, he was kept on the base and never touched a gun.

In 1982, he returned to Moscow and began writing full-time for *Moskovski Komsomolets*. Soon he had an assignment to write a short article about an international peace conference in Moscow. Orlov put in a paragraph about the Soviet Union's role in the arms race. It was cut out. He decided to write a longer story and to sell it to the national newspaper *Komsomolskaya Pravda*. The article was accepted and he saw the proofs with his half-page story the night before the paper went to press. The next morning, when he went to a kiosk to buy the paper, the story was gone. An apologetic editor explained that the timing wasn't right, that someone or other had just made a speech, that he should send them something else later.

"Citizen diplomacy never sold in Soviet newspapers," says

Orlov. "Even when I was writing about sports I tried to give it some human interest angle, to ask an American hockey player, for example, to describe his everyday life at home. But I had trouble with editors. Once one didn't like the way I described an American hockey team as friendly guys laughing on the bus and having a good time. Nowadays this is no big deal, you can read in every newspaper that millions of Americans are common people who want peace just as much as you do. But back then I was very proud whenever I could get this message published."

To get articles past the editors and censors, Orlov knew he would have to outsmart them. In early 1984, he wrote a story about an American woman named Cynthia Lazaroff who had developed a Soviet studies curriculum for American school children. Lazaroff invited him to go on a hiking expedition that she was organizing that summer for American and Soviet teenagers in the Caucasus Mountains. Orlov interviewed the teenagers on the trail and came home determined to sell a long story about the young people's impressions. He approached an editor of an important paper. According to Orlov, the editor at first rolled his eyes and said, "We don't need any more of this peace freak stuff." Orlov asked him to please just read it. The editor was still unimpressed, saying that the story was not sufficiently political. Orlov archly replied, "Comrade, don't you think it's about time our anti-American propaganda became a little more sophisticated? Of course, we could put in something about Reagan and imperialism, but then everyone would know it was propaganda."

The editor looked at the piece again. Orlov seemed so confident that the editor did not want to admit that he did not fully grasp this new sophisticated style. He began nodding his head and murmuring, "Yes—I see what you mean." The editor pointed to a few quotes by the Americans which he considered objectionable and suggested that if these could be changed the story might run. Orlov countered that he had already carefully selected and ordered the Americans' quotes to create a certain effect. "If we alter their words then the Americans will know they have been manipulated. But if we just arrange their quotes in a certain way, then they can't complain." The befuddled editor accepted the story.

In November 1984, the Esalen Institute's Soviet-American Exchange Program brought entertainer John Denver to the Soviet Union during a time when cultural exchanges between the countries had dwindled to nearly zero. Orlov met Denver and Esalen program director Jim Hickman, liked them, and decided to help out by getting them some press. He got a radio interview with Denver on the air by persuading an editor at a Moscow radio station that Denver's homilies about peace were good "counter-propaganda." He also broke an informal ban on broadcasting American music on Soviet radio, which had begun when the U.S. boycotted the 1980 Olympics, by playing some of Denver's songs. "At that time, the American music shelf was limited to about five or six tapes of Paul Robeson and Pete Seeger," he recalls.

Then he wrote an article about Denver and used his wiles to convince an editor to print it. "I was told this editor was a tough person, a hardline Communist. So I immediately told him that I had a good propaganda story. I led him to believe that it fit the usual line about the traditional American enemy, where an American like John Denver who talks about peace is some kind of political defector. So the editor read not what was on the paper, but rather what I put into his mind."

As this went on, even some of his fellow journalists began to wonder if he didn't have some sort of secret clearance. "They don't understand how I publish what I do and get away with it. They think I must get permission from some government agency or whatever. But the reality is that *inner censorship* is much, much stronger than any censorship imposed from the outside. My friends would say, 'Well, you know, we have to think of our careers.' But my philosophy has always been: Let *them* cut it, if they want. At least I won't be the censor. And often things which I'm sure will never be printed are printed." He pauses and grins. "Also, no editor can ever be sure that I don't have clearance from a higher level than they can know about. So if I am confident and relaxed, they figure I know what I am doing."

Orlov's new American friends sent other Americans his way. Soon he was quietly introducing people to one another and giving them insider's advice about how best to beat the system. He read over the Americans' proposals, suggested tactical changes, made a few discreet calls to find out correct phone numbers or to discover which bureaucrats were likely to be more receptive. He also continued to get his American friends into the Soviet press, "because this helped them have more access to officials. It meant that somebody, somewhere, had said they were okay."

Orlov also wrote articles to protect and encourage Soviets who dared to meet with Americans outside of authorized receptions. For years, Soviet families belonging to an informal group called Club Healthy Family had been meeting in Gorky Park to do exercises, play games, swim in lakes, and hold seminars. "They try to educate their children in healthy and cooperative ways, to counteract the competitive education of school. They do things establishment medicine would oppose, like having their kids swim in ice-water in the winter. And this too is a kind of rebellion, a quiet resistance to the state." Orlov helped introduce them to American families, and their kids began flying kites with American kids. When the Club ran into some trouble with local authorities, Orlov managed to publish a laudatory newspaper article about them. "The director of Gorky Park was pleased to hear that something so positive was happening in his park, and things have been smooth ever since."

In addition to the Esalen exchanges and Cynthia Lazaroff's US-USSR Youth Exchange Program, Orlov was soon helping out groups such as Young Storytellers for Peace, Animal Ambassadors, and Children as Teachers of Peace, quickly becoming a kind of jack-of-all-trades at Soviet-American exchange. He designed the logo for *Surviving Together,* the magazine of the Institute for Soviet-American Relations. He and a friend, Nikolai Lamm, wrote the restaurant review section for the guidebook *Information Moscow,* acquiring a number of pounds and hangovers in the process. He was also a behind-the-scenes coordinator and troubleshooter for rock star Billy Joel's 1987 Soviet tour. A visit to his apartment became *de rigeur* for the American citizen diplomacy avant-garde.

His personal life began blending with his politics when he fell in love with an American exchange student studying Russian in Moscow. She went back to the United States, but then returned after they both decided something had to be done about the $1,000-a-month phone bills. They lived together for three months to see how things would work out, but Orlov says this created a no-win situation with his mother. "First it was: 'How can you consider marrying this foreigner?' Then my mother grew fond of her, and when we broke up it was: 'How can you do this to this poor girl who came all the way to the Soviet Union to be with you?'"

The steady traffic of Americans through his apartment raised further suspicions among his friends. "A lot of people thought I must be KGB because I had all these American contacts and I didn't seem to be afraid," he admits. "It's a very bad thing to be suspected of being KGB here. It's not the same as being an American and working for the FBI. I almost lost one of my best friends because of this. Another of my friends at first thought that I must have KGB connections, and then she thought: 'Wait a minute, have I ever known anyone who's been in touch with Andrei to get in trouble? No. So he must not be an informer.'"

As much as he liked and even admired his American colleagues, Orlov found things to criticize in some of their attitudes. "They come here, and they get suddenly opened. They have these amazing experiences that they never dreamed of having, and they think it is because they are in the Soviet Union. When really they would have just as amazing an experience if they went into their local butcher shop with this same attitude of openness and willingness for relationship. Then they go home and they still ignore the local butcher and they give talks about building relationships with Soviets.

"Some of them have told me that they have never felt so alive as when they are here. I am glad they are having that experience, but they didn't have to come to the Soviet Union for that. And let's say they did, let's say they needed to come here to break out of the patterns of their lives—are they going to go home and continue to try to build peace there, to build relationship there? That's what counts—how much people are able to make peace at home, and in their own lives.

"In a way, the words 'I love the Russians!' have as much meaning or truth in them as 'I hate the Jews.' I've never understood someone who tells me, 'Oh, all the Russians are great people.' 'Wait a second,' I say, 'I know at least a couple who I don't think are so great. Would you like to meet them?' They always say no.

"It's another stereotype. People are trying to break one and end up making another. Of course, the image of the enemy is more dangerous for world politics, but I'm not sure that the image of a whole nation of smiling and friendly and generous people is very accurate either. And in the long run, it's not good, because it's not true."

He also thinks that many of the Americans who now lead

"citizen diplomacy tours" to the Soviet Union have lost some of the willingness to take risks that was essential in the pre-Gorbachev days. "Back then, they rode on the subways and met people by accident and ended up in their homes," he says. "Now they get to Moscow and they call their friends and they bring busloads of people there. So the chain reaction is limited. My neighbor is as interesting as I am, if not more so, but Americans don't have his phone number."

Orlov believes there are plenty of new frontiers for those Americans willing to go beyond the currently mapped territory of citizen diplomacy. In 1987, Orlov was given a small collection of children's art by an old Army buddy, Khafiz Bikhayev, who is now the director of a children's art school in the Mordovian city of Saransk. Orlov in turn gave the paintings to Paula DeCosse of CONNECT, a Minnesota-based group that coordinates children's art and essay exchanges, and she began exhibiting them in several U.S. cities. After one of the Saransk children's paintings was chosen for inclusion in an American calendar called "Faces of the Soviet Union," the Saransk girl was hailed as a celebrity in her hometown, Bikhayev was praised by the Ministry of Culture of Mordovia, and thousands came to a Saransk exhibition of American children's art sent by DeCosse. Now DeCosse and Bikhayev would like to exchange people as well as paintings, but there is a problem: Saransk is a closed city to foreigners. One of the reasons, according to Orlov, is that "you can only get there by train, and the only train route goes past miles and miles of barbed wire fences around labor camps."

Still, Orlov thinks that determined Americans can maneuver around such restrictions and spread exchanges to these untouched areas. Since Americans are still banned from Saransk, he travelled there recently to speak to high school children about his impressions of Americans. One little girl asked him: "Why, if America is such a bad country, do their kids draw these happy scenes of their homes and friends? Is this meant just to fool us?"

Given attitudes like these, Orlov considers every exchange a positive step, whether organized by a grassroots group or with help from the government. The concrete effects can be the same, regardless of the organizer's inner motivations. "Even if a television program of Soviet and Italian young people trading questions and answers is just meant for the West," he says, "it's still happening, it still has an impact." And even projects sponsored by the Peace Committee have some effect, he thinks—more, perhaps, than its officials actually intend. He explains with an analogy: "My relationship with my sister-in-law was once very bad. Then I decided to just *pretend* to be nice to her, even though all the feelings I had inside had not changed. I just *acted* in a different way, I *pretended* to like her. And then that led to a change in the relationship. The change on the outside led to a change inside."

Sometime in the future, Orlov would like to walk across the entire Soviet Union, from Vladivostok to Riga, in the company of a few close Soviet and American friends, "so that we could have a chance to really talk and to get to know one another. The more difficulties the other person has that you can accept and live with, the stronger you are and the stronger the connection is. Then after years and years we can come to a point of respecting our differences and all that we don't know and can't know about each other."

Connection and difference, sameness and separation—these are his issues. It is why he went into the Red Army and why he welcomed Americans into his home. It is why he leapt at the chance, recently, to talk with the commander of a Soviet submarine armed with nuclear weapons. "We met by accident at a party, and we were very eager to speak together," he says. "I'd never before met a person who could launch nuclear weapons, and he'd never before met a real pacifist." They went at each other verbally for hours.

The submarine commander wove a scenario: You are a Soviet submarine commander. You are cruising near Los Angeles. You have just received word that Moscow has been fused and flattened by American nuclear bombs. All of your friends and family are glass. You are next to Los Angeles, and you can destroy it. The despairing urge for revenge is hot in you. The order comes from central command to fire. Will you fire?

As he posed the question, the submarine commander smiled in triumph.

"No way," said Orlov. "No way I would fire."

The submarine commander was astonished. Why not?

"Because," said Orlov, "I have friends in Los Angeles. And there are kids there."

"But your family is dead. *Your* kids are dead. Your whole city is glass!"

"So what?" said Orlov. "I won't bring them back to life by killing more. And kids are kids."

And they continued to argue, to thrust and parry, over these simple, important questions. Are kids kids? Are Moscow kids more important than American kids? Is there a difference between "us" and "them"? Are we one family, or aren't we? The submarine commander was as unshakeable in his convictions as Orlov was in his. His loyalty was to his family, his people and his country. People outside of his country merely threatened it, were merely "them." Exhausted and unpersuaded, he and Orlov parted ways at dawn.

With the coming of *glasnost, perestroika,* and the new profusion of Soviet-American exchanges, Orlov's role has changed. He seldom writes about exchanges anymore—"lots of other people are doing that." He seldom needs to finagle access to key bureaucrats for his American friends—the doors are now ajar. Instead he works as a consultant for a number of music-related East-West business ventures, ranging from smoothing out the technical arrangements for a Leningrad production of *Candide* to advising a Soviet cooperative that distributes American music tapes. He produces a twice-monthly national radio program called "Musical Globe" on Western music and keeps up with the rock 'n' roll scene in the Soviet Union and elsewhere. And he still takes on behind-the-scenes tasks such as mediating between Western rock promoters and Goskontsert, the official Soviet concert agency, on the production of a Live-Aid-type concert to raise money for Armenian earthquake relief efforts.

In his own writing, he has largely turned from journalism to the movies. His first script was for a film about the ill-fated hippie demonstration on the "Day to Defend Children" in 1971. Ironically, the script fell victim to *perestroika*—after a film studio had accepted it in 1987, a major shake-up in personnel within the studio followed, and the new people considered anything the old people had liked to be suspect. Orlov is now repackaging the script and working on others. One is about the "legend of the dolphin," which was told to him by an American friend. "The legend says that people can be free and independent and still strong as a group. Like a dolphin pod. They can be as playful and honest and friendly as dolphins are, and share this kind of dolphin good energy." He is also writing a comedy about his two years in the

Army. Another script, which a studio recently accepted, is for a punk rock musical that takes place in a psychiatric hospital.

Perestroika has made his life easier, but he is not about to let his guard down. He created his own reality and lived without fear before *perestroika,* and he would do the same if it were to vanish tomorrow. "I've spent a long, long time creating a space for myself outside the system," he says, drawing a large circle on the table to symbolize the system, and a small circle outside of the large one to symbolize himself. "Now maybe the system has expanded, at the moment, to include my little safe space," he continues, drawing this. "But what if I let the walls of my little circle collapse, and then suddenly the big circle contracts and shrinks back to its original size or even smaller? Where will I be then? By remaining in my little safe space I'm still one step ahead."

Some of his old hippie friends think he's sold out because he writes for official papers, he does radio shows, he belongs to the Journalists' Union, and thus, in their view, he has become part of the propaganda machine of the state. Orlov describes this judgment carefully, without attempting to defend himself. "You know, my path has not been an easy one. I've got a unique place. It took me a long time. It's not for everyone." He lights another cigarette and stares at the crystal in his hand. "Once a woman asked me, 'Why are you fighting so hard to get these articles printed? You must be crazy!' And she wasn't kidding. She really *did* think I was insane. She couldn't believe I took this seriously. That was the atmosphere around me for a long time. But given the standards of sanity today, whereby 'sane' people are admitted to the military, placed in missile silos, and trained to start wars, then I don't mind being considered insane.

"Big movements don't start with a lot of people moving in the same direction. Big movements begin as smaller movements, and at their origin they are created by individuals. It goes back to personal responsibility. It goes back to the relationship between inner peace and outer peace. Everybody creates some kind of aura, some kind of field of influence around them. Each person can do what fits within the range of his or her responsibility. If you only do a small thing, it's better than to do nothing." He pauses and stares out the window. For a moment, beneath the self-control in his eyes, there is a flicker of pain.

6 | Our Policy Is the Policy of Peace

Often it is said obliquely, but it is almost always said, and repeated to make sure the message is clear. For most independent Soviet peace activists, it is a statement of integrity, a litmus test of their own worth. We are not connected with the Soviet Peace Committee, they say. We are something else.

But what *is* the Soviet Peace Committee?

I did not relish the prospect of trying to find out. It was probable that the Peace Committee, which has many reasons to want to control the Soviet peace movement's image in the West, would not be very happy about my investigations. Yet I knew that if I did not understand the Peace Committee, I had little hope of understanding the complexity of Soviet attitudes toward war and peace, or the challenges facing individuals trying to change those attitudes.

At a conference held in Washington, D.C., in February 1988, I was introduced to Mikhail Shein, a staff person in charge of American affairs at the Moscow headquarters of the Soviet Peace Committee. I called him in Moscow a few weeks later and we made an appointment for the following week. All seemed well, until I showed up at the Peace Committee headquarters on 36 Prospekt Mira ("Peace Avenue") on the appointed day at the appointed time. "Shein is not here," the taciturn man at the front desk informed me. I protested that there must be some mistake. With an air of great weariness, the man made another phone call. "Shein is not here," he shrugged, and went back to his newspaper.

I waited a few minutes in hopes he would show, wandering in the meantime through the first-floor lobby and looking at an exhibit of "peace posters" drawn by Soviet artists for a United Nations peace day. The posters were stilted and lifeless, filled with unimaginative assortments of clichés such as white doves, missiles with red lines through them, and children stiffly holding hands.

Twenty minutes later, I went back to the taciturn man. "I am an American journalist, and I want to talk with someone about the Peace Committee," I said. "Surely *someone* must be here who can talk with me." The words "American journalist" produced the desired effect; the man reluctantly put down his paper and began dialing numbers to get rid of me, the morning's problem.

Fifteen minutes later, a soft-spoken and diminutive man, very correctly dressed, appeared and introduced himself as Sergei Stepanov, a staff person in charge of British-Soviet affairs. He politely walked me through the hallways of the Peace Committee, showed me several offices (the American department was, indeed, empty) and answered my questions as we sat on a plush green couch in the lobby. Somehow, although he did not give the impression of evasiveness, when I later listened to my tapes I could not pick out anything he said that was worth repeating. The only time his voice rose above a half-whisper was when I asked him about the Trust Group. "In my opinion they are not sincere, they are not concerned with peace," he said. "Their program doesn't have anything to do with peace activity. Their image as a peace group is the fault of the Western media. What they are trying to do is create confrontation and an enemy image. They are constantly saying—don't go to the Soviet Peace Committee, they're agents of KGB, and so on." After this brief moment of passion, his voice became listless again. An hour later I thanked him and said good-bye. He said good-bye with equal relief, and did not ask any further details about who I was or what I was doing.

After this colorless encounter, I was in no hurry for another one. On my next trip to Moscow I found myself inventing excuses not to call the Peace Committee again.

But as it turned out, I didn't have to—they called me. Genrikh Borovik, the president of the Peace Committee, was tipped off by an American who warned him that my book might portray the Peace Committee as being less than completely peaceful. Borovik alerted his assistant, Alexander Nebolsin, who tracked me down through an acquaintance at the Soviet Committee of Physicians for the Prevention of Nuclear War. "I'd like to talk with you," Nebolsin said pleasantly on the phone. I responded with equal pleasantry, and we made an appointment. This time, I had a feeling, I would not be stood up.

When I walked into Borovik's spacious sixth-floor office in the

Peace Committee, Alexander Nebolsin was sitting behind the president's desk. A large, hearty man chummily dressed in a wool sweater and slacks, he shook my hand, motioned me to one of three leather swivel chairs, and, after speaking of several things in an introductory way, came to the point.

"So, I understand you are writing a book on the Soviet peace movement," he said, and paused.

"That's right," I said.

"That's very interesting," he said, smiling and crossing his arms.

"It certainly is," I answered, meeting his eyes and smiling back.

He swivelled a few degrees in his chair. "How long have you been writing this book?"

"Oh," I looked up at the ceiling, "since about last January, I think."

His eyes registered a moment of surprise, quickly concealed. "And have you come to our Peace Committee before?"

"Oh yes," I said cheerfully, "I was here in February."

His surprise deepened. "And whom did you speak with in February?"

"With Sergei Stepanov, from the British department."

"Sergei Stepanov," he repeated softly, and I swore I could read his thoughts, *Note—tell Stepanov to be more careful next time.* "That's nice," he said aloud, nodding.

"And I met several people at the conference in Washington, including Genrikh Borovik," I volunteered. "In fact, I even interviewed him."

"You've already interviewed Borovik?" A note of alarm entered Nebolsin's voice. I had just palmed his one trump card—access to Borovik, which was arguably necessary for the book's completeness.

We were interrupted, just then, by the arrival of Evgeny Oskolsky, public affairs director of the Peace Committee, a trim, well-groomed, gray-haired man in a gray suit who energetically shook my hand and began presenting me with brochures, decals, mini-calendars, and articles about the Committee. Nebolsin watched us, apparently still thinking over this last piece of information.

"Will you be using the material from this interview with

Borovik for your book?" he asked as soon as the conversation paused, choosing his words carefully.

"Yes," I said, "it was, as we say, 'on the record.'"

"On the record," Nebolsin repeated softly. It was not a new phrase to him. So far so good, I thought to myself. He's off-balance, he knows I already know too much. The best he can do is damage control.

"Now, if it's all right, I'd like to ask *you* a few questions," I said, setting my tape recorder on the table between us and knowing full well that, according to the rules of the elaborate game we were both playing, it would have to be "all right."

For the next hour-and-a-half, Nebolsin, Oskolsky, and another Peace Committee official, Vyacheslav Sluzhivov, who soon appeared at the door and was motioned inside by Nebolsin, robustly set forth a vision of the Soviet Peace Committee that was finely attuned to what they thought I wished to hear. My first question— "So, convince me that you are not just a propaganda cheerleader for existing Soviet policies"—set them off for a full twenty-five minutes. Even if I had wanted to, I would not have been able to get a word in edgewise.

"I don't think the word 'propaganda' is a bad word," Oskolsky began. "It just means advertising. If we're propagandizing the will of the Soviet people for peace, and their desire to live in friendship with everyone, then that kind of propaganda is good."

"It doesn't please us very much when we are called an official movement," said Sluzhivov. "We consider ourselves representatives of the people, and of people's diplomacy. Citizen diplomacy changes people's preconceptions. We're looking for the path that gives us concrete results. We could organize some kind of protest, go out on to the streets, fight with the people, attract media attention, but there wouldn't be any results."

"It will take years to make people really free. The fear is in the blood," added Oskolsky. "The Stalin terror was a terrible thing. There was a guy in Murmansk who in 1947 got a postcard from the captain of an American ship, and he immediately got fifteen years in prison."

"We're trying to correspond with our partners in other countries. We're destroying the concept of enemies. We are showing our people that people in other countries are just the same as we are."

"Now during *perestroika* we're striving so that the Soviet Peace Committee and the Soviet peace movement will become an even bigger channel for the desires of the masses."

"All these years we've been talking about democracy, but we didn't have the slightest idea what it meant. One of the Soviet Peace Committee's goals now is teaching people how to be democratic. . . ."

And so on, in language finessed after years of meetings with tough-questioning Americans. The old terms—"peace champions," "peace fighters," and even "peace activists"—were clearly out. What was clearly in was "citizen diplomats." Oskolsky proudly handed me a brochure: "Want to meet a Soviet citizen diplomat? . . . Drop by the Soviet Peace Committee!" In a reference to their most enduring criticism, one headline in the brochure announced: "ARE WE INDEPENDENT? NO! WE DEPEND UPON," and followed this with a bullet-style list that included the "100 million contributors to the Peace Fund," "bright ideas of peace-mongers from all over the world," and "public opinion in our country."

Oskolsky also handed me a report to the U.N. World Disarmament Campaign summarizing the Peace Committee's activities in the previous year. Compared to the shrill lambasts of the Peace Committee during the Brezhnev era, the report was modest in tone. One phrase leapt out, however: among the main purposes of the joint projects agreed upon at a citizen exchange conference in Washington, it said, was "increasing the sympathy of American public opinion towards the USSR." Nothing was said about increasing the sympathy of Soviet public opinion towards the U.S.

An article by Peace Committee president Genrikh Borovik in *Pravda* on October 18, 1988, was also phrased in reasonable tones. Citizen diplomacy, Borovik said, "is not only rallies, demonstrations and protests." After describing a joint Soviet-American peace walk co-sponsored by the Peace Committee, he remarked that in America there are "enemies, both overt and covert" of these kinds of events "who would do anything to discredit it and the Soviet organizers of the march (by making all manner of hackneyed allegations, including claims that the Soviet Peace Committee is not a non-governmental organization but a government agency seeking to hoodwink Americans by sending specially trained propagandists and bureaucrats rather than real peace campaigners to the United States)." But, he said, "the bolder we are in launching new and off-beat forms of work, the more friends, I'm sure, we're going to make."

Corporate, I thought as the three men continued their litany. Corporate peacemaking, complete with well-paid executives, droves of secretaries, plush offices, slick annual reports, and money. Lots of money.

"One more question," I said. "*Nasha politika—politika mira* (Our policy is the policy of peace). True or false?"

Silence.

"What was that?" said Nebolsin. I repeated it.

Oskolsky jumped in first. "We don't have slogans like that anymore," he said. "They've all been taken down."

The image of a huge banner inscribed with this very phrase, which I had seen not four days before near the Leningrad airport, flashed before my eyes.

"Now, wait a minute, Zhenya," Sluzhivov interrupted quickly, as if he had read my thoughts, "that's not true. They do still exist."

"It's pure nonsense," Nebolsin offered from the president's chair. "It doesn't mean anything. We have a lot of old slogans like that from the period of stagnation, and we're getting rid of them. But not as quickly as we would like."

"So you don't use that slogan in your Peace Committee activities now?" I said.

"Oh no," said Sluzhivov. "We have new slogans now. Slogans like, 'We need common security.' 'Cooperation, not confrontation.' 'The Russians are coming with peace and friendship.'"

Later that evening, as I was drinking tea with a Soviet woman whose projects occasionally compel her to have contact with the Peace Committee, I mentioned my meeting with these three. Her eyes widened when I gave their names. "Nebolsin?" she said, patting her shoulders with the Soviet hand-signal that means high-ranking KGB. "What did you do to deserve *him*?"

But as far as I know, that's as far as it went. I was never called in for another chat. The Peace Committee appeared to forget about me, and I tried to do likewise. I could not ignore it completely—it is too big, still plays too active a role in many exchange projects, and has left too thick a residue on the thinking of Soviet citizens for that. But I gave up trying to go through the front door of 36 Prospekt Mira, and instead pieced together the Peace

Committee's story from Americans and Soviets who have tried over the years to work with it.

The Soviet Peace Committee (the literal translation of its Russian title is "Soviet Committee for the Defense of Peace") was established in 1949, during a time when peace groups were proliferating in many countries. It was probably intended as a vehicle for the Soviet government to send delegates to various world peace conferences, as well as to organize their own under the aegis of the World Peace Council, a federation of openly pro-Soviet peace groups founded the same year. Although initially a number of non-communist groups were involved in the World Peace Council, most of these dropped out in the 1950s when it became clear, as its current president, Romesh Chandra from India, said in 1979, that it "positively reacts to all Soviet initiatives in international affairs."

The Soviet Peace Fund, a separate group set up to receive donations to support the activities of the Peace Committee and other "public organizations," was established in 1961. By the early 1980s, the Peace Fund claimed that it had more than 100 million donors, leading to extravagant statements by the Peace Committee (less often heard today) that its membership was in the millions. Peace Committee officials still point to the Soviet Peace Fund as proof of their "independence," in answer to the frequent Western accusation that they are not a truly public organization but rather a branch of the Soviet government. In 1984, Oleg Kharkhardin, first vice-chairman of the Peace Committee, went so far as to say: "We are really independent, unlike some non-governmental organizations in Western countries which must depend on funds from the government or from foundations."

The Soviet Peace Fund, however, often collects its donations in a very organized way. Sometimes Soviet workers arrive at their factories and learn that one day's pay has been automatically sent to the Peace Fund. Other Soviets may receive along with their wages a list of Soviet public organizations, including the Peace Fund, to which they are "encouraged" to send a portion of their earnings. Many Soviets, however, do voluntarily contribute to the Peace Fund in honor of a loved one lost in World War II or in the genuine belief that activities financed by the Peace Fund will help prevent another war. But in recent years donations to the Peace Fund have slackened, partly because of a perceived lessening of the danger of nuclear war as East-West relations have improved, and partly because the establishment of many new charitable organizations has given Soviets a wider philanthropic choice. Anatoly Karpov, the champion chess player who is also chairman of the Peace Fund, said in early 1990 that annual donations to the Peace Fund had dropped from a peak of about 300 million rubles a year in the mid-1980s to about 180 million rubles in 1989. No one knows exactly how rich the Peace Fund is, but in addition to taking in hundreds of millions of rubles each year it also has custody of many warehouses full of donated art, antiques, and icons. According to Karpov, the Peace Fund primarily assists war veterans and their families, supports a wide range of Soviet ·"public organizations," and distributes money to worldwide humanitarian relief efforts.

That the Peace Committee is not part of the formal structure of the government is beyond doubt; that it is controlled both directly and indirectly by the Party is also beyond doubt. At the highest level, the Peace Committee is directly overseen by a person in the International Department of the Secretariat of the Central Committee of the Communist Party. The formal policymaking body of the Peace Committee is called the Presidium, a thirty-member "board of trustees" consisting of prominent public figures and Party members. Every five years, the Presidium is elected, usually from a provided list, by a national conference of four to five hundred "peace supporters." The day-to-day business of the Peace Committee is overseen by a Secretariat; under it is a paid staff in the Moscow headquarters of about 100 people.

This structure at the national level is replicated at the republican, regional, city, and even institutional level—many large factories, for instance, have their own branches of the Peace Committee. Outside of Moscow, the Peace Committee and the Peace Fund are often functionally identical, and the main activity of the local branches is collecting money for the Peace Fund. In recent years, however, the national Peace Fund has grown more autonomous from the national Peace Committee.

Until about 1987, the main function of the Peace Committee was the propagation, both domestically and abroad, of the Soviet "line" on war and peace. It went like this: We're not to blame for the the threat of nuclear war. It was the United States that first developed the nuclear bomb, that first used the nuclear bomb, and that led the way at every step in the arms race. The arms race is propelled by the American military-industrial complex and its greed for profits. The military-industrial complex controls the American mass media, deliberately broadcasts a distorted image of the Soviet Union, and dupes the common people into believing in a Soviet threat. But all we are doing is trying to keep up and maintain parity so that we can defend our motherland. Soviet people suffered terribly in World War II. Soviet people do not want another war. Soviet people completely support the peaceful policies of the Communist Party and the Soviet state. Soviet people are not pacifists, however; they also unfailingly support national liberation movements in countries seeking to shake off the chains of colonialism and imperialism. Eventually, as capitalism continues to decline because of its internal contradictions, revolutions will erupt in the capitalist countries. But the invincible might of the Soviet Army will protect the Soviet people from the consequences of these wars. In the meantime, people all over the world look to the Soviet Union as the stronghold of peace. The Soviet Union has put forth dozens of peace initiatives and arms control proposals since the end of World War II, all of which have been spurned by the West. The Soviet Union is doing everything it can to prevent war and defend peace.

This line was delivered in a standard lexicon. "The forces of peace" and "Soviet peace champions" were ranged against "the forces of war" and "American imperialist circles." As one writer put it in the Moscow journal *International Affairs* in March 1987: "Soviet peace initiatives have come up against grim resistance from reactionary imperialist forces, which see them as an obstacle to their imperial plans for world domination and social revenge." In contrast, all Soviet people want *mir i druzhba,* "peace and friendship," and they and the Soviet state are engaged in *borba za mir,* "the fight for peace." The irony of the word *borba,* which can be translated either as "fight" or "struggle," has not been lost on ordinary Soviets. According to one Russian joke, "There will never be war, but the fight for peace will be so vicious that every house will be left in rubble."

In school lessons and songs for children, in books and mass rallies for adults, the Peace Committee and other Party organs repeated again and again that the Soviet Union is for peace. Evidence of this propaganda can be found in a small book called

Swords into Ploughshares: The Soviet Peace Movement from the Grassroots,
written by Marilyn Bechtel, an American, and published by the
National Council of American-Soviet Friendship in 1984. It is a
book which, ironically, is meant to persuade Americans of the
authenticity of the official Soviet peace movement. One of its
photos shows a "peace meeting of doctors" in a hospital in Baku,
Azerbaijan, *circa* 1984. A hundred women in white coats and white
caps are sitting in a large meeting hall, holding up pre-printed
banners and placards with slogans in Russian: "No to War!" "Peace
to the World!" "No to the Arms Race!" The women are dutifully
raising their fists into the air and looking to the side of the photo,
following some unseen leader's cheer. One expects to see faces
that match the clenched fists, faces of passion, fear, anger. But the
women's faces are expressionless. Under a mask of outward do-
cility they have hidden their individuality, their personal integrity.
They continue to chant, thinking at the same time about dinner,
about the difficult patients on the coming shift, about picking up
a child from school.

In another photo, a trim young Soviet teacher leads her
elementary school pupils in their annual "peace lesson." Bright
posters with phrases like "Peace to the Planet, Happiness to Children" are pasted next to the chalkboard; one has the word "*Nyet*"
scrawled across the fat black silhouette of a bomb whose tail fins
are separated by a white outline of the Statue of Liberty. Another
photo shows thousands of Muscovites at an outdoor peace rally
waving huge printed banners (untranslated in the caption) that
read: "Our Policy Is The Policy of Peace," "No to Pershing and
Cruise Missiles," and "The USSR Is Coming Forward For Peace."

The Peace Committee has always relied heavily on the memory
of World War II, known in the Soviet Union as "The Great Patriotic
War," as the emotional soil for its propaganda. As Soviets will
frequently remind American visitors, about twenty million Soviets
died during the war, and nearly every family can name a close
relative who was killed. Of young men between the ages of 19 and
21 in 1941, less than three percent survived, producing a whole
generation of widows and spinsters. Apart from the loss of human
life, the country was economically devastated by scorch-and-burn
Nazi tactics, and in some ways it has never recovered. Although the
older generation carries these memories most vividly, even
younger Soviets raised on a steady diet of family war stories,

innumerable television documentaries, films and books about the war, and repeated references to it in school will often speak of the Great Patriotic War when asked about peace. Field trips of school-children to war museums and memorials include the solemn laying of flowers at eternal flames. *Mir* is often described as simply the absence of a war like the Great Patriotic War.

But the prominence of the war in the Soviet psyche has been unnaturally amplified. One factor has been psychological: until recently, while Soviets heard almost every day about the twenty million people who died in the war, there was no public acknow-ledgement that even more died during the Stalin purges and collectivization campaigns. Grief that was actually stemming from a broader and longer-running terror could only be acceptably expressed in terms of the war. For many Soviets, the war became an emotional touchstone for other tragedies in their history that could not be spoken of so openly.

The other factor is political: the deliberate harnessing by the Soviet government of the enormous emotional power of the war for its own ends. Along with constant reminders of the losses of the war go constant reminders that the Soviet government *did* succeed in "defending peace" and fighting off the Nazi invasion. The sacrifice and heroism of the war is frequently held up as a model for the sacrifice and heroism necessary to build socialism. Indeed, some scholars assert that the very legitimacy of the Soviet govern-ment in the eyes of its own people rests in large part on its victory in the Great Patriotic War. "The Party's role as the developer, promoter, and guardian of Soviet [military] power is one of its primary claims to support from the population," wrote military analyst and U.S. Navy captain Steve Kimes in a 1986 *Strategic Review* article. "The Party draws its strongest support from its role in the Great Patriotic War, which is constantly held aloft as the im-mensely successful military expression of the Socialist *political* sys-tem. . . . By manipulating the perceived danger of war in the population, the Party enhances its prestige and power."

Many observers have remarked upon an unwritten social con-tract between the Soviet people and their government: we will put up with a lot, it says, as long as you keep the peace. This helps explain the otherwise puzzling emphasis the war still receives in propaganda, education, and public life five decades after it began. Even if people will no longer sacrifice for communism, they may still sacrifice for peace. In 1988, *World Student News,* published in Prague, printed a poem by an East German student on this theme:

> War is made by people
> Who expect to make a profit on it. . .
> Remember
> Peace is something we have to fight for
> If we want it
> Peace requires effort and courage
> Resistance and, very often, sacrifices too
>
> But, isn't it better
> To make sacrifices for peace
> Than to be sacrificed to war. . .

War is bad, but the Army is good. Tremendous quantities of propaganda were expended to glorify the Soviet Army and the might of the armed forces, and to portray the existence of a huge defense establishment as natural and necessary. For if Soviet people began raising questions about "peaceloving" Soviet missiles, then the legitimacy of Soviet foreign policy might be called into question, and even the legitimacy of the Party's wisdom and the state itself. One propaganda poster, issued to commemorate Red Army Day in February 1988, shows a nuclear missile poised on a huge squat truck shaped out of the words "No one will catch us unaware." A squad of soldiers, with stern and identical faces, grips machine guns in the background. The missile itself is composed of the flattened Cyrillic letters "HAC," which spell the Russian word for "us." A nuclear weapon and the identity of the Soviet people are here fused into one.

The official myth that the Soviet Union is respected around the world as a leader in the fight for peace penetrated deeply into the consciousness of ordinary people. *Not For War We Raise Our Sons,* published in 1987, is a collection of letters accompanying donations sent by Soviet women to the Soviet Peace Fund. The book was published in English for distribution to Westerners, but while the letters were chosen to create a certain effect, there is no reason to doubt they are genuine. "Unlike peace campaigners in the USA and Great Britain, the Soviet people have no need to demand that their government pursue a peaceful foreign policy," writes Zoya Pukhova, the president of the Soviet Women's Committee, in the book's preface. "The Soviet state, ever since Lenin's first Decree on Peace, has always opposed war and the threat of war."

The letters are from women war veterans and pensioners, seamstresses and poultry maids, beet farm workers and shop assistants, lemongrowers and librarians. Some have pooled their funds to send donations of more than 1,000 rubles. The same themes come up again and again: the tragedy of World War II, the peaceful policies of the Communist Party and the Soviet government, the sanctity of children's happiness, the collective duty of all people to work for the common good, and the need to persuade the "transatlantic ringleaders" and "rabid militarists who live for profits alone" to give up their preparations for a nuclear war. Many use the same images of peace—"clear skies," "sunshine," "happy children"—over and over as they repeat their belief that their government is "doing its best to save human civilization from a nuclear catastrophe."

Among their stories are vivid recollections of the war. "How can I remain passive now and do nothing to prevent a repetition of that horror, to prevent a new war?" writes one veteran from Barnaul. "I hate those who are preparing for a war and are hoping to unleash it in space as well. . . . I want children to live, everything living to grow and flourish, birds to sing songs to our children, and the sun to smile down on all people on Earth." A letter from the village of Maloye Pekhovo in the Novgorod region reads: "I am a pig-tender. I am fifty. Like all people, I do not want another war. I was a little girl during the war, but I remember that we had nothing to eat, no clothes and no shoes. It was very hard, especially after my father was killed. That is why I shall contribute what I can to the cause of peace."

Many donations are described as ways of keeping alive the memory of husbands, fathers, and grandfathers killed in the war. The women's understanding of "war" is clearly of a time of starvation, sieges, occupations, the burning of villages, and men going off to battle. Relatively few seem to grasp that nuclear war is anything more than an exceptionally bad version of a "regular" war. Many say they do not want their children to live through what *they* lived through, as if a new war would be similar. Only rarely is an explicit fear of nuclear war expressed: "I am terrified by the thought that a huge bomb could wipe out our city and everyone and everything in it. And if many bombs are dropped, the whole planet would die. To prevent this, I am ready to contribute to the Peace Fund."

Yet concern about the threat of nuclear war appears to be a relatively recent phenomenon. Soviet émigré and former pollster Vladimir Shlapentokh noted in a 1984 article in the journal *Problems of Communism* that while the threat of a third world war was painted as both imminent and real during the closing years of the Stalin regime, beginning in 1953 the government emphasized a comforting vision of growing world socialism and stressed that a new war could be avoided. Repeated references to the protective might of the Soviet Army and the "support for the Soviet Union by peaceloving people throughout the world" left their mark on public opinion. Ninety-seven percent of the respondents to a 1960 nationwide poll answered "yes" to the question "Will mankind manage to avert a new world war?" Public complacency remained intact even during the Cuban missile crisis, which was played far less alarmingly in the Soviet press than in the West. When Shlapentokh conducted a 1968 *Pravda* survey asking readers to "raise any issue bothering them," almost no one mentioned the threat of war. This complacency continued through the days of detente in the 1970s; in both the official and *samizdat* literature of this era there are few references to a fear of a new war.

Then, in the early 1980s, official portrayal of the prospects for peace shifted. President Ronald Reagan's descriptions of the Soviet Union as an "evil empire" and "the focus of evil in the modern world," his offhand reference to bombing the Soviet Union, and statements by his advisors that a nuclear war was winnable and survivable all produced much alarm in the Soviet Union. Visiting Western scientists and activists bringing information about the consequences of nuclear war may also have helped draw attention to the dangers. At any rate, assurances that the mighty Soviet government would never allow another war to begin were suddenly replaced by a public admittance that the Soviet Union was vulnerable to American missiles, followed by almost frantic calls for nuclear arms negotiations. In a March 1983 interview in *Pravda*, Soviet leader Yuri Andropov drew an alarming picture of American military might, saying that the American arsenal had swelled from 4,000 to 10,000 weapons in a few years, and that the Reagan administration "invents new plans on how to unleash a nuclear war in the best way with the hope of winning it."

The resulting war scare was kept alive by daily newspaper articles and television shows painting an apocalyptic vision of imminent nuclear catastrophe. Reagan was frequently compared to Hitler and portrayed as someone "ready and willing to press the button." A map from the 1985 edition of a Soviet publication called *Whence the Threat to Peace,* which hung on the walls of thousands of classrooms and meeting halls, illustrates this terrified view of the world. In the center of the map is a large, pink, tender-looking Soviet Union. Hovering above it is a fierce dark brown North America bristling with nuclear missiles, bombers, submarines, tanks, and fighter planes. Dark patches with more missiles and bases in Western Europe, Turkey, the Indian Ocean, and Japan surround the rest of the pink area, and black arrows with points embedded in pink represent the flight paths of missiles. Next to the map are vivid color photographs and descriptions of NATO nuclear and conventional weaponry. In the lower left-hand corner is a cartoon depicting three Nazi-like generals, with hats identifying them as "$", "NATO," and "USA," attempting to push the Earth off a precipice with a crowbar; the only force preventing their success is a strong muscled arm labeled "USSR."

Letters began flooding the headquarters of the Peace Committee anxiously inquiring what could be done to avert a nuclear catastrophe. The Peace Committee and its local branches were suddenly busy organizing petition drives, peace art and essay contests, and fund-raising events for the Peace Fund, as well as trying to cope with a new flood of American citizen diplomats arriving on peace missions. In 1983, the Peace Committee helped establish a nationwide "lesson for peace" in Soviet schools on September 1, the first day of school. Local peace committees and other groups began arranging mass peace rallies in protest of the neutron bomb, the deployment of American missiles in Western Europe, "Reaganism," and "American aggression." In October 1983, nearly 800,000 people turned out in the streets of Moscow for one such rally.

"People sometimes ask whether it is necessary to hold all these mass actions when an unshakeable moral and political unity exists in this country, when the CPSU [Communist Party] and Soviet state are doing everything to preserve and strengthen peace," wrote Yuri Zhukov, a commentator for *Pravda* and then-president of the Soviet Peace Committee, in the Moscow-based journal *International Affairs* in May 1985. "[But] these actions are of tremendous political significance. They impart a special weight to the peace initiatives of the Soviet state. What government in the West can say that its policy is approved of and supported by the entire nation?"

Of course, as was frequently pointed out by the American press, the themes of these rallies were hardly spontaneous, being already emblazoned on mass-produced posters. The virtues of the Soviet government's peace initiatives were not in question, and the rallies were carefully organized by local peace committees, Komsomol, trade union branches, and other Party-controlled organs. At times, attendence was so strongly encouraged at the workplace as to become essentially mandatory: one's absence at a rally might be noticed disapprovingly. On the other hand, coercion alone cannot account for these sorts of turnouts. In 1984, a Moscow medical student told me wistfully that "we had 800,000 people come out for a demonstration, and the *New York Times* said it was just propaganda." She was disappointed that what for her had been a genuine expression of her concerns about nuclear war had been so discounted abroad. Several years later, an art teacher in Leningrad described these early 1980s demonstrations as "both official and unofficial. The outward form was official, but our feelings were real. The slogans were not what mattered. We were trying to show that we cared."

"RUSSIAN DOVES: SOVIET PEACE GROUPS HAVE OFFICIAL SANCTION TO DENOUNCE AMERICA, BUT NOTHING IS SPONTANEOUS, CERTAINLY NOT THE SLOGANS THE DEMONSTRATORS UTTER," ran the headline of a front-page *Wall Street Journal* article on June 21, 1982. "The desire for peace is deeply felt in a country that lost twenty million of its people in World War II," wrote reporter David Brand. "But many Western analysts believe that the Soviet government carefully nurtures these feelings in a campaign that is aimed partly at creating an image of an aggressive America and partly at justifying the Soviet Union's heavy military spending for ostensibly defensive purposes."

The *Wall Street Journal* article appeared just ten days after a quarter million people had occupied Central Park in one of the largest peace demonstrations in U.S. history. As the nuclear freeze movement continued to gain momentum in the United States, the Soviets decided to hop aboard, proclaiming in late 1982 that they too were for a freeze. Whether this was mere smart politicking, based on an assessment that it was safe to support something to which the Reagan administration would never agree, or whether this reflected a true policy commitment, is difficult to guess: their bluff, if it was one, was never called. Meanwhile, the nuclear freeze movement had difficulty surviving Soviet amiability toward its goals. Peace activists constantly had to dig themselves out of a catch-22: if the Soviets won't agree to an arms control proposal, then it must be unrealistic. If they will agree to it, then it must be a bad idea.

At the same time, the Soviet Union found itself on the popular side of the hottest disarmament issue in Western Europe—the deployment of new American cruise and Pershing II missiles in Europe, ostensibly as a response to the replacement of existing Soviet SS-4 and SS-5 missiles with modernized SS-20s. NATO's arguments for deployment of the Euromissiles, as they were known, sounded weak even to moderate circles of Western opinion, and massive peace demonstrations erupted throughout Western Europe. The Soviet Union did its best to take advantage of this moral high ground, and they were successful enough that some Reagan administration officials nervously proclaimed that countermeasures were needed against the Soviet Union's peace campaign. Charles Wick, director of the United States Information Agency, was quoted in the *Wall Street Journal* on May 17, 1983, as saying: "What's happening? The Soviets are characterizing themselves as the peace party, and we're the bad guys."

The Reagan administration struck back, claiming that the Western peace movement had in fact been inspired by a huge KGB disinformation campaign emanating from Moscow. President Reagan suggested in several speeches that the nuclear freeze movement was part of a Soviet plan to weaken America. When asked to point to evidence for this, Reagan referenced a July 1982 article in *Reader's Digest* by John Barron called "The KGB's Magical War for 'Peace.'" Barron's article relied heavily on selected quotes from a KGB defector: "The trick is to make people support Soviet objectives by fooling them into thinking they are supporting something else, like peace."

Articles also began appearing in magazines such as *Strategic Review* and *Parameters: The Journal of the American Army War College* analyzing the infiltration of Communist influences into the Western peace movement. The new Soviet "peace offensive," wrote West German parliament member Hans Graf Huyn in a fall 1984 *Strategic Review* article, "is novel only in its intensity and pervasiveness." Its success, he said, is dependent on the "recruitment of respected personalities who have no leanings toward communist ideology or Soviet objectives, but who fail to recognize the hidden forces at work. . . . They thus become the involuntary players of an orchestrated score that is finely attuned to Western target audiences."

Many conservative analysts dwelled on the ominous connotations that could be read into the dual meanings of "peace" and "world." The phrase *My khotim mir,* for example, usually translated as "We want peace," could also mean "We want the world." Marxist-Leninist interpretations, they claimed, have also added subtle layers on top of the dictionary meanings of *mir.* "The Russian word for 'peace' and its ideological connotations trace a meaning that is starkly different from what is understood under the term in the West," wrote Dutch analysts J.A. Vermatt and Hans Bax in fall 1983. The Soviets believe that peace "is the harmonious condition that can exist only in a communist society and, as such, is attainable only through struggle and conflict. . . . *Mir* is not to be found in non-socialist countries." According to an entry in the Great Soviet Encyclopedia: "The victory of socialism all over the world will eventually eliminate social and national causes of any war whatsoever. The historical mission of communism, therefore, is to eliminate war and to establish everlasting *mir* on earth."

Despite these warnings, it soon became clear that the Soviet peace campaign was essentially reactive in character, an effort to hop aboard an existing popular movement in the West that was itself a reaction to the renewed Cold War and military muscle-flexing of the Reagan administration's early years. Most Western peace movement leaders took pains to separate themselves from the Soviet camp by calling for the removal of all intermediate range missiles from Europe—U.S. Pershings and cruise missiles *and* Soviet SS-20s. Their strategy was to become a non-aligned movement that transcended bloc politics and placed equal responsibility for the arms race on both superpowers. Many groups, such as END, the European Nuclear Disarmament movement, also issued explicit denunciations of Soviet actions in Poland in 1982 and began extending a sympathetic hand to beleaguered dissident peace groups in Eastern Europe, thus recognizing the artificiality of "peace committee" activity in those countries.

Official Soviet peace champions found the notion of equal blame completely unacceptable. "We believe the U.S. is fully responsible for the arms race and the lack of progress toward disarmament," a Novosti publication stated flatly in 1984. And they indignantly responded to the "massive slanderous attacks," as Zhukov put it, on their indigenous peace movement. "Employed again and again is the libelous fabrication that the struggle for peace is forbidden in socialist countries, and there is talk that 'non-aligned' anti-war movements should not cooperate with the peace committees functioning in these countries," he wrote in 1985. In 1984, the Soviet Peace Committee published a book in Russian for domestic distribution called *Chronicles of the Fight for Peace, 1945-1984,* which attempted to refute the idea that the rest of the world ascribed no significance to the Soviet peace movement:

> Millions of common and honest people in all countries are listening to the Soviet people's voice with great respect. That's why open opponents to the peace movement and the agent-provocateurs who have penetrated it (especially during this period of its increase) are trying to slander Soviet peace fighters and their organizations and to build a very real iron curtain between the anti-war movement in the West and mass public organizations in the USSR and other socialist countries. . . . They began to shout from each corner that all those actions are organized "by command from the top," that this movement has an "official" character and is used only to support the policy of the Soviet government. . . . We didn't and don't have any necessity to organize such a movement "from the top." Who speaks so in the West is either a paid slanderer or an easy believer who got under the influence of slanderers. . . . Some people in the West badly want to believe that the Soviet people are against the policy of the CPSU and Soviet State. But these dreams are unrealizable. There is not a Soviet man in the whole of our country who doesn't approve with all his heart the gigantic work done by our Party on the international stage for a course of peace and happiness for our people and all the peoples on Earth.

Before *perestroika,* Americans who met with Peace Committee officials heard three things: we are for peace, you started it, and Afghanistan doesn't count. Each question had a pat answer. When Americans brought up Soviet human rights abuses, they were harangued about American human rights abuses of blacks and Native Americans. When they brought up Jewish emigration, they were lectured about the difference between "internal" and "international" affairs. The ball was unfailingly batted back into the Americans' court: "What about Afghanistan?" was immediately countered by a defensive, "Well, what about Nicaragua?"

Many Americans found these encounters disturbing, particularly since some aspects of the "line" contained truth. Those who had never thought about the influence of defense contractors in weapons decision-making, the ways American mass media can slant news, or the role of the U.S. military in the Third World were compelled to confront a very different vision of their own country for the first time. But it is hard to be self-critical when the person offering the criticism is at the same time insisting that *he,* on the other hand, is completely right. Americans were exasperated by Soviet Peace Committee officials' refusal to consider that internal dynamics within the Soviet military might also contribute to the arms race, or that the Soviet government's actions in Afghanistan undermined the credibility of its admirably worded "peace initiatives," or that Soviet restrictions on information, travel, and freedom of expression for its own citizens contributed to the "image of the enemy" abroad.

A few American visitors accepted the Soviet explanation of the world made simple and returned home believing that "the most serious obstacle to achieving a new period of detente is the slanted and scanty coverage of the USSR in the U.S. news media," as Alan Thompson, the president of the National Council of American-Soviet Friendship, said in 1984. For some, this "we're-to-blame" mentality produced optimism: if the problem really is us and not them, then our task as peace activists is straightforward. All we have to do is mobilize our democratic traditions, throw the bad guys out of office, and live in a disarmed world happily ever after.

But most of the Americans subjected to these tirades became frustrated and angry. Many of them were no fans of the Reagan Administration, either, but they stiffened at the self-righteous smugness of their interlocuters. "We arrived at the Kiev Peace

Committee with a beautiful handmade peace quilt to present to them," recalls Diana Glasgow, director of the Holyearth Foundation, about a 1984 visit of American women peace activists. "Just before we went in, a man on the street took me aside and whispered, 'I want you to know that these people are not your friends.' As soon as we were seated, a guy got up and started giving us the usual line. He went on for forty-five minutes, never bothering to ask who we were or what we cared about. We were absolutely outraged. These are women who have put themselves on the line for peace. They know what tear gas smells like. And we get this party hack lecturing to us about peace-loving Soviet policies. We stuffed that quilt under our arms and got out of there."

For many American citizen diplomats, distance from the Peace Committee and a similar group called the Friendship Society became a yardstick for judging the authenticity of a new exchange. Others decided to keep plugging away at the Peace Committee; after all, it had money, staff, a telex machine, contacts in cities all over the Soviet Union, the capacity to grant visa support, and an expressed mandate to promote "peace and friendship." Although these Americans often emphasized that cooperation did not mean they were allied with the Peace Committee's political agenda, they were, of course, frequently accused of this in the West. One of the first large co-sponsored events was a five-nation, 1,200 mile ride from Moscow to Washington in July 1983 called Bike for Peace, which was repeated along a different route in 1986. In 1982, a tiny group called Promoting Enduring Peace, run by an American couple, Howard and Alice Frazier, convinced the Peace Committee to co-sponsor a Soviet-American "peace cruise" down the Volga River. The cruise proved so popular that it became an annual event. In 1986, Soviets and Americans cruised together down the Mississippi River, and cruises on the Dnieper River began in 1988.

On the plus side, these trips allowed thousands of Soviets and Americans to meet, discuss, argue, come to a better understanding of one another, and sometimes become friends. On the minus side, the Soviets chosen for these so-called citizen exchanges were often pulled from the ranks of the *nomenklatura,* those who live in the world of privileges conferred by artistic ability, academic prowess, or good Party connections, and who therefore tend to present a rosy view of life in the country. But American sponsors of these events felt that imperfect large Soviet-American citizen exchanges were better than no exchanges at all. They were proud of the way they had compelled the Peace Committee to put its money and time where its mouth had always been. "Sometimes you just want to shake those people [at the Peace Committee] by the scruff of the neck," one American peace cruise organizer confessed in 1988, "but the fact is, it is possible to get certain things done with their help."

In March 1987, Yuri Zhukov, the tendentious Soviet Peace Committee president, was replaced by Genrikh Borovik, a playwright, author, and television talk show host with a genial manner and an apparent willingness to try new things. By late 1987, many Americans were telling enthusiastic stories about a "new" Peace Committee. The atmosphere was completely different, they said. One-way abuse had turned into dialogue. The Soviets were willing to admit that Afghanistan was a problem, that secrecy was a problem, that human rights were a problem. Confrontation was out, cooperation was in.

Not only their rhetoric had changed. As the *neformalniye* (informal) movement in the Soviet Union blossomed (some 30,000 Soviet groups of all kinds, ranging from stamp-collecting clubs to new political parties, had sprung up by the end of 1987), the Peace Committee suddenly opened its doors to many new informal "peace groups." The same officials who had insisted that only one unified peace group was necessary in the Soviet Union were, a few months later, proudly describing their cooperation with Rock Musicians for Peace, Green World, and Travelers in Defense of Peace and Environment. In December 1987, as if to underscore that the most hidden subjects of the past were now on the table, the Soviet Peace Committee opened a "human rights discussion club" and invited leaders of the dissident community to attend.

But voices of skepticism soon arose about this "new" Peace Committee. While "*perestroika* has even gone on in the depths of the Peace Committee," wrote Trust Group leader Andrei Krivov in February 1988, "it is *perestroika* not of thinking, but of tactics." By appearing more moderate, he said, the "more clever" Genrikh Borovik hopes to have access to broader sections of the Western peace and environmental movements. The Peace Committee's friendly adoption of several new informal peace groups "is not moved by a desire to help these groups, but by a desire to co-opt those among them who are willing to cooperate with the Committee in exchange for their independence . . . [and] cave in under the temptation of receiving a number of perks from the authorities. . . . [Then] they can be exploited as the most compliant 'independents' to stage the latest comedy for Western peace activists."

Other observers were more cautious about dismissing the significance of these changes. The authors of a 1987 Helsinki Watch report on independent peace and environmental groups in the Soviet bloc pointed out that while the Peace Committee was now able to keep tabs on these informal peace groups' activities, it had also been forced to recognize a pluralistic approach to peacemaking. The emergence of these groups under the Peace Committee's wing "considerably muddies the political waters and makes it quite difficult to determine the degree of compromise that may be involved," the report said. "But if official bodies are ever to be reinvigorated and if a genuine civil society or public life is ever to arise in the USSR, there will inevitably be those individuals or organizations that must remain in the grey area between officialdom and independent initiative."

Tensions between old and new within the Peace Committee were evident during a citizen diplomacy conference held in February 1988 near Washington, D.C., that was co-sponsored by the Soviet Peace Committee and a Seattle-based group called the Center for Soviet-American Dialogue. Four hundred Americans had come from all over the country to hobnob with a hundred Soviets, one of the largest delegations ever to come to the United States. But the Peace Committee's role in the conference had sparked plenty of gossip in the hallways. The White House's U.S.-Soviet Exchange Initiative office was said to be boycotting the event. One of the recipients of the conference's "Citizen Diplomat Awards" was rumored to have refused to come claim it, and another awardee later confessed privately, "I was tempted to march up there and give it back when the conference director said the Soviet Peace Committee was one of the most sincere and creative groups working for peace today."

There were also rumors that some Soviets had refused to come under the auspices of the Peace Committee and that others had come despite the Peace Committee's best efforts to prevent them.

The Center for Soviet-American Dialogue had initially invited a large pool of Soviet "social innovators," but Peace Committee officials did not take this list seriously; they regarded many of these people as enemies and others as nobodies. They filled the list with their own choices, kicking off a protracted tug-of-war between them and their American partners. On the whole, the Peace Committee won, but at the last minute, the American organizers managed a complicated arrangement whereby two of these "social innovators," Gennadi Alferenko and Rustem Khairov, were whisked to the United States on visas arranged by Evgeny Velikhov, the vice-president of the Soviet Academy of Sciences. With a few other exceptions, the rest of the independently minded Soviets stayed home.

Rama Vernon, director of the Center for Soviet-American Dialogue, made the best of it in public: "Thirty of the people from my original list came, and I would have invited some of the others had I known of their existence." Behind the scenes, the grumbling was more intense, as Americans who had paid a stiff fee to meet with the dynamos of *perestroika* found, with few exceptions, a rather predictable assortment of retired film directors, newspaper editors, political scientists, and Peace Committee bureaucrats. Many of the hallway discussions centered on the question: could Genrikh Borovik—and, by extension, his enigmatic organization—be trusted?

"Borovik? He's a nice man," was all one American leader in Soviet-American exchanges could tell me. Said another, "I assume someone like that has to have been pretty oily to have risen to the top." Borovik's amiable speeches stressing cooperation and the destruction of enemy images were receiving ovations at the conference plenaries. But one Sovietologist in the hallway pointed out that less than a year before, Borovik had hosted a bitterly anti-American documentary on his weekly national television show. His other television credits included shrill-toned "exposés" of the CIA connections of Anatoly Shcharansky, Andrei Sakharov, and other dissidents. At that very moment, Borovik's play, *Agent 00*, a spy-thriller about CIA involvement in the overthrow of Chile's President Allende, was running in New York City off-Broadway with respectable success. Which was all very well, but raised the question: how would a Soviet react to an American Peace Committee if spy-thriller author Tom Clancy were the president?

Borovik consented to be interviewed and we spent thirty minutes together between conference sessions. "We are trying to make our Peace Committee much more open," he said. "In former times, we sometimes believed we were the last truth, that we were always right. We are a more democratic organization now. In the past there was an image that we were strict, we were square, and maybe it was not only an image. Maybe there was some truth to it, because I think the Soviet Peace Committee was too persistent in supporting all of the governmental proposals in the field of international relations. Though I can tell you that with all our mistakes, and big mistakes, in general the policy of the Soviet Union from the very beginning in 1917 was connected with a true desire to achieve peace."

I watched his face carefully as he spoke. His references to past mistakes were disarming, and his voice had a ring of sincerity when he spoke about the need to work together on the pressing ecological and humanitarian problems of the day. It was hard not to like him, and not to want to believe his friendly words.

"I've read a number of articles," I began, "saying that the program of military-patriotic education in Soviet schools is growing now in strength and influence—"

"First of all we don't have any program for military-patriotic education," he interrupted. "There's patriotism, of course, but we try to combine it very closely with internationalism. We never give any chance for people to hate other people. A film like *Amerika* or *Red Dawn,* showing soldiers from the other country shooting children, is absolutely impossible in the Soviet Union."

"So this military-patriotic education program does not exist?" I thought of the manuals I had seen for *Voyenno-Patrioticheskoye Vospitaniye* (literally, "military-patriotic education"), the testimonials from Soviets about the four hours per week of "military training" in ninth and tenth grades, the books for kindergarteners with titles like *Why the Soviet Army is Kin to Everyone* and pop-up designs of Soviet nuclear missiles.

He paused an instant. "Well—it does exist. But I should call it *anti-war* patriotic education rather than military-patriotic education. I wouldn't deny that there is an army, there are the generals, there are the rockets, and so on, but as Mikhail Gorbachev says, to dance the tango you need two." He was back on firmer footing now. "If you want to talk about where the point of blame lies, we made a moratorium for nuclear tests in August 1985, and asked the Americans to join us."

"Alexei Pankin wrote last year in an article in your journal *Twentieth Century and Peace,*" I said, "and I quote, that 'Views in the country [the Soviet Union] on the problems of war and peace are very complicated, contradictory, and dissimilar.' Would you agree?"

His eyes narrowed for a moment. "What was that again?"

I repeated the quote. "No," he declared. "I do not agree. On the question of war and peace the absolute majority is certain that they do not want to have *any* war." But did agreement on goals necessarily mean a uniformity of opinion on how to achieve them? He dodged this and began talking about the U.S. military-industrial complex. "Our system doesn't allow anyone to make money on aggression, on the armaments race. The director of a rocket factory gets the same money as the director of a tractor factory. But this director certainly understands that making rockets is a waste of money and his brains. He would like to produce tractors or some other useful thing. I wouldn't like to blame your system—I don't like to compare—but there is a big group of people here which lives on the military complex. You are afraid of unemployment if some military enterprises would be shut down. For us, there is no threat of unemployment—we need at least 15 million people for the consumer service industries alone. And certainly it is not an easy thing to convert military factories into peace production factories, but is possible, and we are interested in that."

"But does the statement often printed in Soviet newspapers that 'communism, socialism, and peace are indivisible' mean that in order to have a peaceful world we need to have a socialistic world?"

"No, no. We should be civilized, and not kill each other just because you think this chair is red and I think it is brown. Besides, we have global problems which we can solve only together. This great danger unites us. Once Reagan said that we will work together with the Russians only if some people from space come and try to conquer us. I don't think we need that. There is already an invasion of plenty of problems. Gorbachev said that people are ahead of politicians, and I think it's true. So, we can push politicians. It doesn't mean that we can change them, but for some who are very reasonable but not brave enough, maybe we will give them the strength and the courage."

"What does the word 'peace,' *mir,* mean to you, personally?"

"Peace is . . . is . . ." To my surprise, he faltered for a moment. "It means a lot. It means the absence of fear that my children, and my grandson Vanya, would—would ever be—" he paused and took a deep breath, "it's even difficult for me to say, be killed in a war. I would like them to live. . ." And for a moment, like a crack of light through a door, I thought I saw a real person behind the pleasant, neutral face of the Peace Committee president—a father who had not slept well while his journalist son, Archom Borovik, was writing dispatches from the Afghanistan front. Then the door slammed shut again. "And besides, we should come to a new stage of history," he said briskly, recovering his former tone. "We should begin the real history of humanity." My thirty minutes were up; he shook my hand, gave me his card and disappeared.

As one sacrosanct Soviet institution after another came under attack in the Soviet press in 1988, the Peace Committee's turn was bound to come. Tair Tairov, a former staff member of the World Peace Council in Helsinki and a member of the Peace Committee's national presidium, broke the taboo and earned a reputation as the "deep throat" of the Peace Committee when he published an article in *Komsomolskaya Pravda* on June 25, 1988, that lambasted the committee's "regime of personal authority" and "functional closedness and secrecy." He called for open democratic elections to choose a new leadership for the Peace Committee on the national, republican, and local levels and for full financial disclosure of how money from the Peace Fund is spent. Only in this way, he said, would the Peace Committee be able to change its image "as a bureaucratic organization that is summoned without delay to support any foreign policy action of the government and that is devoid of the possibility or the desire to influence the process of forming foreign policy."

Tairov's article led to a scathing reply by Grigory Grechko, a former cosmonaut and another member of the Peace Committee presidium, in which Grechko dismissed Tairov's criticisms as mere revenge for having been abruptly removed from his post at the World Peace Council in Helsinki in 1985 for "his many mistakes." A few months later, I ask Tairov what his mistakes had been. "My mistakes," he replies tersely, "were that I never listened to the stupid orders and instructions that came from Moscow during my years in Helsinki. And that's why I managed to have a very good relationship with the Western peace movements."

No one would accuse Tairov of belonging to the ranks of ordinary Soviet citizens from which, according to him, the new leaders of the Peace Committee should arise. A law professor and member of the Institute of World Economy, Tairov is a tall, aristocratic man of Uzbek descent with a face lined with the marks of inner struggle, who now looks back at his lifetime as a bureaucrat and member of the *nomenklatura* with discomfort and regrets. "I lost twenty years of my life," he says, "twenty years with no chance to speak freely, to implement my ideas and goals and plans—not only me, but a whole generation."

He decided to bring his crusade for *perestroika* within the Peace Committee into the open, he says, only after its leaders refused to respond to his written in-house proposals. "I gave them a lot of constructive ideas, I did not want to criticize and blame them in public, and I expected that they would accept my criticism in a civil way and we would have businesslike discussions. But they declined to do this. They are so confident. They believe that they are invulnerable, that no one can stop them, that this is another zone of silence. Borovik basically represents the anti-*perestroika* camp and the old Brezhnev time. He has made 32 vice-presidents on the committee—they need only write to the Guinness Book of World Records to have it registered!—and a dozen are close friends who have nothing to do with the peace movement. The Soviet people do not know there is such a factory for producing leaders of anti-war campaigns."

I ask him how he managed to keep his job for six years at the World Peace Council in Helsinki if he did not listen to orders from the Peace Committee in Moscow. "I came to Helsinki in 1979, when there was no big peace movement in the West. But a year or two later really great things started happening, the peace movements became very large, and I was doing a good job and was very popular in the West. So they didn't dare call me back. I was invited to many mass gatherings and peace marches in Europe, and I went, even though sometimes Moscow said no, don't go. I was speaking to thousands of people and was very well-known, and I think this is why I survived so long."

While he was working in Helsinki, did he ever feel that he had to make compromises in his personal integrity in order to remain in that position? "Always," he replies instantly. "Always. All these six years, I was always trying to control myself, just for the sake of surviving and doing something good. The atmosphere in the Secretariat of the World Peace Council was horrible—not because the people were bad, but because of all of this tremendous pressure from Moscow: do this, do that, make this, make that."

Did he have to say things which he did not believe? He pauses. "No, I wouldn't say that," he answers. "I never said things which I do not believe. I spoke and wrote articles about disarmament, about pacifism, about the illegality of possessing and stockpiling nuclear weapons. I never spoke against the regime—I preferred not to say anything, when asked, rather than to say something contrary to what I believe. But behind the scenes I was always having big quarrels with the Peace Committee. When Gorbachev came to power in 1985, I thought that now things would really change, and I started to give my criticisms openly." He laughs. "And that, of course, was my real 'mistake'! They gave me three days notice."

Tairov sees little hope for deep changes in the Committee; in 1989 he resigned from the Presidium and threw his civic energies into working for the upstart new Foundation for Social Inventions, one of the Peace Committee's major rivals for Western attention. "Americans are beginning to realize that the Committee is a very small, centralized, rigid organization which does not represent the whole of Soviet society," he says. "And this worries the Peace Committee a lot, because they already have a very bad image in the West European peace movement, so if their image is ruined in the United States then they are finished. But I don't think they will change. There are nice people within the committee, and many share my ideas, but they don't want to speak loudly and lose their privileges."

Some of the Americans who had worked with the Peace Committee for years, and who had known and accepted the old rules, greeted with relief the Peace Committee's increased willingness to participate in new citizen exchanges. Bridges for Peace, for example, a Vermont-based citizen diplomacy group, has been quietly leading groups of Americans to the Soviet Union in cooperation with the Peace Committee and other established Soviet institutions for eight years; its director, Richard Hough-Ross, notes that home visits and other previously unthinkable conditions for their exchanges are now commonplace.

But according to some of the Americans who have tried to cooperate with the "new" Peace Committee, the old ways can surface abruptly when Americans challenge key areas of Peace Committee control over its Soviet-American projects: for example, who gets to come to America on Peace-Committee-sponsored delegations. In 1987, Sharon Tennison, the director of the Center for US-USSR Initiatives in San Francisco, began working with the Peace Committee on an ambitious project called "Soviets Meet Middle America" designed to bring 400 Soviets on visits to small-town and rural American communities over a period of eighteen months. According to their agreement, the Peace Committee would nominate and send half of the overall delegation—200 people—and Tennison and her group would select the other half from among their Soviet friends and acquaintances.

But Tennison had to battle the Peace Committee at every step to get them to abide by this agreement. Her request for a spring 1988 delegation from the Leningrad branch of the Peace Committee, for example, came back with a list of eighteen people selected by the Peace Committee and only two selected by Tennison. According to one of these two, English teacher Valentina Frantseva, they were not informed they had been invited until two weeks before the delegation was to leave, when they were called into the Peace Committee office and told, "You were invited to go, but there's no time to prepare your papers, so it's impossible." Frantseva hurriedly tried to gather the necessary papers anyway and rushed them to the office a few days before the flight was to leave. She was told by Ada Kosygina, the president of the Leningrad branch, to forget it. "Of course I was extremely disappointed," relates Frantseva, "but I thought that was the end of it."

When Tennison discovered that Frantseva and her other nominee would not be coming, she telexed the Leningrad office a message to the effect that, "Either you get those two people over here, or the other eighteen can just stay home." Something in her tone must have conveyed that she meant business. The Leningrad branch hurriedly took Frantseva's papers and managed to do in two days what it had previously said it could not do in five months. A few days later, Frantseva was on a plane to the United States.

In December 1988, Tennison made a last-ditch attempt to

reach an understanding with the Peace Committee by meeting with members of the Presidium, the decision-making body of the Peace Committee, which normally has little to do with executing the Committee's projects. She was astonished to find former president Yuri Zhukov sitting at Genrikh Borovik's elbow; "I thought he had died and been buried." Presidium members listened and promised to try to do better next time. The next delegation list, however, contained eighteen of the Peace Committee's choices and only one person requested by Tennison. Exasperated, she told the Peace Committee that she was turning responsibility for the "Soviets Meet Middle America" program over to the Foundation for Social Inventions and the newspaper *Komsomolskaya Pravda*. "And you should have seen their faces," she recalls. "They *begged* me to give them another chance. But I told them they had cost us $23,000 in delays, cancellations, and extra expenses run up on their American hotel bills, and that they weren't the only game in town anymore."

The American leaders of International Peace Walk (IPW), which organized three Soviet-American cross-country marches in 1987 and 1988, also had their ups and downs with their Peace Committee partners. The make-up of the Soviet delegation on the July 1988 walk across America provoked controversy not only in the United States but also in the Soviet press. Alexander Nezhny, a writer at *Moscow News* and participant in the walk, fired the first salvo in a July 1988 article where he referred to the "bourgeois-mobile," a bus where "Soviet peace champions" rode in air-conditioned comfort while American peace activists gamely walked through Iowa cornfields in 100-degree heat. Praising the "pure-hearted" approach of the Americans, he wrote: "For them, participation in the walk was the result of a deeply personal and responsible decision." And he contrasted this with the Soviet delegation, writing "Alas, many of us turned out to be more pragmatic than the most businesslike Americans. Why walk if a bus is moving behind us? . . . Why talk about the issues that concern humanity, if one has to get another cap or find a less expensive shop? Sometimes I feel utterly ashamed of some of my compatriots—of their greed, of their petty interests, of their lack of principles." Nezhny quoted Allan Affeldt, the American leader of IPW, as saying that the Soviet marchers represented not a cross-section of Soviet society but rather "a cross-section of Soviet bureaucracy."

Nezhny's article produced a flurry of letters to *Moscow News.* "It's no secret that during the years of stagnation these trips were a boon for many high-placed persons," wrote a journalist from Mongolia. "Even today, some functionaries don't hesitate to strike ordinary mortals from the lists in favour of absolutely irrelevant but influential and 'useful' people." A former Intourist guide confessed how "ashamed" she was when she took Soviets around Western countries and saw their obsession with finding "cheap things to buy. No shortages at home can justify that. The only explanation is a lack of dignity."

Izvestia, Trud, and other major papers joined the fray, accusing the Soviet Peace Committee of having stocked the delegation with unqualified, non-English speaking relatives and acquaintances who considered the walk a giant shopping excursion. They pointed out that while two spots on the walk had been reserved for "Moscow high school students," no open competition (through, for example, a peace essay contest) had been held for these spots, and one of them had gone to a young man who spoke no English and had rather low grades, but who happened to be the grandson of a Peace Committee official. Remarked one Soviet journalist: "It's pure sabotage to send people like that on a peace walk. Americans take one look at these people and say, 'Oh, I guess Russians really are a bunch of fat dull bureaucrats,' and that's the end of their interest in citizen diplomacy."

Nezhny's article hit the newsstands just as the walkers were arriving in California. Outraged Peace Committee officials excoriated Nezhny at press conferences and accused IPW leaders of collaborating on the article. Back in Moscow, the Peace Committee rounded up a bevy of journalists likely to write about the Odessa/Kiev walk and warned them that any further critical articles would spell the end of the walks. Relations between the Peace Committee and IPW, already strained at the beginning of the Ukrainian walk, steadily worsened. "Every time we brought up a problem, whether it was too few toilets or too many security guards around the camp," said IPW director Joe Kinczel, "Oryol [of the Peace Committee Secretariat] gave two responses: one, the problem existed only in our heads, and two, if we continued to make a fuss about it, there would be no more walks in the future."

Tanya Pankratova, a bright, personable graduate student of philosophy at Moscow State University, landed a summer job as a translator for the first Soviet-American peace walk in 1987. Like many other Soviets hired to interpret for Americans on "peace missions," she and her friends at first believed that the Americans would speak about peace with the same winks and nods that their own officials did: "Yeah, we're for peace, what's for dinner? Some people want to see the Soviet Union by bus, some by train, and these—by *walking.*" But within a few days, she said, she was converted to believing in the larger goals of the walk. Afterwards, Pankratova showed her slides and shared her impressions with children at several Pioneer camps and schools. "The walk changed my life," she said. "I was just bursting with enthusiasm—I had to tell as many people about it as possible." Meanwhile, two of her American friends, Philadelphia peace activists Bob Alei and Stephanie Nichols, planned to bring two young Soviet walkers to the United States for a four-week joint speaking tour on the East Coast the following spring. It seemed a low-budget way to magnify the impact of the walk in the United States.

But the Peace Committee at first would have no part of it. Alei and Nichols persisted, however, and got the American leaders of International Peace Walk, who were meeting regularly with Peace Committee officials to plan the 1988 walks, to put their speaking tour on the agenda. Hoping for the best, Alei and Nichols booked a hundred school engagements for April 1988. But despite their offer to pay all costs, including the two Soviets' plane tickets, the Peace Committee continued to stonewall them. "They let us know, very bluntly, that they were just not interested," says Bob Alei. "They only relented because of unrelenting pressure from our friends in IPW." Five days before the start of the tour, they heard that Tanya Pankratova and Sasha Kovalev would be allowed to come. Not until she was on the plane did Pankratova believe it was happening. "The only instruction the Peace Committee gave us," she says, "was to 'tell the truth.'" In a whirlwind tour, Pankratova and Kovalev spoke to about 2,000 young Americans, answering the same dozen questions ("Do you get to choose your job?" "What about human rights?" "Do you have vacations?") hundreds of times.

Back home, Pankratova and other young Soviet walkers began trying to organize an informal group that would take advantage of the new "private visa" regulations (Americans can now get visas to the Soviet Union, and vice versa, if they are invited by friends; previously the invitation had to come from a relative). They hoped to become a referral service for Americans and Soviets who wanted to visit each other's countries in a low-cost, informal way. "We want to have no theory, no ideology, no politics at all, but just to be a very practical technical mechanism for more exchange," explains Pankratova. Months later, they had dozens of proposals on paper and "a lot of smiles and friendly words," but little progress despite almost daily meetings with Peace Committee officials. "Every time we bring them something, they look at it and say, 'this won't work, this won't work.' So we revise our proposal and bring it back, and they say it again." Still, Pankratova was undaunted. "The Peace Committee really has changed. It is one of our most progressive bureaucracies. It's still a bureaucracy, of course, but we think they will help us eventually. We have to have a shelter of some sort, and they are better than Komsomol or some other place." Why are they better than Komsomol? She smiles. "You see, sometimes old bureaucrats are better than young bureaucrats," she says, "because they are tired of their jobs."

One Peace Committee bureaucrat who was clearly tired of his old job is Anatoly Belyaev, the editor-in-chief since 1982 of the Peace Committee's monthly magazine *Twentieth Century and Peace*, written primarily for foreign distribution but with a domestic circulation of about 80,000. In 1987, *Twentieth Century and Peace* transformed within a matter of months from a worthless propaganda rag into one of the most radical voices of *glasnost*. Articles appeared sharply criticizing the Soviet people's "nuclear illiteracy," questioning the role of the Soviet Army, and suggesting that Soviet Peace Committee officials should stop toasting to East-West friendship on luxury cruises and start trying to mediate in the Armenia-Azerbaijan conflict. *Twentieth Century and Peace* caused a minor sensation in March 1989 when it published an essay by exiled writer Alexander Solzhenitsyn.

Belyaev is a crusty old survivor playing with new possibilities like a delighted child. "We are some kind of dissident magazine now," he says with satisfaction. "We began by publishing articles from the older generation of dissidents, the 'sixties people' (*shestidesyatniki*), many of whom suffered very much five or ten years ago. And now we have some very clever younger people writing for us. We had to *invent* our magazine. We invented an approach to national problems, invented an approach to the Army. Our writers have fresh thinking and they are not fettered by slogans."

Boris Senkin, the managing editor of *Twentieth Century and Peace*, pinpoints the change in the magazine to an April 1987 article called "Freedom to Remember" by a young writer named Gleb Pavlovsky. "Before this the magazine was very dull and official, with no ideas and nothing to think about," says Senkin. "I used to be envious of the mail departments of Western magazines—such sharp, clever letters, and in such quantity. We had no hope of getting such letters—the letters we received were on par with the magazine as whole. There was only such childish, provincial trash that we could not print. Then, after we published Pavlovsky's article, I was astonished at the letters that began to appear."

Senkin says they have been amazed and gratified by the results of a recent questionnaire sent to their readers asking them to report what changes they had noticed. "Your magazine used to compete only with the 'Agitator' bulletin in dullness," wrote one reader in Tambov. "Now it differs like sky from the earth. While reading it I sometimes feel that we live in a civilized country with long democratic traditions. It's surprising how many clever people there are in our country." When readers were asked to name the best article in recent years, the top vote-getter was a December 1988 essay by Gleb Pavlovsky called "Peace in the World and in the USSR." Wrote Pavlovsky:

> Only a nonviolent world can become a nuclear-free world—and only in this sequence, not the other way around. But for us in the USSR this road is just beginning, and we are on the threshold only of its first, inner stage: that of becoming at peace in our country, living in a nonviolent community, with morally justified order, but not paralyzed by force and fear. Peace in the country and civic peace come *first*—then, as a result, the struggle for 'world peace.'
>
> The peace movement in the USSR was twice broken off and slandered and twice forgotten: at first by punishment, in the 1920s and 1930s, which put an end to alternative military service and Tolstoyist, vegetarian communes . . . . and the second time, in the form of official government pacifism artificially implanted by the end of the 1940s, the so-called 'struggle against warmongers,' i.e., the 'struggle for peace' all over the world—except the USSR. . . .

Today, peace is again becoming a *deed* in Russia. When, at its spring session, the Soviet Peace Committee adopted the course of internal reconciliation and cooperation with informal peacemaking initiatives in the country, although with some hesitation, this was not only a comprehensible striving of an old institution to find its place in the changed reality, but also a sign of the thawing of the will for civic peace. The forms which decorative pacifism liked so much—roundtable conferences, seminars, walks, people's diplomacy—will be of use, but not so much with overseas pacifists and humane millionaires, *as with our own stubborn fellows!*

Peacemakers are needed more in the country than outside. For example, where were our peacemakers during the days in Sumgait: at a seminar in Venice, at a festival in Cannes? As soon as the news about this, alas, key event of the year was heard, the intelligentsia whose number is so big when they have to receive a Western delegation, or when they have a chance to fly to the West, didn't turn up at the Transcaucasia. . . . If the anti-war Soviet intelligentsia could sacrifice—how awful—their summer leave and dachas, and struggle for peace in the Transcaucasia, perhaps there would have been no 'airport crisis' in Yerevan, no shots would have been fired in September. After all, isn't the chance of saving at least the life of one of our countrymen—in a *peaceful* country and in *peacetime*—worth all the millions of the Peace Fund, the efforts of all the staff members of the Soviet Peace Committee? . . .

Most people, naturally, prefer the conditions of peace to the conditions of war—but are almost never ready for peace as spiritual work. Peace is the spiritual thirst for reality, diversity and freedom, and the will to nonviolence as a condition for this. . . . The struggle for peace is always the dialogue of the minority yearning for peace with the majority thirsting only for the advantages of the absence of war. The peace movement, not being the majority, must become a voice heard everywhere: smooth, honest, absolutely in tune and independent. The actions of politicians and the responses of the people will often ignore this voice, and then peacemakers must go into action. . . . Let's repeat Spinoza, and with pleasure: 'Peace is not the absence of war, but a virtue stemming from the firmness of the spirit.'

Articles such as this have provoked displeasure from the ruling elite of the Peace Committee, but the editors of *Twentieth Century and Peace,* buoyed by support from their readers and what Belyaev calls "an inner elation," are so far withstanding the pressures. "It all falls on Anatoly Belyaev's shoulders—the rest of us feel only the tremors," observes Senkin. "Within the Peace Committee there is a so-called executive council overseeing the magazine, but they are all very busy people and so in fact we are fairly free."

Says Belyaev: "Many functionaries from the Peace Committee and the Peace Fund would like to close us, but they can't. Too many people know about us, there would be too much publicity. We have a very strong position. These functionaries cannot answer us on our level. We are above them. They have no ideas, they have nothing to say. And we have very thick skins.

"Just now we are seeing the development of some kind of movement—not an artificial movement—but a *natural* movement for peacemaking. To me, peace is the devotion to human values. We have a lot of problems within ourselves and within our country, and we have to solve these problems before we can say that we are a peaceful people. In this belief we differ, yes, from the so-called 'public leadership' of the Peace Committee. They are show-biz people, and there are some cosmetic changes going on. They prefer to dance for peace, sing for peace, cry for peace. Hugging, kissing, praying for peace—it's okay. Maybe we are too serious in our peacemaking business. But we believe that sincerity, truth, and above all *ideas* are really important. The time has come for division. Let us invent new words to describe all the different positions, so that we can discuss *ideas* rather than just quarrel and fight. Let us get rid of the mask of unity."

In the past, one could count on the unerring sameness of the Peace Committee no matter where it was found: in every humble factory meeting room, provincial town hall, and luxurious palace of friendship there would be the same bottles of mineral water, polished long tables, smooth explanations, and virtuoso ability to hog the microphone. No more. Like other once monolithic Soviet institutions, including the Party itself, the Peace Committee has lost its facade of unanimity. In many places, especially in the Baltics, Georgia, and some smaller Russian cities, local branches of the Peace Committee have become startlingly independent and have begun to work in partnership with grassroots groups. Starting in 1989, local Peace Fund offices have been able to keep ten percent of the money they collect, which is beginning to decentralize the Peace Committee's activities.

There are some other hopeful signs that the Peace Committee

may gradually be moving away from attempting "to express the will of the Soviet people" and toward a more benign role as a Party-supported public affairs office and a funding source for legitimate projects on conflict resolution and citizen diplomacy. In early 1990 the Peace Committee established a national Center on Reconciliation and re-organized its standing commissions to reflect a new emphasis on finding solutions to conflicts between ethnic groups and republics.

When it comes to interacting with foreigners, the Peace Committee's job has become rather easy; it can merely repeat and amplify what one Western analyst recently termed "the best party line in the world." The withdrawal of Soviet troops from Afghanistan, force reductions in Europe, retirement of many Soviet military officers and significant cutbacks in Soviet defense spending have all put Peace Committee officials in a sanguine position when they are called upon to describe the "peace-loving policies of the Soviet state."

Nevertheless, the current palatability of the present Peace Committee's words and deeds does not mean there have been fundamental changes in its structure and purpose. The Peace Committee remains an organ of the Communist Party, loyal to its instructions and designed to serve its interests. It is no substitute for a truly public and independent organization, and unless radical changes are made in the ways its leadership is chosen and its decision-making conducted, it never will be. As long as the Peace Committee claims to speak for "the Soviet people," a disagreeable whiff of paternalism and arrogance will linger at 36 Prospekt Mira. As the peasant says to the snake in the Russian fable: "*Khot ty i v novoi kozhye, da serdtse u tebya vsyo tozhye*—Although your skin is new, your heart remains the same."

7 | Teach Your Children Well

Galina Dolya points to the white terrier mutt sleeping under her kitchen table. "It all began," she says, "with *him*." In summer 1987, she and David Bell, both English teachers in Dubna, a small city north of Moscow, went camping with their families in the Fanski Mountains of Uzbekistan. While sightseeing in Samarkand they visited a mosque, and Dolya's ten-year-old son Kolya waited outside with Jim, the dog. By the time they came out of the mosque, Kolya and the dog had been surrounded by several West German tourists who had discovered that Kolya spoke English. "The others in our tour group only came to the Soviet Union because it is fashionable now, and all they do is complain," Doris Basu, a teacher from Dusseldorf, told Dolya. The Dubna families invited Basu and her husband to ditch their tour and join them for the evening. Soon Dolya and Basu discovered that they both taught English to children. After four hours of eager conversation in a local restaurant, they parted with promises to set up a pen-pal exchange between their students, and within a year, more than one hundred students in each school were corresponding with one another.

"So that really did begin with Jim," says Dolya, smiling at her dog, who has woken up at the sound of his name and is licking her hand. "And the rest began with the other Jim—the American Jim."

In February 1987, James Baumgaertner, the Wisconsin founder and director of the International Peace Lantern Exchange Project, had given a stack of children's peace lanterns to independent networker Vladimir Shestakov in Leningrad. Shestakov's mother lives in Dubna, and while visiting her Shestakov had shown the lanterns to Mikhail Zhokhov, a World War II veteran and retired school director who is the head of the Dubna branch of the Peace Committee. Zhokhov, in turn, showed them to one of his former teachers, David Bell, who wrote to Baumgaertner and asked for more. In fall 1987, Baumgaertner shipped him a box of lanterns made by American children, each decorated with words and drawings about peace and the photograph, address, and favorite hobbies of its maker.

When Dolya and Bell opened the box, they were struck by the children's photographs. "They were so—so open," says Dolya. "All of these smiling faces—it was like a miracle. One lantern was made by a three-year-old child who drew a rainbow and a picture of himself. His footprints and handprints are there, and his mother writes: 'Let my hands grow, let there be peace so that my little hands can become big hands and I can make a lot of good things for other people.'"

Dolya's students at School #6 in Dubna were soon writing letters to the young American lanternmakers and shipping their own lanterns to Baumgaertner. In August 1988, Bell and Dolya organized a lantern-floating ceremony on the Volga River in which 300 children participated. "The ceremony gets the kids involved, and then they start thinking about what they're doing," says Bell. "Galya and I both use a quote that we think belongs to Abe Lincoln. There are two ways to destroy your enemy. You can try physically to destroy him, but then you yourself may be destroyed. Or you can make your enemy your friend."

"When you are writing to someone, and you see his smiling face in a photograph," adds Dolya, "you know that he is your friend, and you would never be able to kill him."

It is snowy November evening in Dubna, a quiet, tree-lined small city on the banks of the Volga River. David Bell, an American-born Soviet citizen whose family emigrated to the Soviet Union in 1931, is a lanky, white-haired, fiery old man with a trace of a Texan accent and the mannerisms of a roadside preacher. Galina Dolya is brown-eyed and graceful, a mother of two teen-aged boys who has a pretty, puggish face and magenta-tinted dark hair. They make, on the surface, an unlikely pair, but their mutual passions for teaching English, for the outdoors, and now for peace work have made them close friends for ten years.

"The main thing is that these exchanges break up stereotypes about Americans," says Bell, explaining that for years official Soviet media depicted America as a place of high crime, racial discrimination, and widespread unemployment, with a disaffected youth and working class that looks to the Soviet Union for moral leadership. In more subtle ways, Americans were also depicted as greedy, self-centered, shallow, and materialistic. Some Soviets believe that from an early age Americans are taught to smile at the world, no matter what their real feelings might be. The phrase *Amerikanskaya ulibka,* "American smile," has a meaning in Russian similar to "crocodile smile" in English—a smile that hides and deceives. Other Soviets believe that Americans are extremely pragmatic and businesslike, to the point of having few moral or cultural values.

"Nowadays the picture of America given by our newspapers, magazines, radio, and television is quite different, and much better," says Bell. "But before *perestroika,* the image was as bad as the image that Americans had of Russians. On TV, all you saw were the blacks going through the garbage, homeless people sleeping in parks, broken windows in the Bronx."

"I used to take the satirical magazine *Krokodil,* and the last page always had a big cartoon about America," says Dolya. "For example, there would be a wolf with a knife wearing an Uncle Sam hat, labeled 'Imperialism.'" But even in those days, she adds, many Soviets made a distinction between the evil deeds and intentions of the U.S. government and the good-heartedness of simple American people, a belief reinforced both by internal propaganda (Soviets should, after all, be in solidarity with "American workers") and by the powerful psychological forces of projection. Since Soviets felt they had little influence on their government's actions abroad, they assumed Americans did as well.

"The officials pounded the image of the American evil empire into our heads," says Bell. "but a lot of people were still sympathetic to Americans."

"Yes," says Dolya, "but on the other hand, the propaganda did its work. The stereotypes did affect people. For example, a couple of years ago I asked my students to write down their images of America and Americans. And some of the children wrote things like racial discrimination, greed for profits, capitalism, poor people. But not all children have these images. Many have just the other tendency—they love everything American, they think America is paradise."

"So now our task is to help the kids get a balanced impression and a balanced knowledge from an early age," says Bell.

"We may not be able to change stereotypes in the minds of

grownups," adds Dolya, "but we must not allow them to appear in children's minds."

David Bell's own story puts him in a unique position to bridge the Soviet-American gap. His father and seven of his father's brothers and sisters emigrated to America in 1911 to escape pogroms against Jews in the Ukraine. As a young man, Bell's father was the "lefty" of the family and was active in socialist politics. In 1931, he was asked to lead a tourist group to the Soviet Union because of his fluency in Russian and English. While in Moscow, he met an official in the Ministry of Agriculture who pleaded with him to stay in the Soviet Union and "help build socialism." Bell's father took the offer and sent a telegram to Texas, and a few months later his wife and three children arrived in Moscow.

Bell remembers his childhood in Moscow as "very cold, very oppressive." But the family scraped by until his father was arrested during one of Stalin's purges. "My father stopped building socialism on March 14, 1938," he says. Surprisingly, his father was not convicted—"they couldn't find anything to accuse him of, which was absolutely extraordinary for those days"—and so he was exiled to Kazakhstan, where he got a job as an English teacher. When the war began, however, many people from the European part of Russia were evacuated to Kazakhstan and his job was given to someone who was not a so-called "enemy of the people." With no job, he soon died from exhaustion and hunger.

Meanwhile, twenty-year-old David Bell had been scooped out of classes at a chemical institute, pushed through a six-month officer's training course, and given a commission in the Red Army. During the war he served as a landmine expert and a "sapper," planting mines and building fortifications in Poland and Germany. Was he in any battles? "What do you think I was paid for?" he snorts. "Of course I was. I was wounded three times. I had some luck. When you step on a mine the probability of survival is not very great, because usually you fall on another mine. So the expression is that the sapper makes only one mistake in his life. Well, I stepped on a mine, and it knocked my feet out from under me and I just sat down right where the mine had been."

I mention that it seems that the memory of World War II is kept alive here in the Soviet Union much more than it is anywhere else—

"—and more than it should be," Bell interrupts. "That's what you want to say, isn't it? That we talk about it too much. 'We fought this war, we defended peace, we must be ready to defend peace again,' and all that. You're right. We do talk too much about that. What about World War III? What about the way our government has built up its weapons? We've never made any direct noises to our government about that, and that always gets your goat in America. We're not out in the streets telling the government to stop building this or that. But slowly, things are changing here. People are demanding to know how their money is being spent, what the military budget is, for example. As the saying goes, *Vnachale bylo slovo*—'In the beginning was the word.' We're starting to have *glasnost* about these things, and that's the first important step."

In fall 1987, Bell was granted permission to go to the United States and visit relatives whom he had not seen in fifty-six years. He had just retired from his career as an English teacher, and his three-month journey across America helped give new direction to his life. "When Abe Lincoln's mother was on her dying bed, she said to him, 'Abe—be somebody.' So, with my trip to America, and with Gorbachev and all the new changes, I said to myself, 'Dave— *do* something!'" After the first box of peace lanterns arrived, Bell began a busy correspondence with James Baumgaertner in Wisconsin and became the letterwriting hub of the Soviet peace lantern network. Lantern enthusiasts in Volkhov, Krasnodar, Novosibirsk, and other cities began relying on Bell for updated information and fresh supplies of lanterns.

"Here's a woman in Krasnodar named Tatiana Megentesova, who belongs to a society called the Torch of Rerikh, and she writes that they dropped leaflets from an airplane to advertise their lantern float last August!" he exclaims, holding up a lengthy handwritten letter. "But she says she has trouble getting the local Pioneer Club authorities to cooperate—she calls them a 'bog.' She writes that the first secretary of their city Party Committee said that lately there are too many of these *mirotvortsi,* these peace-creators, and we should be making the army stronger instead. And the head of the Afghanistan veterans' club in Krasnodar calls her a pacifist and is very opposed to her activities. So she is appealing to me for help."

Bell is grateful that in his own city he has managed to find support among local Party leaders. Without it he doesn't think he would have had the courage to keep going. "You have to understand the psychology of a person like me. Anyone who lives here who was born elsewhere is an alien and automatically under suspicion. I've lived through fear all my life. You understand? I'm fighting fear within myself, doing all this. Listen, do you know anything about the history of this country? I'll tell you the history. Three hundred years of the Czar family. Seven years of Lenin. Then twenty-seven years of Joe Stalin. Eleven years of Khrushchev. Nineteen years of Brezhnev. A year and a half of Andropov. A year and two months of Chernenko. And now we're just beginning to live."

Bell was a catalyst for setting up a sister-city relationship between Dubna and James Baumgaertner's hometown of La Crosse, Wisconsin. When he and Mikhail Zhokhov, the head of the local Peace Committee, wrote a proposal to their mayor about matching with La Crosse, they were careful to avoid the usual verb *prosim*—meaning "we ask, request, beg"—and instead chose words that meant, "we express our desire." "Because we're up to here with begging," says Bell. "That's the mentality we're up against. Always asking, always begging for permission. No—we are expressing our desire. We looked in the big Russian dictionary to find just the right word." The two mayors signed an agreement in summer 1989, and the pairing is now recognized by Sister Cities International. The first delegation from Dubna visited La Crosse in October 1989 and an ambitious series of music, business, and children's exchanges is planned.

"Now this work is everything to me," says Bell. "It's my whole life. People ask me why I don't just go to America and stay there. But that's so silly. I've lived my whole life in this country, I have my wife here, I have my home, I have friends, and Dubna is a beautiful place to live. And besides, things are getting exciting here. I'd like to live up to the year 2000, just to see how it will all end up!"

Galina Dolya's biggest challenge is balancing her peace work with the demands of being a wife, mother, and full-time teacher. Dolya grew up in the city of Donetsk in the Ukraine; her father died when she was fourteen and her mother when she was sixteen, but she still finished high school with a gold medal and earned admission to Kharkov University. She met and married her husband Sergei after only two years at the university and was forced to interrupt her studies when he was sent as a young physics graduate student to work at the Joint Institute for Nuclear Research in Dubna. But she stuck to her dream of becoming an English teacher and managed to obtain her degree by taking correspondence courses and commuting to Kalinin, seventy kilometers away, all while raising her two sons.

Dolya has now taught English at Dubna's School #6 for thirteen years. Last year she received a special award as "Merited Teacher of the Republic" for her innovative methods. But she is often overworked and exhausted, and sometimes a minor congenital heart condition forces her to lie flat for hours. "I am a very bad wife and a very bad mother," she claims. "My husband Sergei is family secretary, shopper, and cook. He always prepares breakfast, but unfortunately he only knows how to make meat and potatoes!"

At first, when letters and packages from foreign countries began to arrive, she and Sergei worried that he might have trouble with his job at the Joint Institute for Nuclear Research, even though the institute is concerned with the theoretical and civilian aspects of nuclear power rather than military applications. "It was very uncomfortable, and we were afraid," she admits. "Maybe if it had been a few years earlier it might have damaged him, but so far everything has been okay."

In winter 1988, after her students had already begun to exchange letters, souvenirs, and lanterns with children in Dusseldorf and the United States, she read in the Soviet teacher's newspaper *Uchitelskaya Gazeta* about what Soviet teachers were doing for peace. "And it was *so* uninteresting, so *dead!* It was just the old boring stuff—the festivals of peace, the competitions of political songs. I did the same things myself for ten years and I knew that other teachers didn't know what else they could do. So I wanted to share with them the materials I had about the lanterns and pen pals." She called *Uchitelskaya Gazeta* and a staff writer gave her the address of a small, newly organized committee called *Pedagogi Za Mir* (Educators for Peace). On her next trip to Moscow, Dolya visited the chairman of this committee and gave him written descriptions of the lantern and pen pal exchanges.

The next development was completely unexpected. "Six weeks later, I received a call from this man asking me if I wanted to go to

America!" Together with the Soviet Academy of Pedagogical Sciences, the American group Educators for Social Responsibility was organizing a summer seminar in Massachusetts on stereotypes, communication, and conflict resolution. Dolya went, and brought back many new techniques and perspectives to use in her work. She also met and became friends with Susan Jones, a leader in Educators for Social Responsibility who was about to start a two-year teaching post at the Anglo-American School in Moscow.

In January 1989, Dolya and Jones organized a "summit" in Dubna for Jones' fifth-graders—children of diplomats and journalists from around the English-speaking world—and Dolya's students. The children got along well, and most of the Western parents who came along were impressed by the warmth and hospitality of the Dubna families, but a few couldn't resist finding something to complain about. London *Daily Telegraph* reporter Xan Smiley, who came to Dubna with his daughter, wrote in an article on January 23, 1989, that School #6 was laden with portraits of Lenin, scrolls of patriotic hymns, and posters about civil defense in a nuclear war. Pointing out that the school had earned "a laurel for giving pupils the best preparation for military service" and that a poster hung outside the gym titled "How to Keep Fit for a Future War," he succeeded in leaving the impression that the long arm of the militaristic Soviet state reached even friendly Dubna.

"It's all true," says Dolya, showing me the article, "all the things he saw really are there. Except that the poster by the gym is called 'Ready for Labor and Defense,' it doesn't say anything about war. But what he doesn't understand is that none of those things work. The children are very cynical about the hymns and the flag, and they don't respect Lenin in their hearts. They have their civil defense courses in ninth and tenth form, but it is just a rest from physics and mathematics. They do exercises, the boys study guns and the girls learn how to put on bandages, but these courses have no effect on them. Just the opposite—they are always making jokes about it."

I ask her if one of the motives of her work is counteracting whatever influence this military propaganda might have. "You are right," she says after a pause. "If not to win—then at least to *neutralize!*" For many years, she explains, Soviets have been taught from an early age to blame all problems, big and small, on an outside enemy. "They always talked about the enemy in order to cover up our own problems and to avoid saying the truth. They said we must put our money into defending our country from the enemies, and that's why we live in such poverty, why we don't have this and that. And the people said, 'Okay, we'll give everything so that there will not be war, so that we can live in peace.' They played such a trick, I think."

But if the children are not very influenced by this propaganda, what exactly is she neutralizing? "These old views, attitudes, stereotypes . . ." she trails off. "Here, I will show you," she says, going to a bookshelf and pulling down two high-school English textbooks. "Here you will read. And remember they are the *only* ones available."

I open the ninth-grade book at random and find a passage titled "The United States of America—Part IV." After a brief description of the structure of the U.S. government, the text continues: "Both the federal government and the state governments serve the interests of the capitalists. . . . Many citizens of the USA, especially black and 'coloured,' have no rights proclaimed by the Constitution."

I pause and look up at Dolya. "The Fourteenth and Fifteenth Amendments," I say, "swept away in a phrase!" She shakes her head and tells me to keep reading. The book, published in 1985, is a collection of wooden vignettes about American life interspersed with passages like "The Soviet Right to Leisure and Rest" and "Lenin Proclaims Peace." One of the latter repeatedly refers to the "struggle of all peace-loving forces for peace and peaceful cooperation." The general picture of American life dates from the Depression of the 1930s—massive unemployment, legalized racial discrimination, and an overall sense of desperation because "the Republicans and Democrats defend the interests of monopoly capital and imperialism in national and international politics." Most of the book's many anachronisms are politically loaded, but a few are simply funny: for example, the assertion that marbles is the most popular game among American boys.

I read some choice sections aloud. "Millions of emigrants from all parts of the world crossed the ocean, hoping to find a better and happier life, but they did not find a country of equal opportunities," says a passage describing the Statue of Liberty. "When Maxim Gorky visited New York in 1906, he called it the City of the Yellow Devil, the city of gold. The Yellow Devil, the power of money, enslaves the people of America today as it did in Gorky's time." Galina Dolya is both wincing and laughing. I put the book down.

"Now you understand what I am neutralizing," she says. "You can see—no games, no interest, no dialogue, no real life. After studying this book the only thing you are prepared to do is stand at the rostrum and make political speeches."

In her classes Dolya uses her own self-published textbook called *Happy English,* which is full of light-hearted rhymes, poems, dialogues, and stories. *Happy English* and a companion book called *Happy Russian* may someday be officially published, but Dolya isn't holding her breath. At the moment she is simply grateful that the Ministry of Education is no longer issuing ironclad curricula and laying down strict rules for what teachers can do in the classroom. "For me it's okay, I have my own method," she says. "But other teachers need help—they don't have any good textbooks, and they don't know what to do."

Dolya is now a member of the twenty-person national coordinating committee of Educators for Peace. The group is producing a newsletter, holding conferences twice a year that attract several hundred teachers, and trying to create a book and a film about new peace curricula for teachers. "Of course, the group is better than nothing, but we are not yet that effective," admits Dolya. "It's only the work of a few enthusiasts, and so we're not widely known."

Now that nearly all of her students—about 200—have pen pals (and some of them have six or seven apiece), she sees her next step as arranging more face-to-face activities. In summer 1989, Dolya and several of her students worked as interpreters for a canoeing trip of Soviet and American artists down the Volga River. During August and September 1989, Dolya and Bell organized three lantern-floating ceremonies in Dubna: one on Hiroshima Day, one at a nearby Pioneer Camp in cooperation with Olga Bazanova from Novosibirsk and two dozen visiting Siberian children, and one that included children from the Ukraine, Georgia, and Yerevan. A few weeks later, Dolya was on a train to Dusseldorf with a group of twenty children eager to meet their West German pen pals.

In December 1989, Dolya and her students visited a hospital in Minsk filled with young children dying of leukemia—victims of radioactive fallout from Chernobyl. "You cannot imagine how horrible the conditions are there," she says. "They don't have enough medicines, enough equipment. The children just lie in bed and watch their friends die one by one." Dolya and her students raised money for medicines by selling crafts at an American Embassy Christmas bazaar, but they understand that the most important gifts they can bring these children are their letters, visits, and love. "If we can save maybe one child's life, or at least make a few children more comfortable and happy, it is worth it," says Dolya. "And this is another way that my kids are learning that what they do makes a difference in the world."

Dolya plans to arrange both inter-republican ("peace within the country has also become very important!") and Soviet-American ecology camps and expeditions during the next few summers. "Having enough physical energy to act is the main thing now," she says. "I am interested in too many things! I have many great plans, but it's necessary not to die beforehand!"

Her work is further complicated by attitudes of suspicion and envy among her fellow teachers. "Perhaps only ten percent of my colleagues really support me," she says. "Most of it is not because of politics but rather who I am as a teacher. I work hard, I try to change something, I am ashamed to come to my students with the old boring things, and that irritates many teachers very much, because they don't want to change. So they say, 'Oh, she is only doing this because she wants to travel abroad.' But when we began working it was forbidden to go abroad! And some of them are irritated that we are always making displays and creating events about life in America and in West Germany." She laughs. "The old ones frown and say I am propagandizing the Western style of life!"

At the moment, she is not afraid of any reprisals, but she is also aware how much she has singled herself out. "It is a very difficult situation in the country right now," she says. "Still the door is open. But I have a feeling it could be shut at any moment. Just like in a prison—the guard opens the door and allows you to come out and walk. Then he says, 'Come on back.'" She pauses. "But I have no time to worry, and that saves me! Our task now is to keep making a lot of personal contacts. And then it will work. We don't know what will be. But we hope."

8 | The Stage Mother

O ne day in July 1986, Nadia Burova received a telephone call from a woman she knew slightly, who told her that a dozen American children were in Moscow to do a play called *Peace Child* with a cast of Soviet children. The play was supposed to tour both the Soviet Union and the United States the following month, and rehearsals had just begun. But all was chaotic. The Soviet interpreter for the children could not understand the American director's instructions and the children were getting impatient and frustrated. "Please come *immediately*," the woman pleaded. "You know theater. You know English. They *need* you."

Burova came and was soon entranced by the spectacle of Soviet and American children rehearsing a dance scene and "just being so natural and lovely together." But language problems were indeed plaguing the cast. As an English instructor at Moscow State University, Burova had for many years staged plays and musicals performed by her students; she thus was able to explain the director's lingo to the children. There were nods of comprehension, and the rehearsal began to click.

Afterwards, a grateful official from the Soviet Ministry of Culture asked Burova to join the *Peace Child* production as an interpreter and chaperone. Burova declined, saying that she had no passport, she had a deadline for a book translation with her employer, Progress Publishers, and, most of all, she had major surgery for breast cancer scheduled in less than two weeks. The official said that it was up to her, but he promised that if she would just go with the children to Yalta and Ulyanovsk, she also could go with them to the United States. "You will be part of the new face of the Soviet Union," the official cajoled. "Why should it be someone else?"

Finally the children in the *Peace Child* cast persuaded her to come. She postponed her surgery and put her translation on hold.

"I paid with a couple of pounds of flesh, and much pain," she says, "but I received great happiness."

A soft-faced woman in her forties, with auburn hair and round blue eyes, Burova has an affinity for children that is clearly reciprocated. "I wanted to have lots of children—that's why I became a teacher. I have tremendous respect for children. Of all human beings, they are the best. And if you can love them and be truthful with them, you can help them grow up into wonderful adults."

Burova's husband, Dmitri Prigov, is an avant-garde artist and poet whose darkly political works were until recently published only in *samizdat* and in the West. Burova kept her husband, son, and adopted daughter fed and clothed by teaching English at Moscow State University for fourteen years. "My boss couldn't understand why my students would do so well," she recalls. "She would scour my desk looking for cribsheets and screaming that it was unnatural that my students only got brilliant marks. But it wasn't my fault—the students liked me and I liked them. We enjoyed being at our lessons together. There was a method I was supposed to use, but it seemed to me boring. So I brought in songs and we acted out dramas, and then we decided to do American and British musicals for audiences. We called it 'English Theater,' and it became very popular."

A few of her colleagues warned her that she needed to be careful about "foreign influences" on her students. "It was during the Cold War," she says, "and America was considered a bit dangerous. But I thought maybe our theater would help make up for there being no Western exchange students. I am sure that lack of knowledge about each other leads to stereotypes and breeds war. And drama, music, theater, literature, and the arts in general are the surest ways to promote understanding and bring people together." Joining the *Peace Child* production, she says, "was an extension of what I'd been doing all my life."

In *Peace Child*, a stage adaptation of the *The Peace Book* by British author Bernard Benson, Soviet and American children become friends and then lead a world crusade of children for peace, taking their message to superpower leaders and to the United Nations. The play was first performed in London in 1980 under the direction of British filmmaker David Woollcombe and was later staged in the United States and several other countries. In July 1985, Woollcombe brought American children to Moscow to perform the play with Soviet children during the World Festival of Youth and Students. Woollcombe and his colleagues at the Peace Child Foundation then tried to persuade officials at the Soviet Ministry of Culture to allow a mixed cast of Soviet and American children to stage the play in both the Soviet Union and the United States. Final permission came only at the last minute and was rumored to have been granted by Gorbachev himself. After some hasty rehearsals, *Peace Child* went on the road in August 1986.

"Watching *Peace Child* convinced me I had been right all this time," says Burova. "When you are with a person from another country, you see the human being without the stereotypes or the politics. The dream of *Peace Child* was coming true right in front of us. There's a scene in the middle of the play where the Soviet and American kids have to separate. And each time they did it, they cried and were apprehensive, because they knew that someday the separation would be for real. I think thousands and thousands of people in the audiences also cried, watching these kids loving each other on stage."

The twelve Soviet children, aged eleven to eighteen, were among the first allowed to travel to the United States, and they were greeted by hordes of journalists and crowds of angry picketers. "The American reporters were very annoying," remembers Burova. "They kept asking questions like, 'Is it true you're kept inside schools all day long?' and 'Did the government issue you these clothes?'" Burova encouraged the Soviet children to answer the onslaught of questions as patiently as possible. "I told them that it was very important they speak to people, because they could be a source of information and truth. And that they should never lie, even if telling the truth would be painful."

But the American and Soviet children eventually became so exasperated with reporters that they made a game out of tricking them. When asked to point to a "Soviet kid," they pointed to an American, who would then answer questions in Russian with memorized lines of Pushkin. "Then I'd 'translate,'" recalls Burova. "'This is Natasha, she's from Moscow, she's eleven,' and so on, when really it was Cristy, or Sarah. And of course the kids were *delighted*."

The sad and angry rows of protesters outside of theaters were less of a joking matter. "There were many Jewish émigrés and Afghani refugees who were quite hostile to the Soviet Union, and quite hostile to the kids," says Burova. "They asked questions about terrible things that the kids had never given a thought to before. It was a really good school for them. These questions made them think. They started questioning, started doubting, and started feeling responsible for their country."

At times the protests went beyond words. *Peace Child* received a bomb threat during an afternoon performance in Boston. In Seattle, the cast returned from an outing to find rotten eggs in their rooms, bootprints on their towels, and suitcases and drawers upended. "So we did feel that someone really evil might be lurking," says Burova. "But so often the kids would just melt away the anger." When the cast visited the school of one of the young American actors, a number of parents and teachers organized a boycott, declaring that this boy was "a traitor and a Communist for participating in this peace thing with Russians," recalls Burova. "But we decided to go anyway. And the kids there just stared at Karina, and Slava, and Natasha, all so lovely, and said, 'You mean you're *Soviet?*'" Within fifteen minutes the American and Soviet children were singing together and the boycott was forgotten.

Burova and the Soviet children returned to the Soviet Union inspired but unsure of what they could do next. Although the Ministry of Culture seemed pleased by the tour's results, an official told them plainly that the children would never be sent abroad again; even if the *Peace Child* tour were repeated, other "more professional" children would take their place. But meanwhile, many friends and teachers were eager to hear their stories, so the children and Burova began going to Soviet schools and talking about *Peace Child*. "And soon we were suggesting setting up a movement of children and parents for peace," says Burova. "Everyone was so enthusiastic, and we spontaneously recruited dozens, and then hundreds, of children. I gave away letters Americans had given me, and that led to pen pal relationships, and then to the twinning of school classes, and then to sister schools. Everyone wanted to write, everyone wanted to express himself, everyone wanted to do their own version of *Peace Child*. It was like an avalanche. And we just started to exist as a grassroots movement, without anyone's permission.

"Some people said to us—why are you wasting your energies fighting for peace when our government is fighting for peace, and when there are so many other things that need doing in this country? But we want to feel like *individuals* in our work for peace, to make our own little individual contributions. People don't want to be just cattle-herded anymore. Everyone is so cheered up by this *glasnost,* and everyone wants to do something, *anything,* outside of the established structures."

A loose network of former *Peace Child* cast members, their parents and families, and newly recruited teachers and children began putting on local concerts and productions of *Peace Child* in schools, Pioneer clubs, and "palaces of culture" at several local factories. "Nadia was a tremendous source of support for the kids, especially in those first few years," says Lucia Effros, one of *Peace Child*'s American coordinators. "She was the force that held them together. She had a vision, she saw what could be done, and she stuck her neck out and plugged away at it despite many obstacles and poor physical health."

The Soviet cast members of *Peace Child* soon improvised their own new musical play called *Underground Travel,* in which children from different countries manage to visit each other by digging a network of underground tunnels. "They were certain that one of the biggest obstacles to world peace is that children are not allowed to travel," says Burova. "Maybe they were still remembering the official from the Ministry of Culture who told them they were not going abroad another time."

Soon the children were staging scenes and songs from *Underground Travel* in addition to *Peace Child.* Karina Chepoi, a nineteen-year-old *Peace Child* veteran, began organizing and directing her own children's "Peace Theater." The Center's network quickly spread to other cities via family and friends; Burova wrote to relatives in Tashkent, Karina Chepoi wrote to her grandmother in Moldavia, a parent wrote to friends in Estonia. "It was so easy," says Burova. "We started by sending the sheet music, the score and the script for *Peace Child.* And many people began putting it on, knowing that children in other cities and other countries were doing the same thing, and with the dream that someday they too would have mixed casts."

Soon Burova's enthusiasm began to attract attention. "Nadia, do we have to call out a fire brigade, and hose you down? There is too much fire and hot air around you," remarked an official from the Ministry of Culture. Undaunted, Burova wrote a long report about the *Peace Child* tour for the Ministry and included in it a proposal for recognizing a new informal movement called Children and Parents for Peace. "We said that we didn't want another mansion," she recalls. "The youth organizations, the Soviet Peace Committee, the Soviet Veteran's Committee—they all have beautiful mansions with grown-ups sitting in them puffing out their cheeks and giving talks to foreigners. Instead we said we would like a plot of land somewhere near Moscow, maybe in a park, where we could build a place called Peaceland for children and adults to come from all over the world and do drama, and arts, and filming, and music, and languages, and global citizenship training."

Burova's vision for Peaceland had been inspired by a visit to Disneyland during the *Peace Child* tour. Asked for her impressions during a television interview, Burova had said that Disneyland was fine, but it was too bad there couldn't be a similar place for children that was educational, cross-cultural, and peace-oriented as well as fun. "And immediately I began receiving telephone calls from Americans who wanted to come to this wonderful place," she says. Before going into a hospital for her long-postponed operation, Burova sent a copy of her report and proposal to Raisa Gorbachev, the executive secretary of the Soviet Cultural Foundation.

While recovering from surgery for breast cancer, she received a call from a staff person on the Communist Party Central Committee, who told her that Mrs. Gorbachev had read and appreciated her proposal. Could she provide a few more details? Elated, Burova spent the next several months in her hospital bed scribbling plans. By spring 1987, the Cultural Foundation had agreed to sponsor her "Center for Creative Initiatives of Children and Adults for Peace," and a wooded area in a northeastern district of Moscow had been set aside for Peaceland. The district Komsomol committee and a large light-bulb factory also signed on as sponsors.

Burova's visions for Peaceland were extravagant: according to one of her proposals, it would "occupy a vast wooded area with a botanical garden and a zoo, areas reserved for ecological and other experiments, a simulated village for folklore studies, a culture center with a convertible theater/circus/concert hall, and adjacent studios." But she and her network of children and parents also continued to work on smaller, more immediate projects, including international summer and winter children's camps focused on music, ecology, and drama.

"Our idea is to promote *oneness,* and to try to turn the globe into a home, a beautiful, habitable home," says Burova. "And we think this can best be done by throwing bridges of knowledge, and thus respect, across the gaps that divide nations and cultures and generations. I saw firsthand during *Peace Child* that when Soviet and American kids do something tangible together, they find it very easy and natural to cooperate. By giving children a place to be together, we can help raise a new generation of people who will know they are part of the global family.

"For Soviet children, the main thing is to revive in them the natural human feeling of pride in initiative, and encourage them to come up with ideas for what they would like to do. Because they're estranged, the younger ones. Some have been corrupted already, and are very self-centered and greedy, but most are just very bored. They are surrounded by all this grimness, shortages, and disillusionment. Everything that was said in the textbooks and newspapers has been shattered, and everyone's looking at stark reality. When you are young you are not so programmed and you can see clearly. So they see this grimness, and they are turning to alcohol and drugs, and going into gangs and killing each other. And all this is happening while the state is *chirping* about peace and freedom.

"Sometimes the Party youth organizations are good, but like the whole country they are stagnant. If the local Pioneer or Komsomol leaders are using their own ideas then sometimes it's fun. But most of the time the kids just don't care anymore. They're bored, and they want to do things *themselves,* and not always be herded into a regimented life. So let's encourage them, and give them the facilities and support they need. We want to work with kids so that they feel they really have the right to their own, individual, human initiative.

"And we want it to be fun, we don't want it to be all that serious. If you read about the Center on paper, it sounds really very serious. We say we want to focus on the arts, and music, and drama, and filming, and the joys and difficulties of growing up. But when you come and improvise your own ideas, and start making your own props and costumes, it becomes something quite different. Working for peace should have some enjoyment in it, not only tragedy and gloom. This country has suffered so much—we *should* have fun! The kids deserve it!"

In September 1987, Burova was invited to chair a task force

during a Moscow conference on "breaking stereotypes" sponsored by the Soviet Peace Committee and the Seattle-based Center for Soviet-American Dialogue. Her children entertained the delegates with their songs, puppet shows, and re-enactments of scenes from *Peace Child.* "It was a real breakthrough in the conference," says Burova. "Before that, there had been nothing but arguments. After watching the children, the delegates were able to reach a lot of agreements."

The Soviet Peace Committee suddenly took an interest in Burova and her Center, and began coaxing her into leaving the Cultural Foundation and joining with them. "'You are a peacemaking organization—look at what kind of role you played in the conference,' they told me. So I asked them to become one of our sponsors. 'But we want to be the *major* sponsor,' they said." Burova sighs. "They simply seduced us. I still don't know if it was a piece of good luck or bad luck. But we left the Cultural Foundation and joined with the Peace Committee as a kind of children's department. They gave us all their projects and proposals which had been piling up over the years that involved children."

The Center for Soviet-American Dialogue invited Burova to attend a citizen diplomacy conference co-sponsored with the Soviet Peace Committee and held near Washington D.C. in February 1988. As one of few delegates representing a grassroots group, Burova was besieged by eager prospective American partners, and after the conference she was whisked to Ohio, Illinois, and California on a speaking tour. A Chicago-based educational group, the Kohl Foundation, presented her with their annual "International Peace Prize." Although this tour laid the groundwork for many of the Center's future exchanges, it also drew the ire of several high-ranking officials in the Soviet Peace Committee, who pulled Burova aside and accused her of "drawing too much attention to herself." Burova never knew if the tenuous support granted by the Peace Committee might evaporate at any moment. "Nadia was scared to death that she might do something wrong and ruin everything," says Diane Gilman, one of her American colleagues. "She is a very free-thinking and independent person, but the pressures to 'tow the line' and conform to outward structures have been enormous. The balancing act she must perform is probably beyond imagining for most Americans."

Still, Burova managed to obtain permission and funding to

send two delegations of Soviet children to the United States in June 1988. One was hosted by a Boston-based group called International Arts for Peace; the children put on poetry readings, created tile murals, and sang at several concerts. The other delegation went to New York to participate in a week-long "Kids' Summit" of 150 children from fifty countries organized by a New York-based group called Kids Meeting Kids Can Make A Difference. Another group of Burova's children traveled across Canada on a "friendship train," and still others joined the 1988 Soviet-American Peace Walk in the United States. In August 1988, her Center and two Moscow schools hosted thirty children from two San Diego "sister schools." Karina Chepoi and her Peace Theater troupe traveled to Carmel, California to act in a new adaptation of *Peace Child.*

Burova and her colleagues auditioned the Soviet children for these trips and selected them for their musical talent, English language ability, and knowledge of current events. "In every group, we try to have children translators, children entertainers, and children discussion leaders. And if a child can speak English, and give public talks, and also sing, that's our good luck!" she says. "We also involve underprivileged kids in our projects, so that all of them can feel part of the fun, and have the opportunity to travel abroad. I have a special feeling for students in the vocational training schools, who are usually considered outcasts. They are often orphans, or children of simple mothers and fathers, and they are put into these schools to learn a trade to support themselves."

Burova also hopes that the Center of Creative Initiatives for Peace will give children from the diverse cultures and republics within the Soviet Union an opportunity to get to know one another. "We want to bring little Tadjiks and Eskimos and Armenians and Estonians together," she says, "because one of the things that irritates many of us is that while we're always talking about ourselves as living in a 'fraternal family of peoples' in the Soviet Union, the reality is quite different. Most Estonian kids have never seen Tadjik kids, and most Eskimos haven't been to Georgia. And there are some terrible ethnic slur words in our vocabularies that we have to purge. It's our task to bring all these children together, so that we can really *enjoy* living in a very multicolored and multicultural family."

Although the Peace Committee helped sponsor these exchanges, Burova has found working under its auspices a mixed blessing. Progress on Peaceland became snarled in red tape, and Burova discovered in late 1987 that her Center had been placed under the supervision of a new spin-off of the Peace Committee called the Association of Peace to the Children of the World. The president of this association, children's author Anatoli Alexin, invited Burova to become his vice-president, but she insisted that her Center remain autonomous. "He wanted to set up a publishing house that will translate his own books and publish them for children in other countries," says Burova. "And that's fine, but he was not really interested in working with the children themselves to encourage their creativity. His principles differed radically from ours."

It was soon apparent that the Peace Committee, in the guise of Alexin's Association, was trying to gain control over Burova's network—perhaps to ensure that its grassroots enthusiasm would be channeled in "appropriate" ways. But the Peace Committee underestimated Burova's popularity and persistence. Her informal network of Soviet children, teachers, theater directors, and other supporters kept growing, and Americans continued to be attracted by her fluent English, her gritty style, and her emphasis on practical projects. After a lengthy internal battle, Burova succeeded in getting her Center separately registered under the sponsorship of the Soviet Peace Committee in February 1988. With this legal status she could open a bank account, raise money, and send and invite delegations.

Her relations with the Peace Committee remain wary. "There are some nice people there who have supported us, but there are others who don't like us. They like what we do, but not *us*. And I'm so gullible, and I've made so many mistakes. What we really want to do is make as many children happy as possible. But it's not as easy as we thought before. There are many egos involved. It's big politics, and we're just children, me included."

In June 1988, Burova and her children arranged a small public fair in the yard of the Peace Committee's headquarters to introduce the Center to a wider audience. They set up booths to sell souvenirs made by vocational school students, and children from Karina Chepoi's Peace Theater began singing on a small outdoor stage. "But all of a sudden, this lady who works for Anatoli Alexin appeared, and she started to *push* the children, literally, off the stage, saying 'Away with you! Clear the stage!'" recalls Burova.

"Then a bus arrived, and kids in red ties and white shirts marched onto the stage and started singing in very clear, inhuman voices. It was the Popov Choir, the official choir of the Party organization. There is no spirituality about their music, they are like soldiers on the march. And when I asked, 'What are you doing?' this lady said: 'You're doing this the wrong way! There are TV cameras here, and the performance should be perfect! Your children are *amateurs*, and these are *professionals!* The Association should not disgrace itself, Nadia! We should have the best in the country! And you're just fussing around, when it's done so easily. You have no skills in organizing. You just pick up the receiver, you call the official choir or the official dance group, and they sing, and they dance. And it's perfect for the TV screens.'

"Those are the Association's principles—making it perfect, showing off. It's contrary to our principles. Our children may sing in completely false notes, but it's *they* who are singing, because they want to sing. Not because someone told them to sing."

Burova's struggles to keep the Center independent and effective have been exhausting, and she has not won them all. "She's had a tough time because she's been operating individually rather than building a lot of alliances, and Soviet society just isn't used to that," says Lucia Effros of Peace Child. Several of her other American partners report that her zeal and her precarious relations with officialdom have made cooperating with her a challenge. "She doesn't spare herself, and so she doesn't spare others," says Judy Woodruff, director of the Boston-based group International Arts for Peace. "And in general it's difficult to work with people who have cosmic vision and no money."

Burova's ongoing battle with cancer has also placed huge demands on her, her family, and her Western partners. Her first operation did not go smoothly, and even with further surgery her health remains uncertain. "But this tumor has given me inner strength," she says. "I realize that probably I don't have much time left to do things, and I want to die a satisfied and fulfilled person. That's why I'm even more energetic than I used to be. I'm very insistent, and impatient, and that's why people get annoyed with me."

Her home telephone rings constantly, and the only time it is possible to hold a sustained conversation with her is after about one in the morning. But this does not seem to discomfit Burova at all. "Ever since the cancer, I've felt no urge to sleep," she says. "There is too much to do. I have too much energy in me. I usually get to sleep around four in the morning and wake up at eight."

Since 1988 she has maintained a grueling international travel schedule, hopping to Australia, Great Britain, Italy, and the United States to lay plans for new international children's music camps, ecology camps, and theater productions. Meanwhile, her husband Dmitri Prigov is at last being recognized for his artistic work and has also developed a busy schedule; in 1989 he traveled to the United States for a series of poetry readings and exhibitions. "Not long ago, Dima had one of his pictures appear in *Sovietskaya Cultura* on the same day that he gave a poetry reading on the Voice of America," says Burova. "That's a sign that things have *really* changed."

Burova's Center now has a fifteen-member board of directors ("I am both the chair and the armchair," Burova says with a laugh), about 250 active members in cities around the Soviet Union, and an estimated ninety cooperating schools with "peace theaters," "peace choirs," or sister-school relationships. At each of the Center's international camps, young theater directors and teachers from cities like Volgograd and Kishinev work as counselors and then go home inspired to develop their own exchanges and peace plays. In Moscow, the Center's amateur music and theatrical groups have put on concerts to raise money for orphanages and Armenian earthquake victims. Karina Chepoi's Peace Theater has been invited to tour Britain and Spain, and one of its concerts celebrated the opening of a Moscow office for the Peace Child Foundation, which in 1989 organized fifteen new joint tours of *Peace Child* involving in its casts nearly 500 Soviet and American children.

In December 1988, Burova and her colleagues arranged for a two-week international children's music camp that brought together 200 children from Great Britain, West Germany, Austria, and several republics of the Soviet Union. Burova invited me to drop by the camp "to feel the atmosphere. I can't possibly describe it to you." When I arrived at the vocational school in northeastern Moscow that was hosting the camp, two young violinists from the elite Purcell Music School in London were accompanying a Mozart chorale sung by a fifty-member girls' choir, all children of workers at an auto factory. The poised London children were dressed in jeans and colorful sweatshirts. The Moscow girls seemed a little awestruck to be on the same stage with them, and were dressed in the drab, ill-matched clothing of the Soviet poor. Nevertheless, their music sounded fine, and the piece was greeted by enthusiastic applause and whistles from the other campers in the audience.

Afterwards, I asked one of the London violinists if she had made any Soviet friends during the camp. "Oh yes—*tons*," she replied promptly. Had language been a problem? She thought for a moment. "No, not really," she said. "Lots of them speak English. And we stay in the same hostel, and eat in the cafeteria, and go on outings together, and have lots of discos." An Austrian choir director confirmed that the atmosphere during the camp had been warm, creative, and caring; he added that he planned to invite the auto-factory girls' choir to Salzburg the following year.

When the music camp ended and the participants went to the airport, "everyone was crying and crying," says Burova. The Soviet children stood on one side of the customs barrier and the Western children on the other, waiting to go through passport control. Then a West German boys' choir formed a circle and began to sing. A hush fell over the airport; even customs officials stopped to listen. "They sang a beautiful song in English about love, about how by loving us you are blessed by God, and we are blessed by your love, and we love you too and are blessed by God as well. It was so beautiful that the border itself paused, and fell silent."

9 | Peace Vigil

The sky is overcast, the air raw and cold, the deserted city park heavy with snow. At noon on February 27, 1988, a single man stands bareheaded in a sheepskin greatcoat in front of the eternal flame of Leningrad that commemorates the losses of World War II. "It is my custom, before beginning the vigil, to spend a few moments with the flame," Vladimir Zhikarentsev says quietly. For several minutes he gazes at it in silence, his hands clasped before him and a small smile on his face.

"It is very strong, the fire," he muses. "Your thoughts can fly away with it. Or you can take it into your heart. Either way, it is a very strong thing."

Zhikarentsev then leaves the flame and walks a few hundred meters across the street to a small white-columned rotunda in another park. A half-dozen others are waiting there. He takes a long blue banner with the words *Vakhta Mira* (Peace Vigil) from his bag and strings it across the front of the rotunda. By the time the banner is raised the number of people beneath the rotunda has doubled.

Soon a discussion is under way about the ecological threat posed by a new city chemical complex, the creation of a cultural club for contacts with English-speaking countries, and the meaning of *mir*. "You see what too much *mir* has done to this country," one man announces, taking in with a sweep of his arm the rundown apartment buildings and the dowdy state slogans. "It is not that there been too much *mir* in our country, it is that there has been too little *mir* in our hearts," a woman replies. Others in what is now a crowd of fifty murmur agreement; the discussion continues.

Zhikarentsev slips out of the center of the crowd for a few minutes. "As you can see, our Peace Vigil is not an organization, it is a form and a method for uniting people," he says. "Our main goal is the building of a nonviolent world by nonviolent methods of struggle. And we hope that every Saturday afternoon all over the world people will make such a peace vigil, so that we can create peace waves, waves of love and light, that can travel around the world."

In March 1987, Zhikarentsev, a computer engineer, and Yuri Gorbachev (no relation to Mikhail), a philosophy professor and Party member, read about a hunger strike by American physician Charles Heyder in protest of the continued build-up of U.S. nuclear forces. Impressed by Heyder's commitment, Zhikarentsev and Gorbachev decided to collect signatures of support for him from Leningrad citizens. For two months they held placards on Saturday afternoons in Palace Square, gathering nearly 4,000 signatures and a cadre of fellow vigilers before the police told them to leave. But by then Peace Vigil had gathered momentum, and a core of interested people continued to meet for discussions about *mir* every Saturday in a section of Mikhailovsky Gardens that became known as the "Hyde Park Corner" of the Soviet Union.

"The main idea of Peace Vigil is peace creation, or rather *mir* creation, because peace is only one side of our life," says Zhikarentsev. "What will we do when there is peace on earth? What will our life and our relationships be like? Nobody knows. We know what war life means much better than what *mir* life means. So we call it *mir* creation, *mirotvorchestvo. Mir* means ecology, peace, community, nature—it is a very complete word, in our language."

Given the way times have changed, it is difficult to remember that in the Soviet Union of early 1987 such open-air meetings were rare and forbidden and their organizers subject to arrest. What made Gorbachev and Zhikarentsev take to the streets? "You see, every man has a moment in his life when he matures," Zhikarentsev explains. "We had reached a point where we knew either we had to act, or we had to stop growing as human beings. The key idea of Peace Vigil is tolerance. Without tolerance we cannot continue to exist in the world. Tolerance will cross the borders between our souls, between our countries. First there will be tolerance, and then disarmament."

Zhikarentsev is a dark-haired man in his mid-thirties with a humble manner and large, bright green eyes. Although he is employed at an engineering institute, his real passion is Eastern philosophy and languages, and he reads in four languages, including Japanese and Chinese. For ten years he studied karate on his own, using a photographed copy of a book brought back by someone who had visited the West. Eventually dissatisfied with what he calls the "war character" of karate, he turned to aikido and meditation, and he read every book on metaphysics and spirituality he could find: classical texts of Buddhism, Taoism, and Hinduism, psychological works by modern writers like Jung, and the books of suppressed yet revered Russian mystics like the early-twentieth-century philosopher and painter Nicholas Roerich (Nikolai Rerikh).

Like thousands of other Soviets, Zhikarentsev kept his spiritual explorations to himself, sharing them only with trusted family and friends. "In our society we are atheists and materialists," he says. "We do not like to think about thin things. We believe only in dense, material things that we can touch through our senses. Because you cannot touch *chi* [Chinese for "life-energy"], the Communists say it does not exist. Our spiritual life has been completely discounted and suppressed."

Yet Zhikarentsev, and many other members of Peace Vigil, belong to a tradition of Russian spiritual seekers inspired by homegrown sources: classical writers such as Tolstoy, modern philosophers such as Roerich, Fyoderov, and Vernadsky, the mystical aspects of Russian Orthodox Christianity, and the reverence for the natural world still preserved in many Russian folk customs and beliefs. They have also been influenced by Eastern religious traditions, by German romanticists like Goethe and American transcendentalists like Thoreau and Emerson, and, more recently, by an influx of "New Age" books from the West.

Although quite diverse in their practices and viewpoints, many of these spiritual seekers share several beliefs. One is that the content of our thought creates our reality, meaning that human beings must take responsibility for creating their own lives and the world around them, rather than passively accepting that they are victims of fate, "the system," or God's will. Another belief is that the purpose of life on earth is to evolve, both as individuals and as a species, toward a higher level of consciousness and to develop loving, harmonious relationships with our inner selves, with people around us, with other living beings, and with the world as a whole. Followers of this tradition believe that the individual soul, "the God within," is the ultimate source of spiritual guidance, and that each person must discover and try to follow his or her own path in life. This means remaining loyal to one's own inner truth despite the pressures of outside conformity, while at the same time understanding that no one way, no one answer, is right for everyone.

These beliefs are antithetical in almost every way to the dogma of orthodox Communism. They emphasize inner growth while Communism emphasizes outer struggle. They teach that we ourselves are responsible for both the good and the bad in our personal lives and in our world, while Communism teaches that all bad things can be blamed on someone or something else, on external enemies and oppressors who must be resisted and overcome. They see the evolution of the individual as the primary purpose of the world, while Communism sees the development of the individual as secondary to the evolution of the collective. They maintain that individuals can each discover their own highest truth, while Communism says that the truth has already been discovered by the great men of Communism and all that is now required is hard work to manifest it in the real world.

Not surprisingly, such philosophical tendencies have been traditionally considered dangerous by the Soviet state, and have been given pejorative labels like "cosmopolitanism" and "cosmism." It is not hard to see why adherents of such ideas made very poor *vintiki*, or "little cogs," in Stalin's famous description of the social machine. They had the potential to cause far more trouble than followers of the hierarchical and doctrine-oriented Russian Orthodox Church, which has structurally more in common with the Communist Party than either would like to admit.

In the early years of Soviet power, these spiritual independents were systematically weeded out, killed, silenced, or forced to flee. Among them was the artist-philosopher Nicholas Roerich, who with his wife Elena remains one of the most revered and influential of modern Russian spiritual leaders. Roerich left the Soviet Union in 1916 and lived most of the rest of his life in India, where he and his wife wrote a number of dense mystical texts called *The Books of Living Ethics*. In the 1920s, Roerich launched a world peace campaign under the "banner of culture" that gained many followers, among them U.S. Vice-President Henry Wallace. The Roerichs' written works trickled back into the Soviet Union and their influence lived on. Today many Soviet cities and towns have active

"Roerich Societies" whose members promote their ideas of culture, peace, human potential, and inner harmony.

"The Roerichs were very great people of humanity," says Zhikarentsev. "They wrote about their conversations with great spiritual teachers, with Mahatmas, and they taught how to use flame imagery to center our souls in this world. Because flame and thought are of the same material. And all things in this world—tables, chairs, stones, people—all consist of this energy. But usually we see things more thickly. They wrote very interesting books, and, as far as I know, they are only in Russian. And the language is very strong, very poetic and somewhat archaic, even in Russian."

Peace Vigil was thus a new shoot on hardy roots that had lain dormant in Soviet society for decades. "But very often during the peace vigils, when I tell people about our heart, they laugh," admits Zhikarentsev. "They say the heart is an organ for making the blood go through the body. When I talk about the heart as a place of wisdom, very few people believe me. They have never heard of such a thing."

"They haven't heard about love?"

"They know about love, and they have felt love in their hearts, but they think it is something like reflex. It is the legacy of materialism. But still, a few people respond. And we have our peace vigils on the streets because we must find such people. We cannot talk about these things in newspapers or magazines, so we have to find our friends on the streets. And the next problem is that most of the people who understand about the heart are not ready to work to create *mir*. They do not understand that we must do something with our hands and feet. They are working only for their own self-improvement, to increase their personal power. Maybe only one person in a thousand both understands the heart and understands that it is time to work."

By the end of 1987, Peace Vigil had appeared on the streets of six other cities. At the Golden Gate of Kiev, at the entrance to the Lenin Library in Moscow, and at the plaza facing the main cinema in Novgorod, Soviets gathered on Saturday afternoons to discuss and debate *perestroika*, ecology, and the Peace Vigil mottos: "From peace in oneself to peace throughout the world," "Peace through culture," and "From a healthy body—to a healthy way of life." As one of their pamphlets put it, their overall aim was to spread "the new way of thinking about PEACE, through Tolerance that is non-critical; about HUMANISM, through Inclusiveness that is Love; about HEALTH, through Service for the good of the whole."

Although each group held Saturday vigils, their other activities varied. The Novgorod and Volkhov chapters began working to restore churches and other historical monuments. The Zhukovsky chapter, led by a former drug addict, opened seminars for drug users. The Moscow chapter generated most of the movement's pamphlets and written materials. And the Leningrad chapter became famous for its enormous public meetings; at their peak, in summer 1988, several thousand people gathered each Saturday afternoon in Mikhailovsky Gardens.

Why were members of Peace Vigil able to take to the streets at a time when other groups, such the Trust Group, were still being routinely arrested for open demonstrations? For one thing, Peace Vigil's slogans and platforms never aimed direct criticism at the Party or the government. Most Trust Group members therefore considered the group spineless and a little flaky. Nikolai Khramov of the Moscow Trust Group dismissed Peace Vigil because "they make no concrete proposals." Ekaterina Podoltseva of the Leningrad Trust Group called Zhikarentsev "a nice guy with good intentions, but his concepts of strategy are not worth discussing." Zhikarentsev says about Poldoltseva: "She is a good woman. But the Trust Group's methods are not our methods. They struggle and create confrontation, and confrontation is violence."

What most disarmed authorities, perhaps, was Peace Vigil's philosophy of inclusiveness. Unlike the Trust Group, which avoided contact with official agencies for fear of compromising its independence, Peace Vigil sought out dialogue with the Peace Committee, Komsomol (the Young Communist League), and city and Party authorities as a matter of principle. "We believe it is important to be in relationship not only with groups which are close to us, where everything is smooth and clear, but also with groups who are very distant from our ideas," says Zhikarentsev.

In Leningrad, the relationship with the Peace Committee never got off the ground; after several fruitless meetings, Zhikarentsev concluded that it was only possible to work under, not with, the Peace Committee. He had somewhat better luck with Leningrad city authorities, for eventually they legalized Peace Vigil's public meetings in Mikhailovsky Gardens. "The officials gave us permission because they believe our nonviolent approach is good for them," says Zhikarentsev. "They see us as a buffer between them and the anger of the people. But I think we are not as harmless as they think."

Peace Vigil's strongest contacts with officialdom were through Komsomol, whose representatives appeared to be both impressed and perplexed by the group. Komsomol co-sponsored a national Peace Vigil conference in March 1988, but took care to distance itself from what one internal document termed the group's "ideological vacuums." According to a report published by the Komsomol Central Committee's Department for Propaganda and Agitation, Peace Vigil was to be admired for its "social energy" and "attempts to appeal to the best human qualities and to defeat political indifference among a certain part of our youth." But Komsomol suspected that behind Peace Vigil's "camouflage of basic humanistic principles" was "some sort of political position that differs from Marxism." And the report stated that "we cannot put up with elements of cosmopolitanism, pacifism, and denial of the class approach which can be traced in some of the group's vague wordings. Komsomol has never supported religious positions. That's why the slogan, 'From peace in oneself to peace throughout the world,' is shared by us only in its second part."

Zhikarentsev admits that the connection between personal values and world politics is a tough one to convey to the skeptical majority of Soviets. "We must organize seminars to teach people what inner peace means," he says. "Because most people have no idea of such a thing. They do violence to their inner nature, and when they do that they do violence to the outside world. The inside and outside are related. It is a very hard and important concept for us to explain."

From its earliest days Peace Vigil attracted the attention of the Soviet press. In February 1988, the weekly *Moscow News* compared Peace Vigil and the Trust Group and found the former more to its liking. A mostly favorable article in the magazine *Sobesednik* in May 1988 described Peace Vigil's activities in several cities in some depth, but concluded with a critique by a man identified as a "Moscow scientific worker" who derided Peace Vigil's principles as "a strange blend of Eastern and cosmic philosophies with the new thinking." A Leningrad newspaper, in an article headlined "Citizen Diplomacy in Action," also generally praised Peace Vigil's activities but expressed displeasure at the occasional presence of "anti-Soviet propaganda" during the vigils, which reduced them to "the level of a tribune for demagogues."

After the large and heated Saturday meetings in Mikhailovsky Gardens during summer 1988, Zhikarentsev himself began to worry that Peace Vigil was becoming too confrontational. "During the vigils many people are saying: 'Let's kill our enemies and live in a new happy world,'" he tells me in October 1988. "They believe we must determine who are the true enemies and kill them, whether these enemies are Communists, Jews, bureaucrats, or democrats. For example, many people say the Communist Party is our enemy, and their leaders have done a lot of evil, and we must kill the Party. And at the same time these people say that non-violence is their ideology. I say, 'Why? How can you say you are building a nonviolent world if all you can see is killing enemies?' They reply, 'We don't mean kill them with a knife, we mean only that we must struggle with them and crush their power.' They don't understand that when we struggle, when we create enemies, we are also creating violence. They can't understand this, because they hate. They hate very much. Some of them were dissidents and in prison, and they hate the KGB and the Party so much that it is difficult even to speak with them."

"How do you try to change their thinking?"

"It is too hard to change them, and I don't even try," he replies. "I only make a discussion with them to give the people who are listening an understanding of this problem. I use them as a platform to explain these things. But it is difficult. And many people who come to Peace Vigil hear all this talk about enemies, and they leave because they don't want to create violence yet again."

To address this problem, Peace Vigil members have begun translating and distributing materials on nonviolence and conflict resolution given to them by American groups such as Peace Brigade International and the American Friends Service Committee. "These groups are proving that the methods of Gandhi and Tolstoy can work. This is very important, because in our country, our propaganda says that Tolstoy was. . ." Zhikarentsev makes a circle with his index finger next to his head. "Because Tolstoy said that if somebody gives you a strike on the cheek, you must give your other cheek for his strike. And our books say, such a funny man! Of course you mustn't give your cheek—you must struggle, struggle, struggle. In a way, they are right. But they have insisted too much on this, they have poured out the baby with the bath-water. They have removed all nonviolence, all spirituality, from our life. And so we have very, very, very much violence in our country. And very, very few people feel we must do something other than struggle. They don't even know nonviolence exists. They think that only struggle, only revolution, can change the world."

I admit that while I had read *Anna Karenina,* I had not read Tolstoy's works on nonviolence—where would he recommend I begin?

"Ha!" he snorts. "I myself even do not know! In this country we know *War and Peace,* and his other literary books, but his works on nonviolence are very little known. There is only one edition of his complete collected works, and the print run was very small."

"So you'd heard about them, but not read them?"

"I hadn't even heard!" he exclaims. "I learned about the real Tolstoy when I studied Gandhi, because Gandhi wrote that he was a student of Tolstoy. I read in the works of Indian, Chinese, and Japanese philosophers that they were very respectful toward our Russian classics." He shrugs. "You see? What has emerged from us here in Russia has simply not been communicated. So people don't even know that we have a deep spiritual life inside our culture."

Peace Vigil's "no enemy" principle was put to a test in July 1988, when twenty Peace Vigil members from five cities attempted to join a peace walk from Odessa to Kiev co-sponsored by the American group International Peace Walk and the Soviet Peace Committee. At first the Peace Committee refused to allow them to participate. Undaunted, the Peace Vigil members scheduled their vacation time during the walk and arrived in Odessa with their sleeping bags and tents. According to Marina Prilutskaya, a Mos-cow leader of Peace Vigil, "The Peace Committee was very angry and the KGB ordered us off of their bus. But because we had two small children with us, they finally agreed to take us to the gates of the camp where the walkers were staying." There, officials relented and said the Peace Vigil delegation could join the walk if it paid its own way.

Most of the Soviet walkers were staff workers of various re-gional and city Peace Committees, "who work for peace and make money at it," says Zhikarentsev. "And you can feel that some do not have deep feelings for their work. They simply came and took part in an activity of the central Peace Committee. So they did not like us very much, and when we led discussions with the Americans about spirituality, about cosmic ideas, they would interrupt our meetings and start laughing at us. But the Americans found these discussions very interesting, of course! And eventually some of the Soviets listening began to feel that there is something in it, and began to have discussions with us. They were officials, but still they felt something. It was very good. The years of terror have suppressed our people's feelings, have suppressed our spiritual life, but the potential is very strong and good."

The two small children on the peace walk belonged to Alexander and Svetlana Supronenkov, the coordinators of Moscow Peace Vigil. When I visit the Moscow vigil near the main entrance to the Lenin Library in early November 1988, their small blue banner is dwarfed by enormous red streamers hung by the city in preparation for the anniversary of the October Revolution. Supronenkov, who resembles a short, personable Solzhenitsyn, is facilitating a lively discussion with a dozen people. Other passersby linger in front of the display boards propped against the wall: a photo exhibit about the previous summer's peace walk, the text of the United Nations Declaration of Universal Human Rights, several magazine clips about Soviet endangered species, a chart showing the percentage of Soviet GNP spent on the military, and three stuffed animals perched on broken toy pistols and machine guns.

The most popular display is a large posterboard called "Toward a Healthy Way of Life," which summarizes the teachings of the contemporary Russian guru Porfery Korneevich Ivanov. The advice in Ivanov's "manifesto for children" is direct and unpretentious: take cold baths, walk in the open air, fast once a week, think positive thoughts, don't smoke or drink, "greet people always and everywhere, especially old people," love nature, believe in people and help them, and "let your thoughts and actions coincide." At any one time during the afternoon about twenty people are reading and taking notes from the poster, including many young men in military uniform.

Alexander Supronenkov, a lighting manager at the Taganka Theater, visited one of the Leningrad vigils in spring 1987 and decided to bring Peace Vigil to Moscow. The first vigils began on Pushkin Square in June 1987, but they were quickly booted by the police to the Arbat, and from there quickly booted to the Lenin Library, where they have remained since. "We just get out in the street and start talking with people about what they think about peace," says Marina Prilutskaya, an interpreter at a society for the blind.

Moscow Peace Vigil has been among the most successful in establishing a working relationship with the Soviet Peace Committee; in fall 1988, it received permission to hold a weekly meeting of informal peace groups in the lobby of the Peace Committee headquarters on Prospekt Mira. "The Peace Committee is always complaining that we never do anything, that we are just words," says Alexander Supronenkov. "But when we proposed a very detailed, concrete plan for a week of activities around the International Day Against Military Toys in November, they refused to have any part of it." Why? He shrugs. "They were afraid. They said they did not have the authorization from above to participate in this activity. But it's better not to darken the situation by dwelling on negative things."

"Our idea is to appeal to the feelings and the humanity of the bureaucrats," adds Prilutskaya. "We try not to treat the Peace Committee or KGB as enemies, but rather as groups of human beings. We just go inside the stuffy official organizations, and make a friend. And it works. For example, we photocopy our materials with the help of a person inside the Department of Censorship!"

Just then a woman carrying a large shopping bag approaches the vigil. "Are you from the Peace Committee?" she asks shortly.

"No," says Prilutskaya.

"Are you from the regional Party committee?"

"No."

"Are you from the KGB?"

"No," says Prilutskaya, "we are just a movement."

The woman looks hard at Prilutskaya, her eyes mistrustful, and walks away without another word.

Prilutskaya shrugs. "As you can see, many don't believe that we are not hired to do this for money. But all we can do is stand here and be ready to give information. If they want to label us demagogues and KGB, that means they don't want the information."

A man with a briefcase interrupts one of Supronenkov's discourses about inner and outer peace. "Your approach is too general," he complains. "The level of culture of an individual doesn't really affect peace in the world."

"When a person shoulders you rudely on a bus or in a queue, this is due to a deficit of peaceful harmonic existence within oneself, and with nature, children, old people, and all of life," says Supronenkov. "As long as we have this deficit we cannot truly make peace in the world."

"But we need concrete solutions to these problems," replies the man. "For example, we need to cut the military budget. That would be the greatest step toward solving ecological problems, starvation, ignorance. I don't say that you don't have the right to stand here, but it's only decoration, a window-display."

Another Peace Vigil member, a young Army officer out of uniform, speaks up. "Let us decrease our spending on the military, but we should also stop shouldering our way in buses."

"That's not a problem of war and peace," replies the man.

"I think it's exactly a problem of war and peace," says the young officer.

"But we must move forward by dealing with concrete and real problems," insists the man.

"You have your viewpoint, and you have a good position in wanting to reduce the military budget," says Supronenkov genially. "We can support your idea and discuss it as much as you like. Because Peace Vigil is not mine—it belongs to everyone. And everyone has the right to express his idea and try to push it forward."

Another man who has been listening speaks. "Who are you?"

Supronenkov turns to him with a smile. "Are you interested in surnames?"

"Who is paying for this? Because it is very artificially done, and very naive. It is only meant to impress foreigners."

"What would you do if you wanted to improve life?" Supronenkov asks the man, who quickly mutters "*Chepukha, boltovnya* (What a lot of nonsense)," and walks away.

A third man who has been listening then speaks. "I live in Kalinin. When I get on the bus quietly and meekly, nobody pays attention to me. But when I muscle my way on and stand up straight, people respect me and like me."

"They don't like you," says Supronenkov. "They are afraid of you."

The man does not reply. There are murmurs of approval from the crowd.

"We do not need to be strangers to one another, closed to one another," Supronenkov continues. "When you greet someone and say hello, *zdravstvuitye,* be healthy, you can *mean* it, and in this way actually help them to be healthy. Honest human connection—it is the only way out."

At five o'clock, as they are packing up their display boards, Prilutskaya and Supronenkov insist that I join them for dinner. "In Sasha's home you will see with your own eyes the true nature of Peace Vigil," says Prilutskaya. "You will see his beautiful children and the way we pour cold water on them."

Supronenkov lives in a northern Moscow suburb beyond the end of the metro, in a modest first-floor flat with no telephone. It is customary in Russian homes to remove one's shoes at the door and don *tapochki* (houseslippers), but I am surprised when Peace Vigil members ask me to remove my socks as well. "It is the custom of our—our sect—to go barefoot in this room," says the young Army officer with a sheepish smile. The room is simply furnished with bookshelves and a few paintings.

"Do you believe in God?" Supronenkov asks me as we sit down on the couch.

"It depends on what you mean by 'God,'" I say.

"In your God."

"Yes, of course."

"Then everything will be all right," he beams, pointing to a painting on the wall of a man with flowing white hair and beard. "Here is the God of Russia," he says.

Porfery Korneevich Ivanov "came to us in 1898 and left us in 1983." Supronenkov claims that millions of Soviets know him simply as "The Teacher." Ivanov was born in a small village in the Voroshilovgradsky region of the Ukraine. A simple, uneducated man, he gained his wisdom "directly from nature, in the Russian language." During the last fifty years of his life he wandered on foot throughout Russia and the Ukraine, preaching and healing, always wearing only short trousers—no shoes, no shirt—in every season.

"He had the ability to heal without laying on hands," says Supronenkov, adding that he had been a disciple of Ivanov for thirteen years and had traveled with him on many of his journeys. "He could make the lame walk, the blind see, the deaf hear. And people who had heard of his healing powers came to him." The

KGB also came to Ivanov, and imprisoned him in a psychiatric hospital for eight years. According to Supronenkov, Soviet doctors performed "experiments" on Ivanov to try to determine the source of his healing powers, and tortured him by various manipulations of his spinal cord. Released only when he was near death, Ivanov revived himself by lying on the snow and lived many more years.

Supronenkov shows me a treasured scrapbook of reproductions of Nicholas Roerich's paintings and texts. "Roerich and Ivanov never met, but Roerich predicted Ivanov's coming—he wrote that God would come to Russia." He then begins telling me a long, very esoteric parable about "the beast in the cave," only a small fraction of which I can follow. It is clear he wants me to understand the underlying essence of Moscow Peace Vigil, although this is a side of the group which they understandably keep muted during their public vigils.

Just then his two children—a boy of six and a girl of four—run into the room and jump on their father's lap with unrepressed glee, their healthy little bodies still glistening from their cold water bath. The girl puts her arms around me and kisses me with disarming enthusiasm before both of them run to the kitchen for their vegetarian dinner.

"You see?" says Prilutskaya. "That is the true nature of Peace Vigil."

A few months later, I ask Vladimir Zhikarentsev in Leningrad whether all members of Peace Vigil were also followers of Ivanov. "No, not all, but many people respect him very much," he says. "I consider him one of the Mahatmas, who came to Russia to give us the next teaching. His words and his deeds were on a very high level—they were not the words of a simple man."

By January 1989, the Leningrad Peace Vigil meetings in Mikhailovsky Gardens had been closed down by city authorities, supposedly because of restoration work going on in the park. "Of course, the real reason was that there were too many sharp speeches about our Party," says Zhikarentsev with a soft chuckle. He does not seem at all perturbed by this turn of events. "In fact, Peace Vigil was no longer developing itself through the meetings in Mikhailovsky Gardens," he says. "With every Saturday meeting Peace Vigil took the wrong way over and over again. There was violence in the speeches. People who visited us thought we were not a citizen diplomacy organization, or an organization for a new way of thinking, but simply a democratic organization for *perestroika* and *glasnost*. I felt very clearly that the situation was wrong."

Zhikarentsev had suggested to other Peace Vigil members that they stop for a few months, or perhaps change the location, but his friends disagreed and the meetings continued. "At last the situation was so bad that everybody saw it, including our officials," he says. "I knew very well that if we kept meeting in another place, all of these people who wanted to speak would follow us. So now we organize our Peace Vigils as meditations. We meet every Saturday at twelve on Palace Square for a short meditation, and then we talk among ourselves. In this way we don't need permission. We are free, and we feel free. And all the people who like to speak, don't like to meditate!" he adds with a laugh. "So they went away. And now we have pure Peace Vigils!"

Since early 1989, the Leningrad branch of Peace Vigil has been registered as a social organization under the auspices of the Soviet Red Cross Society. This legal status has allowed Peace Vigil members to open a bank account, rent halls for public lectures, and expand their activities. In summer 1989, Peace Vigil sponsored a residential summer ecology camp near Volkhov. Zhikarentsev now hopes to organize regular seminars on nonviolence and to train teams of "peace brigades" that will travel to hotspots of ethnic violence and attempt to mediate in local conflicts. He also wants to create a joint business venture with a Western peace group to produce cooperative toys and games that might earn enough money to finance their own magazine on nonviolence and citizen diplomacy.

"Street demonstrations play a good role, but I feel something weak in these events," he says. "We need another tactic just now. We need to create, to build, to gather the power. The meetings are a way to become visible to people, to speak after seventy years of silence. But gathering the power is an invisible activity."

"What kind of power exactly?"

"The power of citizens to create some kind of alternative. Not simply to cry that we are *free*, and you are our *enemies*, but to create a basis for relationship with each other. To find our creative power. It will take, I believe, five to ten years of very intensive work. But if we remember that we are united, that we are one, there will be evolution and mutual activity, and we will find this power."

10 | The Disturber of the Peace

I n colloquial Russian, a *vozmutitel spokoistvia*, a "disturber of the peace," is someone who persistently challenges the status quo and thus does not permit others to live quietly. The term comes from the title of a novel about Hoja Nassredin, a folk hero in Central Asia who is, according to a dictionary of Russian slang, "a wag and a wit, a boon companion, a merry and kind-hearted fellow, and an eternal vagabond who is always on the side of the poor and the downtrodden, speaking out against despotic rulers, corrupt judges, and the cringing hypocritical rich."

Gennadi Alferenko is a *vozmutitel spokoistvia* deep to his bones. He is the founder and director of the Foundation for Social Inventions, a new Soviet institution which eludes easy classification. Some have called it the Soviet Union's first non-governmental, non-profit philanthropic fund. Some have likened it to a cross between the United Way and a start-up venture capital firm. The Foundation for Social Inventions is indisputably official; it is registered with the Soviet government, housed in the offices of the newspaper *Komsomolskaya Pravda,* and entitled to organizational privileges such as its own bank account. But no one has yet been able to paste the word "official" on Gennadi Alferenko and make it stick. He has fought against everything the word "official" represents all his life.

Five years ago, Alferenko was an obscure geophysics researcher at Novosibirsk State University, a dance buff, and a self-proclaimed "social inventor." No one, least of all Alferenko, could have predicted that soon he would be plucked from hot water in Siberia—some say, by Gorbachev himself—and given a post at a powerful national newspaper and the opportunity to make his dream of establishing a "fund for social inventions" come true. His is the quintessential *perestroika* success story, a modern fairytale

complete with bureaucratic monsters slain and rewards be-
queathed by a wise king.

"There have always been social experiments ahead of bureaucratic reality, and they have always been absolutely unattainable,
insane, grandiose and global," says Alferenko. "But while the bureaucracy is coping with this, you've already accomplished something small. And you go on to the next thing, without pause,
ceaselessly creating, ceaselessly inventing. If you stop and think
about it, and try to protect what you have, you'll get hung up—and
you've lost. Because this pause gives birth to attack and destruction. Just create and go forward without asking permission—just
go forward."

Alferenko has the lithe body of a dancer and the chiseled
profile of an Apache chief. With Americans, he communicates
with his body as much as with his limited English; his movements
are quick and expressive, his hands eloquent, his eyes deep brown
and shrewd. When he grins he can seem boyish, or at least younger
than his forty years. But his forehead also has deep lines etched by
years of being a "disturber of the peace." He has a heart condition,
and often speaks matter-of-factly about how little time he has left
to live. He considers this all the more reason to work eighty hours
a week now.

"My function is to fight. The dirtier and wilier the bureaucracy,
the better. Because it trains you, it gets you in shape. You don't
weaken. You have pain, but you also have energy for life. It's a
battle, and it can be dangerous. You can suffer. And you have to
act without hope of reward. It's a war of ideals. You have to accept
that you'll never end this game, that you'll never win, because even
in the best possible circumstances you only stay alive. Because the
bureaucracy is mercilessly strong. Because the concept of permission is the privilege of its power. But if you travel an unknown path,
if you find green grass and breathe it in like a young child smelling
the air of the mountains and the rushing streams, and you see the
far horizon—then you open up a new path for others."

Alferenko's own social invention—the Foundation for Social
Inventions—is simple in concept and grand in scope. Any Soviet
with a "socially innovative" idea can send a proposal to the Foundation. Alferenko and a small staff select what they consider the
best projects, publish articles in *Komsomolskaya Pravda* describing
them, and ask for monetary contributions from the newspaper's

readers to support them. By the end of its first year, the Foundation had received more than 30,000 project ideas and collected more than three million rubles on behalf of about a dozen main projects. Alferenko once summarized the Foundation's entrepreneurial philosophy thus: "Reward someone, don't be stingy, and he will roll up mountains and break the horns off the devil."

Since the Foundation's mandate is nothing less than the support of innovation itself, an eclectic batch of projects has wound up in Alferenko's care. Some are aimed at improving the quality of life, such as encouraging new teaching methods and designing ecologically sound "villages of the future." Some are civic service projects, such as establishing a network of private foster homes for orphans. Some are business-minded, such as seminars aimed at teaching Western management principles to heads of cooperatives. And some are sheer glitz: the training of young Central Asian women for participation in a London "Miss Asia" beauty pageant, a stunt flight across the Soviet Union by "the world's youngest pilot."

But these projects are not what Alferenko is known for in the West. He is also a seasoned citizen diplomat with a gift for organizing once-impossible exchanges. He has, among other things, arranged for American Vietnam veterans to meet with Soviet Afghanistan veterans, Alaskan Eskimos to meet with Siberian Eskimos, and American children to meet and live with Soviet children in summer camps. He works closely with a dozen top American leaders in Soviet-American exchanges; one of them, businessman and philanthropist Henry Dakin, has maintained a San Francisco support office for the Foundation since 1987.

Around Alferenko, people dream bigger dreams. He projects an infectious belief that there are no limits to human creativity and resourcefulness. He paints broad strokes on large canvasses; he is not a detail man. Negotiations with him are not for the faint of heart or the picayune of mind. He thinks big—very big.

"Our old way to live was to believe that every step that you took needed to have permission. If I see an open door, I ought to get permission to go through it—even though it's open. And thus a whole generation was raised. This is the Stalin paradigm, a paradigm of fear, a paradigm from a time when society had total strength. And people held this fear in their memory, on a conscious and unconscious level. The parents, the grandmothers and grandfathers, brought up their children to believe: 'Move slowly, and ask everywhere for permission.' So this fear of an open door continued. Here people are very happy if they feel a closed space around them.

"But then suddenly you sense the space that surrounds you, and you feel it—I really am free! I can fly! If you feel free, then you are free. The only limit is that your freedom to wave your arms stops at the end of another person's nose. That sensitivity to the other person is a factor of freedom. You can wave your arms, but you should think of my nose. In society there must be those people who go ahead, knowing that it will not be personally profitable for them. Others will follow. It's a kind of skillful sacrifice. You don't have to destroy. You simply have to win. That's what all your actions and thoughts should be aimed for."

When I first met Alferenko in February 1988, he was sharing a tiny office with another journalist, a cartoonist, and a seventeen-year-old volunteer on the sixth floor of the behemoth Moscow building that houses *Komsomolskaya Pravda* and several other Soviet publications. The room contained three desks, two stately manual typewriters, and one telephone. The tag outside the door merely said: "Special Correspondents." The only outward signs of the Foundation for Social Inventions were a few labels with the Foundation's logo stuck on some cupboards.

But it was soon evident that this unprepossessing room was a veritable pressure-cooker of *perestroika*. During the next few hours a parade of aspirants to the title "social inventor" tromped in and out of the room. An architect in a pin-striped suit explained his new housing concept of "clan-dwellings." A young man dropped off a long typed proposal for a "Center for Practical Esthetics" and fled. A somber-faced engineer from Byelorussia appeared with designs for "non-rocket space travel" via an enormous metallic tube encircling the earth. Alferenko, who had evidently heard of this project before, signed a letter of support for the engineer with barely a grin. He was aware that the concept was pure madness. But he was attracted by its audacity, by its sheer immensity. "This project would cost five hundred *billion* dollars," he said in reverent tones, sketching the zeros on a notepad. The engineer was, at least, thinking big.

Between visitors, Alferenko exclaimed "I will show you!" and pulled out newspaper clippings, project proposals, and fat little envelopes full of donation receipts. The Foundation had by then collected 103,000 rubles, most of them directed toward construction of a new home in Zagorsk for deaf/blind/mute children. Contributions from individuals ranged between 10 and 200 rubles. A few people had pledged to give 10 rubles a month. One envelope contained receipts for 15,000 rubles sent by Soviet children toward the building of a memorial to Samantha Smith. An elderly woman in Irkutsk had written that she wished to give 35,000 rubles toward the printing of a Soviet astrological almanac loosely based on Hesiod's *Works and Days*. And one man had donated a single ruble for "the building of a monument to the founder of the Foundation for Social Inventions." Alferenko palmed this one with a grin: "It's a start!"

Meanwhile, the phone was ringing with little pause. The other journalist and the cartoonist were entertaining visitors, and the hodgepodge of people and conversations was dizzying. Messages steadily accumulated on Alferenko's desk pad. "You see, it is a very crazy place," he said distractedly between calls, "but my job is *wonderful*."

Eight months later, Alferenko had moved operations down the hall into a spacious and sunny room hung with posters of hot-air balloons. His staff had swelled to five full-time assistants; one of them hooked a laptop computer into a modem and checked for electronic mail from San Francisco. Alferenko proudly displayed their most recent article in *Komsomolskaya Pravda*, which announced that his Foundation had so far received 3,625,428 rubles and 60 kopecks in donations from readers. "These 60 kopecks," he added, "are also very important." He then held up a copy of Donald Trump's *The Art of the Deal* and announced: "Today this is my favorite book."

The room was bigger, but the flow of visitors unchanged. A shy young man with a mohawk sat nervously on a chair, waiting to discuss his project: publishing an anthology of Soviet rock poetry. Three Afghanistan veterans walked in for a meeting with two of the staff. The phone rang; it was *The Washington Post*. Two young men in suede jackets—an independent film producer and the director of the film *Little Vera*—dropped by in order to meet a well-known American management consultant who had, at Alferenko's invitation, paused in Moscow for a few days between New York and Singapore. The phones rang and rang. "If we had one hundred phones," Alferenko said with an amused, puzzled smile as he dashed out the door to a meeting, "they would *still* always be ringing."

It is impossible to have a sustained conversation with Alferenko in his office. For our interview we went to dinner in his home together with his ballerina wife, Varya, and his twelve-year-old daughter, Olyesia. Alferenko loves to talk, and although he prefers talking about the future to the past, he soon understood that I wanted to hear his own complex story. He spoke in Russian for four uninterrupted hours, his words underscored by his mobile, dancing hands.

Alferenko's parents died when he was small, and he was raised in an orphanage in a small Siberian village about 400 kilometers north of Novosibirsk. He was well into his teens before he first visited a city and saw such marvels as televisions and trolleybuses. The orphans' sole contact with the "outside" was a radio owned by someone in the village. Alferenko and his friends would sneak out of the orphanage late at night and gather around this radio, listening to the news of the world.

"I went through a school of survival in the orphanage, and also a school of goodness. It was a unique model of humanity. We lived like one family, and we looked after each other. We were of different nationalities, but we had a common sorrow—everyone was without parents. And we had common enemies: the bad teachers and the bad caretakers. We fought against these enemies artfully, talentedly, and collectively, and we preserved our feeling of inner freedom. We *survived*, in spite of the people who wanted to subject us, who did not want us to be free. And we were free the whole time. We organized our own children's council, and discussed all the questions that arose in the orphanage, and independently resolved our problems."

A bright student, Alferenko was admitted to Novosibirsk State University. To earn his pocket money, he organized a construction team of young people to handle small building jobs. "All the time I had to survive on my own strength," he recalls. "I believe that you have to go through a kind of school of difficulties, so that you always feel like your next step is going to be your last. This feeling of danger trains you most effectively. And it kept me in good condition. I always felt that there was a lot of strength concentrated in me."

While at university, Alferenko came upon a book by the great

Russian literary critic Mikhail Bakhtin called *The Problems of Dostoevsky's Poetics*. "This book changed my life. I read it on trolleybuses, on trains, during every spare moment. It struck me very deeply. His basic principles and concepts are not just a key to worldwide artistic culture, they are also a key to many of our political processes. Bakhtin believed in a polyphonic structure of independent initiative. His book forced me to think up several social experiments." Alferenko was also influenced by Albert Schweitzer. "I read about his attitude of reverence for life, and how he discarded his life as a great philosopher and musician and went to Africa to save and heal sick children. Schweitzer wrote that if you talk about doing something, then you should actively do it. A great philosopher is not just a thinker but a doer."

Alferenko graduated with a degree in geophysics and took a job as a researcher at the university. But he had little interest in seriously pursuing a scientific career. "I felt that if I took that path, I would have to make compromises. I would have to adapt myself. I would have to paint my face red." Instead, he became smitten with the idea of founding some sort of independent local organization. "I wanted to organize an experiment that would prove to others that it's possible. I wanted to show how to do it in accordance with the law, to show that it wasn't frightening, and thus to move our society in a direction of independence. I wanted to change the monologue, the one voice of the hierarchical pyramidical organizations directing everyone, into a dialogue, a polyphonic structure of independent voices."

In 1970, he began to organize an independent dance and choreography association called Terpsikhora. Alferenko had always loved dance and had performed Siberian folk dances since he was a child. As a student he became involved in the university dance club, learned ballroom dancing, and traveled to different cities to participate in dance competitions. "Dostoevsky believed that it would be exactly beauty that would save the world. If goodness and beauty grow, then they will defeat evil. And dance is beauty. It's a way to preserve your physical health. It's meditation. It's a ritual, a global ritual. It's a feeling about the world. Dance allowed me to live out what I needed to live, and the bureaucracy could not immediately tell what I was thinking and creating and expressing. That's why I worked with dance. But in actuality I was working on a social, economic, and political experiment.

"I decided that if I was going to walk in the mountains I had to go with good equipment. Alpinists don't try to climb without good hooks. The equipment I needed was a knowledge of history, of our constitution, of the right to assemble, of how to make these voluntary associations legal within our society. I studied this, and I found an old, forgotten law about voluntary organizations from 1932.

"If you understand our society, you know there exist many centralized social organizations, and they're all bureaucratized. And you have to contribute to them on your payday. It's like a tax. For example, my daughter was forced to join a life-saving organization in her school, and she doesn't even know how to swim. Not everyone who joins the society of booklovers knows how to read. So you have obligatory membership in all these obligatory, government-run societies. And of course people are alienated from them. Then there are voluntary amateur clubs, but they don't have any legal rights. They're like dogs on short leashes. So I decided our group would develop a new position for amateur associations, so that they would have strong rights, so that they would be independent and free to go in the direction they wanted to go in.

"Of course, you can't explain to Americans what it meant to me and my friends to found a dancing society. A dancing society, they say—so what? They don't understand what it means to found a jazz club in our country. Or to found a society for sporting pigeons. There's a guy who wanted to do this, a World War II veteran. He just loves pigeons. He loves to watch how birds fly. And he wanted his birds to fly around the world. But a bureaucratic official said, 'You know, what if these birds don't come back? What would it mean if a Soviet pigeon, a dove of peace, were to run away? Then the Western press would write about us!' And the man said to the bureaucrat, 'Listen. The sporting pigeon has several characteristics. One, a complete faithfulness to his home. And two, an ability to orient himself in space, so that he doesn't get lost. Therefore, he always comes back.' And the bureaucrat said, 'Look, even Communists have gone to America and stayed there. Even Communists haven't come back. Your dove could betray us.' So, even until now, this person has not been able to organize a national society of pigeon lovers. Someone in the bureaucracy decided that it was dangerous, strange, and un-red.

"But we organized Terpsikhora, and we presented our own experimental ballet performances. We organized dance competitions and discotheques. We started giving ballet courses and dance appreciation courses for children and for grown-ups, earning our money by way of this. And to open an account with the bank, to keep ourselves going, to do every normal thing, was a battle. It took me three years to persuade and overcome the mayor's office of Novosibirsk so that we could get a bank account. And then we battled to be able to invite dance performers from many different countries—from Cuba, from France, from Bulgaria, as well as from Moscow and Leningrad. It took me sixteen years to create this organization, and to protect it from the pressure of the bureaucracy as one would protect a very small child or a tiny flower. Because it could easily die. You can lay a lot of asphalt around a flower and drive a steamroller over it. But if the flower is pulled to the sun, then the asphalt will be broken apart.

"And then some leader somewhere in the Party—this was toward the end of the Brezhnev era—decided that it was awful, it was very dangerous, that an independent association existed in Siberia. They were afraid that people would learn from it, and that it would start a movement of social innovation. They knew this would undermine the cult of official organizations. Some big person in the Party heard an interview with us on the radio, and he called and said: 'All social innovation stopped in October 1917. That was enough. There's no need for more.'

"So they decided to stop us. The Ministry of Culture, the Ministry of Finance, and the Ministry of Justice all sent commissions to us in Siberia and tried to find a way to close our society, to show that we weren't correctly founded, that we hadn't correctly handled our finances. There was no need for me to go from Novosibirsk to Moscow. A lot of people came from Moscow to Novosibirsk, just to talk to me. 'Gennadi, *why* did you organize this voluntary association? *What* do you want, really?'

"In our society, anything that appears selfless is always under suspicion. If you do something selflessly, not thinking about your own profit, not just in order to get yourself privileges, then the bureaucracy thinks, 'Oh, he must be getting *some* sort of profit and just hiding it.' And so they check you, and they say, 'We still don't see it. How much did you steal?' And a commission takes a look at you, and then another commission. And then a third, a fourth, a fifth. And that's how it continued, for fifteen years. If I had made one mistake, I would be in prison. But I studied bookkeeping and

I checked every document before I signed it. I studied history and philosophy and psychology, especially psychology, because I needed to understand concretely the kinds of powers that were against me.

"It has to do with breaking the old paradigm, and bringing about a presumption of innocence in our society. Our society is built on a presumption of guilt. 'What does this mean?' the bureaucracy asks. 'Who are you, where did you come from, where's your passport, where's your permit, where's this, where's that?' You can see this presumption of guilt everywhere—in schools, in hotels, on public transport, everywhere in civic Soviet life.

"Very slowly, official consciousness is beginning to accept that initiative in a person is not cause for suspicion, but rather is healthy for society. Before, the bureaucrats simply felt that if a person took the initiative, he was infringing on their power. Even consciousness gets bureaucratized if you don't realize that every person has the right of free initiative, if you don't recognize that we're like the free birds. If you, in the bureaucracy, don't trust a person's creative potential, then a feeling of absolute power arises and you think you're God, and you have to mess with it, and you destroy it.

"So the bureaucrats began a long financial and legal war, which we called the 'milk-choreography' war. In 1980 our association received a beautiful building from the mayor's office in Novosibirsk. But there was a milk factory nearby that wanted this building. And the representatives of the mayor's office were told to take this building away from us and give it to the milk factory. So they kicked us out. And for five years we fought for this building. For five years they would take the building away from us, and we would take it back, and they would take it away from us, and we would take it back. Once there had been ten families living in this building, but now there was only one family left, an elderly couple. And the old woman said it was just like in the Civil War: first the Whites occupy the building, then the Reds, then the Whites, and so on.

"In 1982, they set fire to the building on purpose. I had taken my whole archive there—15,000 different documents, famous photographs, gifts from great masters of the ballet and great personalities, unique posters, invaluable historical material. And they set it on fire on purpose, so that our organization would be hurt, so that we'd close down quickly and split up. They set our rooms on fire and they took the building away from us. At the same time they closed our bank account and a financial commission came from Moscow to check us out. Suddenly there are some violations which mean that it's possible that we can be tried and sent to jail for fifteen years.

"I arrived that day at the building and I saw the damage from the fire and learned that the Ministry of Finance and the Ministry of Culture had sent commissions to close down our society. And what was harder for me than anything else was that the archive had been destroyed. They'd taken away my memories, my documents that I'd collected for many years. I felt sick, and woke up in the hospital. Something had gone wrong with my heart.

"But I knew it was my fault that something had gone wrong with my heart, because it meant I was weak. If I'm so weak, if I suffer so much, if the bureaucracy can so easily play with me and defeat me, then that's my fault. So I became determined to learn special ways to struggle with the bureaucracy, to study literature and political science, to learn the historical process, to think more. At that time there had to be a special social technology of survival, a way to preserve creativity in the face of violent, backward, closed social conditions, when there's no *glasnost* or democracy, when there is total suppression of freedom of thought, movement, speech, and so on. It was this way during the time of Brezhnev. It was a very dark time for me. I only survived because Andropov opened the door and I received fresh air.

"In addition to Terpsikhora, I also started a Fund for Youth Initiative. This took me fifteen years. The goal of the Fund was to support local youth projects, so that young people could receive money for their ideas without asking permission from the bureaucracy. We used newspapers, television and radio to reach the population of Novosibirsk. You present your idea, which is not connected with personal gain but rather with a gain for society— making parks in the city better, for example, or saving a species of fish that's going to be wiped out by a dam. The inhabitants of the city, if they like your idea, send in two rubles, or five rubles, or twenty, to support the idea you have advanced. And with that money you can take the first step.

"Our Fund for Youth Initiative was the first independent local fund. Now there is a network of about fifty of these funds in the cities of the USSR. But they're all local funds, they're not central-ized. And I had the idea that there should be a national Founda-tion for Social Inventions. Where projects of social innovation would be published in the newspapers, and then readers who liked these projects could send in money to support them.

"Then in November 1985, at the beginning of the Geneva summit, an article was published in *Komsomolskaya Pravda* entitled 'A Patent for Social Invention' where they wrote the history of our handful of independent Soviet organizations—Terpsikhora, the Sverdlosk Youth Living Complex [a large independent com-mune], the school-factory 'Seagull,' and others. It was shown there the difficult fate of the organizers, including myself, and how hard it had been for us to live and work under Brezhnev. And the newspaper published my idea of a Foundation for Social Inven-tions, and invited readers to send in their ideas. Almost immedi-ately the newspaper received 15,000 project ideas in the mail.

"When he returned from the Geneva talks with Reagan, Mik-hail Sergeyevich Gorbachev read this article, and this article moved him. He immediately understood that social inventors were vital to the success of *perestroika*. 'Please help us!' he said. 'We need you!' So the editors of *Komsomolskaya Pravda* invited me to come to Moscow to develop this idea further, and to create a Foundation for Social Inventions in order to finance and support all the new crazy ideas and projects that were being sent to the paper.

"Siberia is a very special place. Many people in the 1800s, the Decembrists, for example, were sent there because they followed their hearts and went after the supreme goals of their life. They didn't go for little compromises. This Russian maximalism made Siberia into a unique place. Under Brezhnev there was no reason for me to come to Moscow. In Siberia I could work better and more easily because I was farther from Moscow.

"But when I heard that I had the opportunity to come to Moscow, and to work through a national paper with a readership of eighteen million, and to create a national Foundation for Social Inventions—my head spun with the possibilities. Possibilities to reach out and help millions of people. Possibilities to create a new ritual. People receive inspiration and fresh hope from ritual, from the rituals of birth, death, marriage, the rituals of nature. And I thought, 'There are many dark terrible powers in us at this time. We need a new ritual to combat them.'

"So I changed my profession. I left Novosibirsk University, where I had worked thirteen years as senior scientific researcher in geophysics. I came to Moscow with my wife and daughter and became a 'special correspondent' to the paper. My job was not only to report to the paper about people with new ideas and to defend them. My real function was to be a social entrepreneur, to undertake and organize new social experiments, to help people to take part in them and prove that innovation is possible."

Alferenko had first met Americans in the 1970s, through dance. When American ballet troupes toured the Soviet Union, he made trips to Moscow and Leningrad to see them. On one of these visits, a Soviet choreographer introduced him backstage to Robert Joffrey of the Joffrey Ballet. In 1982, Joffrey invited Alferenko to an international ballet competition in Jackson, Mississippi. Relations with the Novosibirsk mayor's office were in a warmer phase than usual and the mayor helped Alferenko secure the necessary exit permissions. Alferenko paid for his airplane tickets and traveled alone, attending every dance performance he could and poking behind the scenes.

One day he and an American friend, dance administrator and Soviet ballet expert Olga delaGuardia-Smoak, decided to organize an international association called Friends of Soviet Ballet. "We didn't ask permission, we were in agreement with no one. This was a risk. She was in the kitchen, and I asked her: how many times have you been to the Soviet Union? Seventeen times. How many people have you taken there? About 500. That's already an international organization, I said. So she called everyone, they agreed, they chose us as presidents and we formed the Friends of Soviet Ballet. Now we have a museum of the Bolshoi Theater in Los Angeles, and members from 15 countries, and we've helped send and receive many dance delegations."

These dance contacts helped put him in touch with other Americans visiting Novosibirsk, many of whom were surprised and delighted to discover an autonomous dance company flourishing in central Siberia. In 1985, Alferenko again received an invitation to the United States, and he spent two months in spring 1986 touring America with a delegation of Siberian dancers, making contacts with a number of leading citizen diplomats and telling them about his new post at *Komsomolskaya Pravda*.

While in New York in May 1986, Alferenko met David Gershon

and Gail Straub, the organizers of the First Earth Run, a UNICEF-sponsored world peace event planned for fall 1986 that featured passing a lighted torch around the Earth as a symbol of global cooperation. They told him they were having a hard time stirring up enthusiasm for the run among Soviet officials. Alferenko was entranced with the project's global dimensions and invited Gershon to fly back with him to Moscow. Within days Alferenko had leveraged the lukewarm support granted by the Soviet Sports Committee into top-level meetings with the Ministry of Culture, the main Soviet television agency, a film studio, and other bureaucratic wheel-greasers. Gershon found Alferenko's ability to work the system mindboggling: "He would tell one committee that another committee was already behind the project, and we would go from there. And he seemed to have a whole network of transformationally minded people scattered in different positions that he could mobilize." When the First Earth Run arrived in the Soviet Union in October 1986, it was greeted by a crowd of 100,000 people; runners carrying torches lit in Leningrad by the First Earth Run flame eventually traveled through sixty-five Soviet cities, Bulgaria, and Romania.

The success of the First Earth Run and his increasing contacts with American citizen diplomacy groups such as Young Ambassadors for Peace and the Esalen Soviet-American Exchange Program won Alferenko both friends and enemies as he maneuvered to set up his Foundation for Social Inventions within the framework of *Komsomolskaya Pravda*. Among his powerful friends were sociologist Tatiana Zaslavskaya and physicist Evgeny Velikhov, the vice-president of the Academy of Sciences. Among his powerful enemies was playwright Genrikh Borovik, the president of the Soviet Peace Committee, who was courting some of the same American contacts. By late 1986 Alferenko had moved to Moscow, and in March 1987 he helped coordinate, with Barbara Marx Hubbard and Rama Vernon of the Center for Soviet-American Dialogue, a small conference on "Socially Innovative Approaches to the Third Millenium." In summer 1987, he assisted Velikhov in organizing a Soviet-American youth camp in the old Russian city of Pereslavl-Zalesky, and he traveled to San Diego later that summer for a reciprocal camp in the United States.

Meanwhile, he continued steadily navigating his Foundation for Social Inventions through the pinnacles and ledges of high-level Soviet bureaucracy. By early 1987, he and his powerful friends had managed to persuade the USSR State Bank to allow him to open a bank account for the Foundation. On July 22, 1987, *Komsomolskaya Pravda* published a full page of articles introducing the Foundation to its readership. "Noisy, inconvenient enthusiasts are the main stimulants to scientific and technical progress," wrote Alferenko. "During the long years of stagnation we got used to having every initiative punished. How did the first ones survive in that situation? By drawing fire on themselves and covering those who were weaker in spirit. They broke through walls and knocked foreheads under a noisy verbal accompaniment—Long live initiative!

"We generally heard the following. . . . All funds are already committed. Apply again at the appropriate time. The circle of administrative tidiness closes. The author of an idea, growing weary of his own enthusiasm, once again falls into the crevices of the administrative apparatus. The energy of creation flows instead into the energy of the struggle for existence." Alferenko invited readers both to submit proposals for projects and to "take part in, criticize, evaluate, and finance" the projects that would appear in the newspaper. "So—something new, and, in our opinion, interesting," concluded Alferenko's article. "Shall we give it try?"

Soon letters and donations made out to the Foundation's account were deluging Alferenko's office. But the Central Committee of Komsomol, which publishes *Komsomolskaya Pravda*, reacted with less enthusiasm. "There were problems," admits Alferenko. "I thought it had taken much too long to establish the Foundation. But it seemed to others that we had hurried." An internal memo of disapproval to the editors of *Komsomolskaya Pravda* from the Central Committee of Komsomol, dated August 17, 1987, and marked "not for publication," complained that the July 22 article was published with "extreme haste" and that "there was no mention of the role of Komsomol in encouraging the initiatives of young people. Does this mean that the newspaper does not intend to work with the Central Committee?" Next to this paragraph Alferenko scrawled an exclamation point.

So what happened? "For three months we published nothing," Alferenko says. "Then we organized a lot of support, from Velikhov and so on." When Alferenko was in the United States in late summer 1987, he told American businessman Henry Dakin that he feared the Foundation would be wiped out when he returned. Dakin quickly printed and distributed an English version of the Foundation's initial articles, and Priscilla Huber Cotler, who helps coordinate the Foundation's San Francisco office, recalls that this publicity in the United States "helped keep Gennadi from being squashed." Alferenko has little interest in dwelling upon the details of this behind-the-scenes war. "Now everything is okay," he says cheerfully. "What is important is that we survived, and we preserved this structure.

"You see, our organization works in the zone of risk. We give our project authors money, but money sometimes isn't everything. We also support our project authors against the bureaucratic cold and wind. We protect them, we help them, we try to work out some agreements with legal and economic organizations in order to make it easier for them. In this sense we're middlemen. It's not an ordinary fund's function. In America, committees and funds just give out grants. In America, money is everything. Here, no. A thousand rubles won't help you buy anything if what you need to buy is a limited product. There are many old economic complications. And so our fund plays the role of a defense mechanism, an umbrella. We set up our project authors, let them go, and protect them economically and legally in the zone of risk."

The Foundation's current structure guarantees that a few projects receive spectacular publicity while the majority receive nothing at all. Alferenko is trying to set up a mechanism that could make obtaining support from the Foundation into less of a winner-take-all affair. In the meantime, he is frank about the whimsical nature of their selection process. "It's very simple. First of all, we read this material. And we have our personal opinions—oh, I like this project, oh, I like that project. It's only personal opinion, and maybe it's very bad taste. So then we invite experts, and the experts make recommendations. But still it's only the experts' personal opinion." In December 1988, Alferenko organized the Foundation's first conference in Moscow, attended by about two hundred "social inventors," where a hundred project ideas were introduced, discussed, and voted upon. Now the Foundation works with a cooperative called Evrika that runs a computer database of socially innovative ideas and publishes a newletter listing all of the proposals the Foundation receives and soliciting feedback from other "social inventors."

What really *is* a social invention? "I'm the enemy of all definitions. Definitions lead to dogma and dead knowledge," Alferenko
replies. "But social invention is the breakthrough to something
new, something humanistic, that has not existed before in a given
social context. The concept of social invention includes the concept of preserving our common human ideals. I don't have to
define those because they are known in world-wide culture: goodness, beauty, fairness, faith, and so on. Letting out the devilish
powers of evil is not social invention. Destroying the planet and all
human knowledge is not social invention.

"Social inventors are people who have a particular knowledge
of survival. Even in the very most difficult circumstances, they will
suddenly *see* a future, which they see as a very real thing. They feel
it in their hands. And they quickly create this new vision that
they've seen. It's a gift. The social inventor is an artist, he has an
artistic gift. He can quickly draw a model of what he wants to
invent: a new life in society, a new kind of communication, a new
kind of industry. It's a creative vision. He works along the same
lines of creative law as any other artist. He has a sense of freedom,
a healing feeling.

"A social inventor always feels how much he is part of human
society. No matter what country he is from, he feels part of a global
society. He feels the needs of humanity, he selflessly works to give
what he sees to all humanity. When a person has an intellectual
product, then he has power, and he either gives it or keeps it for
himself. The technical inventor quickly wants to hide his secret
and receive profit from it. So the technical inventor is working for
profit; he wants to get things from his invention. He doesn't think,
'Is it good for human society?' but 'Is it good for me?'

"The social inventor doesn't get money for his inventions.
That's why we need a special law that will protect the rights of
social inventors. We pay the people who devise destructive devices
for the world. We have to reward people who work to save it. We
need a law to protect their rights, to protect their intellectual
capabilities, and to preserve this 'know-how and show-how.' That's
why we want to start a project that will recognize the highest level
of creativity on our planet every year. We'll develop a worldwide
process to give an award to the ten best social inventors on the
planet of the year, and organize special open worldwide seminars
to share the experiences of new projects and new realizations.

"It's very important that we preserve the memory of who was the author of new social ideas, in order to personalize the whole process. Personalities are born, personalities talk, personalities receive awards. But officially Soviets only have organizations, collectives, group structures. And personality is a crime. Personality is not allowed to appear. The preservation of intellectual authorship is considered dangerous, because it destroys the monopoly of hierarchic centralized organizations. All the roses, all the flowers of social innovation are brought about by a person, not a group. When people who belong to these enormous organizations see that a flower can grow in another place, they get upset. The smell of this rose coming to their nose, but not being in their hands, throws them into a tizzy. And here is where the cult of organization begins. What does the cult of organization mean? I give permission, I give permission, I am in power. That's what organizations do. In our new epoch, in the opening of our society under Gorbachev, we have the historical opportunity to personalize initiatives.

"The influence of social inventors is growing over the whole world. I'm glad that this concept is pleasing to many people. It means that they understand the spirit of our times. The idea is becoming more and more powerful. Many organizations are coming to the conception of social innovation and bringing this idea forward. And this is the culmination of a long historical process.

"I am a maximalist. I want to demand more of our epoch. There is a breakthrough into the future taking place, a visionary consciousness moving toward the third millenium. We're waking up from the 20th century into the 21st. It is a great moment in our history, it is a great honor for us. And of course people are feeling the rhythm of this change-over. People love the smell of it, like wolves smelling something very sharp and hot."

However random the Foundation's assortment of projects may seem to Westerners—and the juxtaposition of "gardens for health, long life, and beauty," a private automobile repair service, and a bike caravan across the country can indeed be perplexing—the pattern makes sense to Alferenko. Still, some Soviets have criticized him for choosing to back only politically neutral ideas. When asked about Alferenko, some Muscovites grumbled that so far the Foundation has been long on fancy words and short on results. Others assumed that his meteoric rise to prominence and power could only have been boosted by compromises. Alferenko dismisses such criticisms: "There are a lot of people who want only to stay in the kitchen or go out in the streets and shout and oppose. Only talk and oppose. It's the old way. It's not my style. Maybe it was okay before, but we have a new process now, a new historical opportunity."

And given the Foundation's precarious existence, Alferenko's caution in picking his shots is understandable. In January 1988, he again came under fire from the Central Committee of Komsomol and other high-level officials when the Foundation published in *Komsomolskaya Pravda* an idea to build a center for physical and psychological rehabilitation of returning Afghan veterans. Gorbachev had yet to announce Soviet troop withdrawals from Afghanistan, but "we knew that sooner or later, Soviet forces would pull out of there," explains Alferenko. "And we knew that the people who had been wounded there would need humane attention in order to come back to a normal life. They return without arms, without legs. They feel handicapped, deprived, humiliated. And their consciousness is different—they have been through something we haven't."

The article led to "lots and lots of angry phone calls and letters from high officials," recalls Alferenko with a grimace. "They told us: 'Afghan veterans are national heroes. We should give them medals and glory and honor, not rehabilitation centers. Veteran rehabilitation centers are only for Vietnam killers.'" Readers of *Komsomolskaya Pravda* reacted differently. Of the six and one-half million rubles in donations that the Foundation had received by January 1989, five and one-half million were for the Afghanistan project.

In summer 1988, Diana Glasgow of the Seattle-based Holy-earth Foundation proposed bringing a small group of Vietnam veterans with expertise ranging from post-traumatic stress to designing prostheses to meet with a small group of interested Afghanistan veterans. "I knew it was very important just to organize this project immediately," says Alferenko. "And not to ask permission of *anybody*, because if we ask for permission we'll *never* receive it. Absolutely never. So I decided to organize this event in our style. We had just received the possibility to organize visas, and so we got visas for the delegation, we arranged the hotels, and we spent maybe 30,000 rubles. We arranged meetings with military people, with the Ministry of Defense, with military hospitals. It was not simple.

"But when we and the Afghan veterans received the Vietnam veterans for the first time in Sheremetyevo airport, these people just immediately became friends. They hugged each other and began friendly conversation. I never expected this, because the Afghan veterans had been very eager to meet the Vietnam veterans, but also very afraid. The Vietnam veterans explained to me: 'For us the Afghan veterans are younger brothers.' And they talked and talked together, and sometimes cried together. And the veterans told me kind words about how this meeting was for them a very profound thing. Then I understood that I did not organize the Foundation for Social Inventions in vain. To be able to organize something to change profoundly people's lives—it happens very seldom."

Some Soviet press articles about the exchange referred to the visiting Americans as Vietnam "specialists" rather than "veterans" to avoid the embarrassing assumption of symmetry between the two wars, but at least one article, in the Soviet weekly *New Times,* did not hesitate to draw parallels between "the war syndrome" in both Vietnam and Afghanistan. Still, Alferenko says that two decades of fierce propaganda stressing the atrocities of the Vietnam War had left its mark: "A correspondent on a national radio program asked me, 'Why did you invite these killers from America? Afghanistan was our special internationalist duty, it was another kind of war. Our veterans are national heroes.'" One of the young Afghan veterans associated with the project, a Moscow policeman, was told by his superiors to quit meeting with the Vietnam "hired killers." When he refused, other policemen, among them other Afghan veterans, wrote letters complaining about him to his supervisors.

By comparison, Alferenko found arranging for a visit between long-separated Alaskan and Siberian Eskimo relatives in summer 1988 to be merely a logistical nightmare. The International Polar Society had been trying to obtain permission for a shipload of aging Alaskan Eskimos to land in northeastern Siberia—a closed area for foreigners because of the large Soviet military presence in the region—for more than a year without success. "So Gennadi Gerasimov [spokesman for the Soviet Foreign Ministry] asked me to help these people. I said okay, and I prepared electronic mail and sent a message to Alaska. They thought it was an invitation, and they immediately telephoned me and said, 'Gennadi, thanks for the invitation.' And every day, for two weeks, I received at midnight a telephone call from the Americans. 'Gennadi, have you prepared the visas and permission? The old people are crying, we are running out of food, and everyone is very tired, and we have been waiting one month.' And I thought, Uh-oh.

"So I decided I had to find a way to organize this trip without a special governmental decision, because that would take at least six months. But even so it was necessary to involve thirty-five governmental organizations for this project. Thirty-five. I asked the leaders of these organizations to help us, and they explained: the problem is the Ministry of Defense. Have you asked for permission? I said. Yes, they said, but it's a secret area, there are many problems, no one will help. It was terrible for me, because every day I am receiving telephone calls from Alaska. The old people are very tired and disappointed, and people are crying on both sides. I called to the local authorities in the city of Magadan, and they said: Yes, we're ready, but we need permission, permission, permission. Each second, each minute, each day, I hear: Permission, permission, permission.

"Finally I decided that I will call to the high-level people at the Ministry of Defense and KGB myself, and ask directly. So I found out the number, and I called on a special line to the Kremlin reserved for communication with top leaders, and explained: everyone in the thirty-five organizations are saying that they are ready, but they say that you, the KGB and Ministry of Defense, are the problem. And these top leaders say, No. It's not true. A lot of people have been asking about this? It's the first time we've heard about it. It's a wonderful project. We're ready to give you permission." Alferenko shrugs. "And we received permission *immediately*."

By January 1989, about half of the Foundation's projects involved some degree of American participation. In December 1988, Sharon Tennison of the Center for US-USSR Initiatives abandoned trying to work with the Soviet Peace Committee and turned her "Soviets Meet Middle America" exchange over to the Foundation. Together she and Alferenko arranged for nearly 100 entrepreneurial Soviets to visit the heartland of America. Alferenko's other Soviet-American projects include placing Soviet young people in the Semester at Sea program, facilitating direct flights and telecommunication links between Alaska and Siberia, arranging for American and Soviet scientists to study dolphin communication together in the Caribbean, and publishing a Russian-language version of a board game called "Give Peace a Chance" invented by a twelve-year-old American girl.

Alferenko is also trying to help Ben and Jerry's, Inc., a Vermont-based ice cream company known for its maverick marketing and social conscience, sell "ice cream of the twenty-first century" in the Soviet Union. "The ice cream parlors would have computer technology, so that people wouldn't just be eating ice cream, they'd be communicating through computers and making electronic newspapers through the new technology of the screen," enthuses Alferenko. "So that every day, at certain points, you'd feel yourself in the net of global communication. Something unseen would be going on in these places. You're eating ice cream and at the same time taking part in a global act of communication. This would be the birth of a new ancient ritual. In the old days, everything great was connected with times of eating. The tribe gathered, watched the fire, ate, and great ideas were born. This is why I like the ice-cream idea. It's an old ritual, but it's the new campfire of our new communications technology. And a great tribe would be gathered around it. Only it's a cold ice cream fire."

Alferenko is reluctant to link the movement for social invention with the "peace movement" since, like many Soviet intellectuals, he associates this phrase with tasteless mass propaganda rallies organized by Party functionaries. "The peace movement is a very specific movement that has both good and bad traditions," he says. "Right now the global military-industrial complex has outdistanced world-wide consciousness. They are ahead of us. You don't have to fight with the military-industrial complex, you have to *pass* them and outdistance them. With your strong, large, great social inventions you have to get out in front of the military-industrial complex, in front of these people with their impoverished knowledge of destruction.

"Tolstoy wrote in *War and Peace* that if bad people unify in order to realize some awful goal then good people also need to unify. If the militaries are using new technology and information to destroy, using all our strength and powers of communication, then we need to do the same thing for the preservation of beauty and good. But this is a new type of joining together; this is not manipulation, this is not coordination. This is an independent, creative, and strong system, a live system. It hums, it works. Out of all those flowers the bees bring something good so that the honey is tasty, and that's what we are doing with our knowledge. The bee works and brings the pollen, and there are different kinds of flowers with different leaves and different petals—and the bee brings something from each of them.

"And we must think, what does 'peace movement' now mean on our planet? Because a lot of people, a lot of organizations and foundations—and not only in the Soviet Union—continue the old style. They invite the workers, organize a special demonstration, make special advertisements and special speeches. They continue to march for peace. It's okay, and maybe it was effective before. But now we have another process. The political situation has changed, but people continue to speak about friendship, peace, friendship, peace, crying and hugging each other, and explaining, 'Oh, it's wonderful, I met them, they're the same people. . . .' It's stupid! It was okay, maybe, during the Cold War. But it's not enough now. We have now an historical opportunity to do—to do *everything*. Not only to march and to fight.

"Citizen diplomacy is first of all a very concrete matter—for example, Soviets and Americans going to the city of Novosibirsk, and meeting there, and planting a tree. Or simply riding on the Moscow metro and meeting people. That's also an opening of the world. But citizen diplomacy should also include very large global things. Although I do not love the word 'global.' You can sit in the warm sand in California and make up some global society, and even make up business cards, and never do the simplest thing, not even plant a tree.

"When people act bravely and strongly, when we work together, that's when changes will come. There must be changes in the inner consciousness of the society. Citizen diplomacy is not like the story of Sleeping Beauty. It's not like Americans can come to the Soviet Union and wake up the beauty who was sleeping for a hundred years. Kiss her, wake her up, and all of a sudden, Wow. Soviet-American relations. No. If the princess slept for a hundred years, she'll continue to sleep for another hundred years. The kiss won't wake her. She'll only wake up because she wants to, because she wants to dance, to express herself. And to feel music and rhythm and beauty. And to move about without limits, in a movement of joy.

"The more different kinds of people and organizations you have working to establish what they want, the less of a risk of monopoly you have. Everybody's looking for a new project and all the organizations are competing to do it best. It creates a polyphony. And then, for the Soviet person, there's a terrible fearful problem—the problem of choice. Which organization to work with. Which organization to give money to. Which organization to travel with. And it's hard and bitter for us, and we remember the old days, when we just sat and waited to be told what to do. It's a difficult time, with difficult moral and intellectual problems. Our society doesn't know what choice means. We must learn ourselves how to become the prince that kisses the beauty.

"Citizen diplomacy is a secret resource of humanity. If the strengths of kindness and beauty can be concentrated, the planet won't be destroyed. Let the military-industrial complex exist. We will outdistance it. In these voluntary organizations all over the world the qualities of good-heartedness and kindness will be preserved and built-up. And this will save the world. This is the meaning of great citizen diplomacy."

In late 1988, a new editor-in-chief with a somewhat cooler attitude toward the Foundation took over *Komsomolskaya Pravda;* sensing that his days there might be numbered, Alferenko successfully established a beachhead for the Foundation within a number of other publications, including the newspaper *Argumenti i Fakti.* He has broadened decision-making within the Foundation by creating separate "boards of directors" to oversee each of their major projects, and he is working on developing branch offices in other Soviet cities.

But he is torn between wanting to establish a permanent structure that can survive shifting political winds, and wanting to avoid creating yet another organizational pyramid. He is wary of an objective process that could become impersonal and bureaucratized: "I like to make immediate decisions after immediate meetings." But already he must rely on his staff to answer many of his calls, and he is appalled by the way the system is beginning to turn him into the very sort of person—the omnipotent bureaucrat with the power to make or break fortunes with a wave of the hand—that he has fought against all his life. "When people call, they refuse to talk to my staff. They are used to the old mentality, the old style, when the only way to get anywhere was to talk to the top leader. So they only want to talk to me, and they want to monopolize my time. And I feel empty, I become very tired."

Alferenko is still a *vozmutitel spokoistvia* in Soviet society. "He's really a sprite," says his American co-worker Priscilla Huber Cotler, "who now has to wear these big baggy bureaucratic clothes." Some of his American partners worry that he is driving himself too hard and that his health is deteriorating. Without his peculiar combination of vision and savvy, the Foundation for Social Inventions might not survive long; many are astonished it has lasted as long as it has.

What is Alferenko's secret? Why was he able to remain a social inventor through all the "years of stagnation," when so many others were not?

"The secret is very simple. It's the secret to success in a state of total bureaucracy. Why was Klimov able to make a revolution in cinematography? Why was our fine director Anatoly Vasileyev able to start his independent theater? How did Vysotsky—after his death, it's true—preserve his voice and continue to be heard in our society? How was the film 'Repentance' made and released, and how has Yakovlev succeeded in publishing *Moscow News,* no matter what? How was Gorbachev able to put forward his conception of *perestroika* and move with it?

"The first trait that these people have in common is a *feeling of inner freedom.* A feeling of inner freedom, which you carry with you always, no matter what happens, no matter what politics or the bureaucracy does to you. And you must search for the path to protect this feeling of inner freedom. You don't go into any compromises, because compromises mean that you will be crushed. You don't cooperate with dishonorable people, because that also will crush your feeling of inner freedom. You don't go absolutely for career or for success, because when you close doors to preserve your privilege, then you're cutting off your own inner space and your inner freedom. This is the most important quality, the feeling of inner freedom. If you don't have it, you'll lose everything.

"It's easy to say that there are bureaucratic limits. It's easy to criticize other organizations, like the Friendship Society and the

Soviet Peace Committee, and make oneself look better. It's easy to say, 'Look how great I am. These organizations just interfere with my work.' No, the obstacles lie with the self. If I don't do something, I and only I am guilty. If I'm not smart enough to use this new social technology, I'm to blame. It's something lacking in my upbringing, in my spirit, something inside me that's putting the brakes on. And I need to think, 'What's going on inside me?'

"I don't see obstacles in the outer world. If some talented bureaucrat defeats me, that means I didn't do something right. Of course there are difficult people, but if I feel myself to be free, and abide by my inner laws of honor and fairness, and I lose, then I'm the guilty one. If we lose the war with the bureaucrats, it will be our fault. It will mean we weren't good enough at this war. To be victorious we must use and concentrate and strengthen all the intellectual powers of our society. If we lose, it will be the fault of me, of my friends, and of all those smart and honorable people who are spending their evenings discussing how difficult, sad, and terrible it is that the bureaucracy is defeating them.

"This doesn't mean that you don't see reality, that it isn't cruel and strong. There are personal and historical limits to the phase the world is located in right now. But at the same time we have what Tolstoy called 'the energy of delusion.' This is a great quality. To have vision, and an understanding of historical limits, but also to have the kind of energy of delusion that will allow you to make a breakthrough. It's not just romanticism. You see the powers of evil, and you see what kind of moral blows they will strike to defeat you. There's only one way to beat them, and that is not to take part in their evil. Not to take part in lies. Not to have anything to do with the evil people in society, not to read bad newspapers, not to read bad books. Lies always surround you, but you have to preserve your energy of delusion by not taking part in lies. It's a very simple principle, the consequences of which are endlessly difficult.

"Therefore, what's my major obstacle? It's this. I'm not good enough at preserving this energy of delusion in myself. Every day, every month, I still have some kind of compromise which takes away my energy. And not to give in to these things is very complicated. I'm a living person, I feel the world, I like beauty and flowers in my life. But to limit this in order to concentrate oneself on the important things—that is the most basic limit that one has.

"I feel the strength in society multiplying. And the process

Gorbachev has started can't be broken. You just can't do it. Society would not rise again. This is the last time. If this fails, then there will be a fearful process of disintegration. Now I see that our government is changing, and so I say, okay, I support you. I support you, Mikhail Sergeyevich. I'm on your side. I'm open to working with you. If you change your opinion, though, I won't change mine. I go my own path. I won't adapt.

"We have gone through a very dark time. Now I know what it means sunshine. Now if the political situation in the Soviet Union were to change, I would still remember. I know what it means sunshine. I know what it means imagination. I know what it means life. You see? And I will celebrate life each moment. In prison, in the dark, in bad weather—I will still know what it means, sunshine in life."

11 | The Mountain

A few feet away, her face illumined by candlelight, a woman with a guitar is singing. Above us, a ridge of the Caucasus Mountains has darkened against a violet sky. It is cold, and we are hunched over with fatigue, stiffly gathered around a candle someone has placed in the ground.

The woman is singing a ballad in Russian, a wistful melody all the more bewitching in its incomprehensibility. It is a relief to sit quietly together, to be free of the burden of trying to make conversation. All day we have been struggling with the language barrier, climbing up and sliding down its slippery walls. We are belaying each other with smiles and an occasional squeeze of the hand, but it is hard work. At times, we wonder whether we will ever scale these walls, and grow doubtful about the possibility of what we are trying to do.

But we are in a valley now, a place of rest. And the woman with the guitar keeps singing her ballads, soothing our tiredness with a voice that belongs to this meadow, this alpine night, as comfortably as the purl of a mountain stream.

I know little more about her than a few facts: her name is Evgenia (Zhenya) Alekseeva, she is 31 years old, she is a pediatric anaesthesiologist from Moscow, she speaks very little English, and she has two daughters aged seven and ten. She is tall and slim, with wide blue-green eyes and a quick smile. But like the other ten Soviets we Americans have traveled eight thousand miles to meet, she is a light behind a closed door. She speaks, rapidly and with great intelligence, a language that is as unknown to me as mine is to her. We are both scrambling to learn the bizarre code wired in the other's brain. Sometimes we astonish each other with a flash of understanding, but more often, the task seems hopeless. The words will take years to find. And we feel we do not have years—we have only these three weeks in the mountains, this one chance, before the borders between our countries split us apart once more.

After a time one of the American women takes the guitar and

strums up some Appalachian ballads. For awhile we swap songs, trade languages, handing the guitar around the circle, smiling and clapping hands. But there are still words between us, as one half of our group can only listen while the other half sings. We are still divided into Russian speakers and English speakers, into Soviets and Americans, and that gulf is precisely what we want so much not to feel.

The candle is almost out. Softly I begin to sing, without the guitar, a Native American chant that has no words. Suddenly everyone is singing. Together we sit up and belt out the spine-tingling harmonies. The lack of words puts us on an equal footing; the circle draws close. For a moment the candlelight on our faces binds us together into a single clan gathered around the hearth.

I look across the circle at Zhenya. Our eyes meet in recognition. And we are thinking, in our different codes: *It's going to work.*

Nearly two years later, in May 1988, Zhenya and I are sitting on a stage in a Kentucky auditorium, dressed in skirts and heels, microphone in hand. A woman in the audience asks Zhenya: "Why did you get involved in the peace movement?"

"At first it was by accident," Zhenya answers through an interpreter. "There was a time when, like many others in my country, I never thought I could do anything to stop the arms race. I only hoped that our leaders and our official social organizations were already doing enough to solve this problem. On the other hand, what I read in the newspapers and saw on television made me start thinking about the fate of the planet. My heart sank when I realized that a nuclear war threatens my children and all the children of the world."

An older man raises his hand. "I think what you girls are doing is great. But I wonder what real good it can do. How can your getting to be friends make a difference to our leaders in Washington and Moscow?"

"Nothing is worse than inaction," Zhenya replies, looking at him intently. "Maybe we can't do anything, but we have to try. And what can I do personally? I will be happy if I can bring information to as many people as possible about the danger that threatens the whole planet."

Later that evening, we are guests on a three-hour call-in radio talk show at a large station in Louisville. The face of the gruff talk show host melts into amiability as Zhenya handles every question with wit and candor. Topics range from the Afghanistan war to current Soviet fashions. Questions come in from Alabama, Georgia, Missouri, Ohio. No one is hostile, and many people thank the talk show host for "this real nice opportunity to talk with a real Russian." Between questions, Zhenya pulls out her guitar and sings ballads by the Soviet poet Bulat Okudzhava. I close my eyes and see these songs blossoming like alien flowers in thousands of American living rooms, truck cabs, convenience stores.

At the one-hour break, I hug her and tell her, "You're doing great."

"I hope not so great that the KGB will call in," she replies with a laugh.

It is one of our rare jokes about the fear. Westerners tend to imagine that police states function by erecting signposts: "This is forbidden. . . This is permitted. . ." Not so. There are no signs; there are only rumors. No one knows how far one can stray off the path of approved behavior; no one can be sure where the path stops and the minefield begins. All that is certain is that keeping to the middle of the road is the safest way.

After the show is over I tell her that if she could do shows like this for six months the Cold War would collapse. "If the KGB calls you, remember—*you* call *me*," I say.

It is a continuation of our joke, but it is also a promise, a pact, and we both know it. I am the one who has put her on these shows, who has encouraged her not to be afraid. She has danced out on this cliff and I must follow her, belay rope in hand.

Later, a nightmare comes.

I am racing through the rooms of a large, strange house, looking for Zhenya. She and Slava have been gone all evening. At first I supposed they probably were taking some much needed time to themselves, relaxing from the whirlwind of questions. Now, around midnight, Slava has returned without Zhenya, saying he has not seen her. I pick up a telephone and speak with a woman operator. "Please, my friend Zhenya is missing," I say. "Please help me find her."

There is a long pause on the line. The woman's voice is cold and grim. "I think you had better talk to someone at the Committee for State Security," she says carefully.

"The what?" I am incredulous.

"The Committee for State Security."

"You mean the KGB? What do they have to do with this?" For an answer, the woman hangs up.

Now frightened, I search the house again, running down long corridors and into what looks like laboratories. But my physician husband David finds her first. She is lying on a short cot, her feet dangling over the end. She is wearing her pink cotton T-shirt, her blue shorts, her Adidas sneakers. There is blood on her face and bloodstains on her shirt. Her arms hang limply and her eyes stare at the ceiling, heavy-lidded and dulled. Yet she is conscious. She is telling David what to do as he bends over her, washing, checking, his face hidden and shadowed with shock. Her voice is light and choppy, with an odd hollowness, as if it were being filtered through a speaker. Her mouth is filled with dark slugs of clotted blood; her teeth and gums are torn.

For a long time we work quietly, the shock combined with the relief of immediate activity overwhelming other feelings. She lies so still that I am afraid she has back injuries. Her dark curls hang damply around her face. Her calm manner lulls our horror. Then David looks into her throat, and begins to scream. I look at him and look at Zhenya's dulled eyes, and suddenly I know, too, even without looking. Her voice—her beautiful voice. The bastards have cut her vocal cords. They have taken away her voice. I back away in horror and want to kill them, now, for doing this to her. Behind me I think I see the leering face of a man with slick dark hair and thin lips. I pick up something large and glass and with both hands, screaming, break it over the man's head. But just before it strikes, the man turns into a machine with a protruding dark knob of instruments for a head. The glass shatters harmlessly. The last image I remember is of Zhenya's large, opaque eyes, staring with no recognition into mine. . . .

I wake up, my chest tight and my heart racing. I know that I am not, by the light of day, afraid that Zhenya will be tortured by the KGB. I know this is preposterous. But all the same, the fear is there, born of history and of the awareness that even today throats are cut in some parts of the world for singing the truth. I also know that there are other, more subtle, sometimes no less effective methods of silencing. No matter what, there are no guarantees. No matter what, the risk she takes is greater than mine.

Our 1986 expedition to the Caucasus Mountains of the Soviet Union was an attempt to make a difference, a bottle tossed in the ocean. At the time, it seemed as good a thing to try as any.

For several years my husband David Kreger and I had been working with International Physicians for the Prevention of Nuclear War (IPPNW), a group founded in 1980 by a handful of American and Soviet physicians, whose offices were located across the street from David's medical school in Boston. In July 1985, a few months before IPPNW won the Nobel Peace Prize, we had led an exploratory mission of Western medical students to the Soviet Union, hoping to link up with Soviet medical students who also were interested in IPPNW. Although Gorbachev had been in power for four months, no one had yet heard of *glasnost* and *perestroika,* and we were surrounded by evidence of what Soviets now ruefully call "the period of stagnation." We were unable to tell if the "student sections of IPPNW" to which we were introduced were anything more than paper appendages on existing Komsomol (Young Communist League) bureaucracies. Few of the Soviet students knew anything about the nuclear issue, and we were often dissatisfied with the stiff atmosphere of our formal student meetings. Despite long-winded speeches about the need for more friendship and understanding between our countries, once the sanctioned meetings were over most of the students chose to flee rather than be seen walking with us on the streets. Almost no one gave out a home telephone number or address.

When the chance to organize a Soviet-American mountaineering trip for IPPNW medical students fell into our laps a few months later, it seemed the perfect opportunity to answer some of our lingering questions. It was, in its day, a radical idea. Few young Soviets and Americans had ever been permitted to spend time together so intimately. Leaving the long polished tables and stuffy meeting rooms behind, we would share the same tents, cook meals together, and attempt to climb the highest peak in Europe.

The Soviet affiliate of IPPNW, the Soviet Committee of Physicians for the Prevention of Nuclear War (SCPPNW), surprises us by accepting the proposal for the trip. The Soviet co-president of IPPNW, Evgeny Chazov, even suggests a symbolic goal: burying at the summit of 18,481-foot Mt. Elbrus a "message to the world" signed by himself and American IPPNW co-president Bernard Lown. Later, however, a staffperson for SCPPNW will tell us that the trip was seen as "just another crazy American idea" that they could not gracefully refuse. The SCPPNW office recruits a famous mountaineer and sports physician in his fifties named Vyacheslav Onishchenko to be the Soviet leader of the trip, and gives him the task of finding nine other Soviets—half physicians, half medical students, and half women—who know how to climb mountains.

Slava Onishchenko soon assembles a group of his climbing buddies and children of his climbing buddies. Because SCPPNW does not take the idea seriously, they do not interfere with his selection, and no effort is made to pick people with good political credentials. In this way we are spared the usual fate of visiting American groups. Not until a few days before we arrive do Komsomol leaders at a Moscow medical institute get wind of the trip. Although they quickly try to organize a coup, insisting that they should go rather than the children of Slava's friends because of their superior experience in dealing with foreigners, Slava refuses to take them, using their lack of mountaineering training as an excuse. When an older acquaintance backs out due to illness, Slava remembers once meeting a young woman mountaineer and doctor who had a nice singing voice, and he asks Zhenya Alekseeva to come along.

Our first days in the Caucasus, we are caught up in the romance of our nationalities. That we have been kept apart so long makes our sudden closeness forbidden and glamorous, and we become fascinated by this interaction of labels with people attached. He is playing cards with a *Russian*. She is slicing cabbage with an *American*. We tend to see metaphors everywhere, and to take our fledgling relationships rather seriously. Our smallest interaction seems freighted with implications. If we cannot cook breakfast together successfully, what chance do we have for world peace? If we cannot communicate well enough to set up a tent, how are we going to end the Cold War?

This preoccupation with significance magnifies our little failures but also enhances our small triumphs. And it makes us all try very, very hard. We force our way through tangles of words, laughing somewhat desperately at half-understood jokes. Tremendous feelings cross in a smile or an offering of food. Together we admire asters, harebells, rhododendron, and dozens of other wildflowers we cannot name. We glissade down snow couloirs, slipping and catching ourselves with our ice axes. We gather wild strawberries and mushrooms, throw frisbees and snowballs.

One day we stand before a group of a hundred sunburnt young climbers at a mountaineering camp and talk, through a translator, about why we have come. After the meeting the climbers shyly gather around us, their smiles and body language speaking volumes. Then someone plugs an American rock tape into a sound system. "When I saw the Americans and Soviets dancing together," Lyosha Kalashnikov says later, "when I saw us holding hands, smiling, crying, singing, it seemed so impossible to me, so unimaginable, and yet here it was happening before my eyes. And I had a vision of our children also dancing together and laughing, also holding hands, and no one thinking it strange or impossible."

To cross the glaciers and gain a pass before the snow softens, we plan to leave camp the next morning at 5 a.m. But not everyone gets up in time, and before camp chores are finished Slava sets off with about two-thirds of the Soviets and Americans. The others are left behind to clean pots and pack stoves. The climb is steep and slippery, and a twenty-minute gap materializes between the lead group and the clean-up crew. When the first group stops to rest, the second group almost catches up, only to see the first group sling on their packs and take off.

It seems to members of the second group that the first doesn't want them to catch up, and they slog on, resentment building with every step. No one wants to be pegged as a member of the "slow group," and those in the rear feel unfairly treated. An American walking between the groups falls into icy water while crossing a stream because no one is nearby to help him. As soon as they gain the pass, five members of the first group bound down the snow and offer to carry the packs of those still climbing. But tensions are already so high that this is interpreted as a further rubbing in of their "strength" compared to the others' "weakness." We are reunited at the pass, but eight people are sullen and angry. Analogies to the arms race course through their minds.

My husband David calls a meeting and explains that it is extremely important for group morale that we stick together. Slava defends his action as simply an attempt to get as many people up the pass as possible before the snow softened. Members of the first group admit that there has been some competition but dismiss it as natural and inevitable. David says that's precisely the point: We are here to prove that cooperation is a stronger force than competition, to demonstrate a different way to climb a mountain.

During the ten-mile descent, everyone makes an extra effort to stay together. But exhaustion amplifies the bruised feelings, and dinner that night is eaten in language-based clusters. Almost everyone feels tired, cranky, and misunderstood.

Two days later we are staring at a river in dismay. The bridge has been washed away in the spring melt. *Cuckoo-grinya*, says Slava, raising his palms with a faint smile. (Roughly translated, *cuckoo-grinya* means "well, that's that, Charley.") Reluctantly, we take off our boots and socks, roll up our pants, loosen the straps on our backpacks, and eye the river that stands between us and four more miles of climbing to a 13,500-foot pass. The river is wide, unruly, waist-deep in places, and icy. *Cuckoo-grinya,* indeed.

While most of us linger on the bank, gathering our nerve, a few doff their packs and plunge in, hopping from rock to rock in the swift waters. They then join hands, balancing on submerged rocks and logs, forming a living bridge for the rest of us. One by one, as we inch into the deepest channel, we reach for Slava's hand while he holds on to Yura, and Yura holds on to Jeff, and Jeff wedges himself into the bank. Encouragement in both languages is shouted above the river's roar; cheers and applause erupt as each person splashes safely to land. We put on dry socks in high spirits. The way to Elbrus, our final challenge, is clear.

On a cloudless day we reach the base hut at 13,800 feet, where a television crew, newspaper reporters, and Dr. Evgeny Chazov, the Soviet co-president of IPPNW, are waiting to hold a press conference. We pay little attention to the wind that starts blowing at sundown, but by midnight it has gained strength and a lenticular cloud hangs over the mountain. Beginning an ascent is out of the question. Instead, we spend the day playing cards, talking, and writing in our journals. As the storm becomes a blizzard, we have plenty of time to contemplate the possibility that the weather may prevent us from taking a single step further. We think about what this trip has meant, and what, if anything, failing to climb Elbrus would change.

The following midnight I open the door to the hut, prepared for an icy blast of wind, but the door opens on silence. No wind, and stars. The summit smolders under a full moon. Soon we dress, put on our crampons, and move into the silver landscape outside of the hut. Behind us, clouds fill the valley, blanketing all but the highest peaks.

Slava takes his place at the head of the line and at 2 a.m. we begin to walk. Our boots sink into deep fresh snow; our ice axes and crampons clang against rock. We are like dark pearls strung on the white throat of the mountain. The wind picks up and at rests we huddle together like buffalo, shoving chocolate in each other's mouths and chipping ice in our water bottles.

Slowly the mountain rolls into day. A hidden sun burns its shoulder as the full moon drops into a crimson haze. I am walking between Yura Teryokhin and Volodya Nikoda, and every ten minutes, during some brief rest, we exclaim to one another about the beauty of the dawn. Three members of the group turn back, unable to handle the altitude. The rest of us slog on.

Hours later, we are still climbing. A dozen of us wait at a clump of rocks for six others still below. The altimeter reading: 18,000 feet. We wait for ten, fifteen minutes, the chill stiffening our bodies, common sense telling us to go on. But we are determined to climb the mountain as a unified group. At last, a half-dozen more climbers trudge to the rocks.

Only 500 feet to go. Each step now takes will. To our right, where snow and sky meet, the sun at last escapes from the heavy shoulder of the mountain; we are dazzled and grateful as rock and ice become edged in fire and color returns to the world. Onward. It cannot be much farther. I concentrate on my breathing and keep going, a few steps behind Volodya.

Then I look up and see he is waiting for me. "Galya, we will go together," he says firmly, taking my hand. "Only twenty steps to go." His steps are faster than mine; we take nine or ten and are both gasping. Our fingers cling together through layers of mittens. "Only fifteen steps to go." The sun, the glare, the air—no, no air. Volodya is going too *fast,* we ought to catch our breath. He tugs on my hand insistently. "Only ten steps." I lose my balance for a moment and feel his hand tighten as I stumble. He brings me back to my feet. "Only—five—steps," he huffs, and I gasp back, "Yes, yes, *da, da,*" feeling my body yelling in protest, feeling my strength gather, feeling my steps coming more rapidly, the odd flatness, suddenly—

There.

Our team is hugging, half-sobbing the words "together" and *vmestye,* gazing at the vast array of mountains to the south, the valley and plains to the north and east, the twin peak and still more mountains fading to the west toward the Black Sea.

"In the nuclear age, the nations of the world are all climbers on a mountain, depending for their survival on the rope of tolerance. The bonds of friendship forged in the wilderness are threads spanning the chasm between countries long separated by fear and ignorance." The words of our message will be reprinted in *Pravda* and the *Associated Press,* broadcast on radio and television. But as we bury our declaration in the snow and shout each other's names, all that matters is that the words are true.

Our last night in Moscow, Zhenya surprises us by inviting us home. She and the other Soviets throw a farewell party in her apartment, full of dancing, food, and rapid introductions to parents, children, and spouses. We are deeply touched by this immersion into their personal lives. It is one thing to gallivant with Americans in the mountains for three weeks on an officially sanctioned expedition. But bringing them home means overcoming the almost instinctual fear that surrounds unpermitted contact with foreigners. Later Zhenya will tell me that before our trip, she would never have considered inviting Americans to her apartment. "But I felt that you were good people," she says. "I had an intuition that I could trust you."

We dance and sing late into the night; it does not feel like a conclusion. The trip refuses to end tidily. Something hangs unfinished and half-born between us.

Back home, we give slide shows, honing our experiences into parables and using them as tools for reaching audiences. Rick Donahue, a medical student at the University of Massachusetts, and his wife Amy, a biology student training to be a teacher, take a year off from school to roam thirty states giving slide shows to nearly 200 audiences. In Moscow, the Soviets give presentations as well in their institutes and clinics. We start studying each other's languages in earnest, determined to meet somewhere in the middle. Letters go back and forth. We know we want to see them again—but how? Rick, Amy, David, and I confer one afternoon in October 1986. Let's invite them back, we decide. Let's invite them *here.*

It is another crazy idea; as far as we know, few Americans have ever succeeded in inviting a specific, named group of Soviet friends to the United States—and certainly not for a camping trip. But after months of negotiations, organizing, and fundraising, SCPPNW agrees to send seven of our climbing companions to New England for two weeks in July 1987. Since we have no 18,000 feet peak handy, we choose sea-kayaking on the Atlantic Ocean as our wilderness challenge.

The Soviets arrive in a daze, unable to believe they are really in the United States. It is a rushed, hot, and exhausting trip on a shoestring budget. We try to pack in too many things at once, squeezing in time for the wilderness, public presentations, and showing the Soviets America. Still, the four days of paddling fifty-five miles among pristine Maine islands are idyllic. Our slogan is "cooperate or capsize," and local newspapers run wild with head-lines like "THE RUSSIANS ARE COMING, AND ARE ARRIVING IN SEA KAYAKS."

The two weeks pass quickly and the Soviets fly home, but once more this does not feel like an ending. The trip has taught us how powerful joint Soviet-American presentations on our potential to transform the Cold War can be: we had received widespread press coverage, and more than a thousand people had come to our five public events. Our time in the wilderness has given us a wealth of shared experiences to draw upon in presentations, and our re-lationships are far more than metaphors. We realize it is time to take this show on the road.

Soon Amy and Rick Donahue, my husband David, and I hatch a plan to join four of our Soviet friends for a month of public speaking in the Soviet Union and a month in the United States in spring 1988. It is the hardest project we have yet tried to negotiate, and we almost fail. It takes an avalanche of telexes and letters from American IPPNW leaders before the Moscow office of SCPPNW agrees to a scaled-down version of two weeks of speaking in the Soviet Union and three weeks in the United States. We dub the tour "Moving Mountains: A Campaign of Hope," and write press releases saying this is the first time young Soviets and Americans will travel together through both countries jointly calling for an end to the arms race.

Our expectations for the Soviet leg of the tour are not high. SCPPNW, we know, is an organization largely confined to a handful of prominent physicians, scientists, and administrators in the major cities. Remembering our experience in 1985, we are prepared to face small, selected gatherings of Komsomol student leaders, with their bland questions and penchant for disappearing as soon as formal meetings end.

To counteract what we suspect will be a complete lack of awareness about nuclear and ecological issues, we prepare a six-page fact sheet on American and Soviet military forces, global environmental problems, and the impact of the arms race on the Third World. The facts are taken from Ruth Leger Sivard's *World Military and Social Expenditures* and Lester Brown's *State of the World*. How many long-range submarine missiles each country has. How many people have died in the Afghanistan and Nicaraguan wars. How much money is spent on the world arms race compared to what is spent on world health. How many hectares of forest disappear from the earth each year. A friend translates it into Russian and we make a thousand copies. We arrive at the Moscow airport with almost a hundred pounds of information to give away; SCPPNW staff meet us and customs officials let us pass.

Our first day in Moscow, we show the fact sheet to our Soviet team members—Zhenya Alekseeva, Slava Onishchenko, Olga Korshunova, and Volodya Nikoda—and wonder if they will feel comfortable handing out this officially unpublishable data. Their reaction is to ask for extra copies to give to friends and colleagues. "Distributing this may be the most important thing we do," Zhenya tells us during a late-night conversation in her kitchen. "What we need most of all is information. Especially the young people. We can't do anything without information."

For the next eight days we give presentations to students and physicians at medical institutes in Moscow and Tbilisi. We hand out fact sheets, show slides of our expeditions, tell stories illustrating how we learned to work together, and use a pitcher of 17,000 metal beebees, each representing one megaton of explosive yield, to demonstrate the immensity of current nuclear arsenals. The atmosphere at the medical institutes has dramatically changed since 1985. The students want to talk about environmental problems, about nuclear power, about religion, about how they can get involved in SCPPNW. When we offer to find them American medical student pen pals, we are deluged with hundreds of home addresses.

At times we sense a vibrancy in the air, a belief that change is possible. At other times the students seem to want to believe in their own helplessness. "We can't really do anything, because we would have to get permission from our Komsomol Committee," we hear several times. As together we try to persuade them otherwise, a new dimension appears in the relationships among our team members. We had started out as hiking buddies and moved from there into friendship. Now we are co-activists in a cause.

Sometimes we feel we are pushing the students, hard. Other times, it is we who are taken by surprise. In Tbilisi, a dozen medical students bring us to an ancient Georgian church that is now a museum. It is a cheerless place that has seen much trouble. Occupying Turks once used the eyes of the painted icons for target practice. Other frescoes were whitewashed around the time of the Soviet revolution. We stand in the sanctuary, subdued, unprepared for what happens next. The Georgian students bring in candles, light them, and cross themselves. A warm yellow light glows where none had before. Three students, including the Komsomol secretary of the medical institute, begin singing Georgian hymns in harmony. Zhenya and I hold hands and are silent as the music flows into us. We and the Georgians spend the rest of the day in old churches, awakening them with our candles and songs.

The next day we fly to Kaunas, the second largest city in Lithuania, and are met by two Kaunas medical students: Arnoldas Doviltis, a tall, coltish twenty-two-year-old with thinning hair and an incandescent grin, and Elena Bayeliene, a future surgeon and the mother of a six-year-old son. We know, almost immediately, that we have met kindred spirits. Elena had attended the 1987 IPPNW Congress in Moscow, and the information she had brought back had helped goad Arnoldas to action. A few months before, in February 1988, they had tried to hold a meeting at their institute of students interested in forming a local student section of SCPPNW, but their rector had broken up the meeting and told them to go home. Ten students, undaunted, met anyway in one of their apartments, which they nicknamed "Boston" in honor of IPPNW's central office.

Arnoldas and Elena are frank about the difficulties they face. Arnoldas calls the Lithuanian head of SCPPNW "the president of a paper empire." The Kaunas students have many ideas for joint projects with Western medical students, but they have no chance of traveling to IPPNW's international meetings as student delegates; "the Komsomol leaders in Moscow circle all those opportunities like sharks." But their biggest challenge is apathy. When they distributed a questionnaire about nuclear war to high school students, they found that the teenagers didn't think it would probably happen and that they believed there was nothing they could do about it anyway. And their fellow medical students say they have too much else on their minds to worry about nuclear war. Most believe that Moscow makes all those decisions, anyway, and who cares what a bunch of Lithuanian students think or do?

Our first night in Kaunas, Arnoldas shows up at our hotel with a set of paints and a twenty-foot length of white cotton. "I think maybe 200 students will come to your presentation tomorrow at the medical institute," he says. "But if we make a banner and hang it in the lobby, maybe 300 will come." We stay up past midnight taking turns with the single paintbrush, laughing and creating passable renderings of American and Soviet flags while rock 'n' roll wails over our tape player.

The next day, 300 students appear, and there is excited discussion about pen pals, sister schools, and a Soviet-American kayaking trip in Lithuania the following year. Afterwards, even the news that the KGB has caught up to us cannot dampen our spirits. The story we hear is just funny enough to be believable. After we had been in the Soviet Union eight days, a distraught KGB agent visited the Moscow SCPPNW office. "Why didn't we know about this speaking tour?" he complained, accusing the staff of failing to fill out the proper paperwork. But paperwork was not the issue. The KGB had been unable to take seriously a bunch of young people who had met while backpacking. And they had not expected us to hand out a thousand uncensored fact sheets to people in airplanes, schools, and hospitals. The agent's chief concern: "What am I going to tell my boss?"

So we receive a KGB tail on our second day in Kaunas. Who are you? David asks the middle-aged man trailing our hospital tour. The man says he is an engineer whose sister works in the clinic. From then on we call our KGB agents "the engineers." We treat them like the clumsy anachronisms they appear to be and invite them to dance with us at our parties. Our attitude disconcerts them; their power comes from fear, and we do not seem to be afraid.

Arnoldas and the other Kaunas students have organized a small conference of students from seven other medical institutes to coincide with our visit. About thirty students from Leningrad, Riga, Vilnius, Moscow, and Kiev have arrived with their enthusiasms and frustrations about SCPPNW. Many complain about too much interference from Komsomol; in some institutes, students can only become "members" of SCPPNW if their local Komsomol Committee approves. Careerism is also a factor: it is not always easy to tell how genuine a commitment students have to the issue, as some join SCPPNW only in hopes that someday this will allow them to travel to the West. Other problems include a lack of funds, a lack of communication between schools, and a lack of basic information. Two women students from Riga clutch a copy of Sivard's *World Military and Social Expenditures,* a gift from us, with tears in their eyes. "You don't know what this means to us," they say, over and over.

Listening keenly to the debates is Yuri Dzhibladze, a young cardiology resident from Moscow who is the new SCPPNW medical student chairman. At first Yuri and Arnoldas impress us as opposites: the competent, savvy coordinator from Moscow next to the impetuous local firebrand. Yuri prefers to go around obstacles; Arnoldas to flatten them. And at first Yuri's narrow tie, tweed coat, and obvious Komsomol connections raise our suspicions. But we soon discover in him a passionate zeal to decentralize SCPPNW and turn it into a working domestic peace group. Despite their differing personalities and tactics, Yuri and Arnoldas have similar goals. But it is inevitable that initially there is mistrust between them. During these days in Kaunas, we do more diplomacy and mediation between Russians and Lithuanians than between Soviets and Americans; that enmity runs far deeper.

Arnoldas keeps us busy. Presentation follows presentation, all to large audiences. We ask if we can speak at a local high school; the next day, we are showing slides to fifty teenagers and teachers. Later, one of the students will write me: "These few hours which we spent together made a very great impression on me. I must confess that my attitude towards the peace movement had been rather ironical up to your arrival." We speak at a school for physically handicapped children, and physicians at a hospital pepper us with skeptical and intelligent questions. The excitement generated by our talks is heightened by the fact that until a year before, Kaunas was a closed city to foreigners. We are "the first Americans" almost everywhere we go.

But all this isn't quite enough for Arnoldas. He wants media. He wants to go bigtime.

He tries to get a permit from city authorities for an outdoor peace demonstration. They turn him down. So instead he gets a permit for an outdoor wedding.

An outdoor wedding?

"I've put a notice in the newspaper saying there will be a 'Marriage Between Nations' at five o'clock Saturday in Rotushes Square," he explains that evening. His idea: the four Americans will marry—symbolically, of course—two of the Soviet speaking team members and two Lithuanians. There will be a microphone and opportunities to speak. The Kaunas Polytechnical Institute Marching Band will perform and attract a crowd. "The rest of the plot," Arnoldas says, "is up to you."

At five o'clock on Saturday, April 9, 1988, we wait with twenty medical students in front of the Palace of Marriages, talking in little clusters. A cold April breeze blowing through the square smells of newly thawed streams and the unwrapping of leaves. Oak trees and brick-and-shingle storefronts brace themselves against the sky. Children on bicycles ride past and covet the balloons tugging at our wrists.

Our words are hushed, light, a little concerned. We are already facing a major setback. Although it is five o'clock, the marching band has not appeared, and a rumor is circulating that the Lithuanian Minister of Education has found out about the wedding ceremony and has ordered the band to play elsewhere. Arnoldas is trying to remain cheerful. "We won't have a crowd, but we will still have a wedding," he says. But we can see his disappointment. We'll sing, we reassure him.

At that moment a bus pulls up to a corner of the square. Out comes a forty-piece marching band and a dozen drum majorettes in sassy powder-blue mini-skirts. Arnoldas beams and we applaud madly as the band members file past us and take their places, all of them trying not to mar their professional dignity with grins. One of the KGB men standing on the periphery of our cluster turns to David in bewilderment. "Are they here to play for *you?*" he asks.

"We'll see," David answers, as enigmatically as he can.

The band strikes up an energetic tune; the majorettes stamp their white boots and fling their pompons to the sky. Soon the number of people in the square doubles, then triples, then multiplies into a crowd of about five hundred. Arnoldas is now in constant motion, disappearing to set up some last-minute detail, appearing to give me a bouquet of flowers and a squeeze of the hand, disappearing again. I see a new look of tension in his eyes. There is no turning back now.

It is one thing to joke about "the engineers" in the staid atmosphere of an institute or the comfort of a private home; it is another to discover them standing behind us in the open air, their hands shoved in their trenchcoats. Although we know that we are invulnerable, that the demonstration, thanks to Arnoldas' creativity, is technically legal, it is still disconcerting to watch them watch us. A raw gust of wind claws under our coats, and we shiver; we keep shivering after the wind has passed. To ease our tension, we go over the plot. David will marry Zhenya; Amy will marry Volodya. Rick will marry a stunning Kaunas medical student named Giedre Ribikauskaite; we tease him for being so obviously pleased with the looks of his bride. And Arnoldas will marry me.

At last the band plays its final fanfare and the majorettes lower their pompons. All eyes are on the microphone in the center of the square. The moment has come when someone must break out of the protective anonymity of the crowd and begin. Where is Arnoldas? I wonder. Then I see him, off to the side, pacing back and forth with long strides. His brow is furrowed; he is poised on the edge of decision. The crowd waits. The band waits. The engineers wait, and the only sound is the murmur of the spring wind.

Arnoldas is walking to the microphone. He looks so young and unprotected that an unreasonable voice whispers within me: *Someone could shoot him, now.* But no one moves. He begins to speak, and his voice is strong and confident. Listening to his welcoming words in Lithuanian, our anxieties melt away. We feel invincible again. The crowd relaxes; the mood shifts to that of a festival. The long wait is over.

Arnoldas comes back and takes my hand. We and the other three Soviet-American couples walk into the center of the ring as trombones and tubas belt out a swingy tune. Elena Bayeliene speaks next, in Russian.

"What kind of earth is this? It is a fragile, bluish little ship. We are all part of the same crew. And if every one of us, if only for a moment, admitted and contemplated this, we wouldn't break holes in our ship's hull. We would work to save the beautiful oceans, the rains, the dawns of our ship. Who are we to each other on this earth? We have no need to harm one another, to stab each other in the back. Let us smile at one another."

On cue, we exchange the painted wooden rings Arnoldas has produced. Zhenya and David beam and raise their hands high. Volodya kisses Amy's hand. Rick offers a courtly bow to Giedre, and she responds with a curtsey; the delighted crowd claps and someone plays a harmonica accompaniment to their little show. Arnoldas and I just hug each other awkwardly; we are both too moved to try any theatrics.

Then Rick steps to the microphone, his arm around Giedre. "Giedre and I met yesterday. Today, we are getting married." The audience laughs. "We are marrying each other's cities, peoples, and countries. The global family today is not a healthy family. With our brother and sister nations, we argue, and we point fingers, and we threaten one another.

"We can build a healthy family relationship, where differences are addressed peacefully and without violence. Today we have enough nuclear weapons to blow up the world more than 200 hundred times. By becoming family, we recognize a new approach to our relationships, relationships which will go on for generations in the future.

"Giedre and I do not know yet where we are going for our honeymoon. But I think we'll take it right here in Kaunas." There is much laughter and applause.

Amy and Volodya bring the pitcher of beebees and a metal bucket to the microphone. Their voices are calm and matter-of-fact. Amy drops in the bucket one beebee: a single megaton. Volodya drops four beebees: the equivalent of all the weapons and bombs used in World War II. He pours in an aspirin bottle's worth: the amount of megatonnage to be taken out of action by the Intermediate Nuclear Forces (INF) treaty. At this, the crowd breaks into spontaneous applause, then quiets as Amy hefts the pitcher and explains its meaning. She asks people to take hands, close their eyes, and imagine, as she pours the beebees, "that this is the last hand you would be holding if this were a real nuclear war."

One minute later, after the last beebee falls, the only sound is the wail of a baby, somewhere in the crowd.

Amy takes a deep breath. "This is not a bucket of hopelessness. It's a challenge to us, as a species, as humanity, to overcome this as a way of resolving our differences. I look forward to a long, happy, and healthy marriage, with all of you."

She kisses Volodya on the cheek and he raises their hands high. The crowd cheers and applauds, a student chorus launches into a Lithuanian folk song, and we beckon the crowd to join hands with us. Soon a hundred people are dancing in a circle three rings deep. The band plays and the drum majorettes march resolutely into the center of the circle. All of the tension has given way to complete abandon. Coats and bags are flung to the pavement. Middle-aged men skip next to medical students; high school girls next to matrons clutching their children. "Is Moscow ready for this?" I shout over my shoulder to two Moscow students dancing behind me. "No!" they shout back. But I can tell they are wondering the same thing.

After so long a wait, the people are not ready for it to end. Song follows song, and it seems we will dance forever in the cold spring wind. But even as we dance, our Soviet-American team is thinking about our fact sheets. If we give the crowd only rhetoric and symbolism, the sense of power will eventually fade into memory and be doubted. In a nod to the "engineers" still standing outside the ring, we quickly confer and decide that, this time, only Americans will hand them out.

Between songs, Rick announces that we have brought "medical information" about the arms race, ecological problems, and other aspects of planetary health. While the others link arms and sing "We Shall Overcome," I take a stack of 200 fact sheets and walk to the back of the crowd. A little girl is the first to ask me for a copy; she runs away as soon as I give it to her, clutching it under her arm. Within seconds I am surrounded by a ring ten people deep. I cannot hand out the copies quickly enough, and I soon place my hands under the pile and let people reach for their own. Within seconds I am staring at a blur of hands, polite yet starved hands, hands shaking with an eagerness to know. The people press close, reach, nod, and disappear; the pile melts away. The white sheets of paper shine and flutter and are gone.

Dimly I hear people singing, "There'll be no more war. . . ." Their hands continue to reach for information, information that can make them powerful. Something lets go in my eyes. In two minutes the pile is gone. The last man takes his copy, nods, and vanishes. I stare at my empty palms. They are light, and trembling.

Two days later, we are sitting in a reception hall of a Moscow medical institute with Bernard Lown and Mikhail Kuzin, the American and Soviet co-presidents of IPPNW. Our team is supposed to be presenting a report to them about the Soviet leg of the Moving Mountains tour, but Kuzin is consuming what little time we have with a long, puzzling speech about why the Soviets had to invade Afghanistan. Everyone is impatient and edgy. There is an unspoken debate in the air.

Two years before, Kuzin, an elderly academician and administrator, replaced Soviet IPPNW co-founder and co-president Evgeny Chazov when Gorbachev asked Chazov to become Minister of Health. Kuzin and Arnoldas eye each other with suspicion across the table. Kuzin wants SCPPNW to be a tidy and civilized group of high-ranking Soviet doctors who attend international conferences and handle visiting delegations. Arnoldas wants to light a fire of public opinion under Soviet military and foreign policy. They represent two sides of a schism being played out in so many ways in the Soviet Union today: the split between old and new, the Brezhnev era and the Gorbachev era, tight and orderly control from the top versus creative and sometimes disorderly action from below.

The success of the wedding has given Arnoldas a dozen new ideas. His latest dream is a bicycle ride around the Baltic Sea, with medical students from each of the Baltic nations riding together and holding weddings and demonstrations along the way. That neither he nor any other non-Moscow student activist will be included in the small Soviet student delegation to the IPPNW World Congress in Montreal next month seems to us an outrage.

"Do you want to speak?" I whisper to Arnoldas.

"I think I am too shy," he whispers back.

Five minutes later, as Kuzin continues to drone on about Afghanistan, Arnoldas nudges me. "I think I will say a few words," he says. "But you start."

Kuzin finishes at last, and the rector of the institute tries to close the meeting. I jump to my feet and introduce Arnoldas before anyone can interrupt. In slow but clear English, he describes the wedding and the student conference, then makes his plea. "I must say that the point for real work is the local place, and not the centers, not the tops, not the meetings near the table," he says. A frozen grin settles on Kuzin's face. "I think that we must look for the possibility to send to Montreal a large number of students who work on the local level, students from Leningrad, Riga, Kiev, and Kaunas, who will be inspired by the Congress. Because now it is only five positions, and all these positions are for students from the Committee in Moscow. I think that if we would like to make this movement in the Soviet Union effective and creative, we must send many students from the local places."

Kuzin is standing up. If looks could kill, Arnoldas would be dead. "The delegation of students will be more than five—approximately fifteen or maybe twenty persons," he says smoothly. We all gasp at the lie. "So you may establish good contact with the students from Canada and America and the developing countries."

Arnoldas is trembling. But he does not sit down. "But I know that no students from Leningrad, from Kiev, from Riga—nobody will visit."

There is shocked silence, followed by much muttering up and down the table. No one is supposed to challenge authority this directly. Lown tries to come to the rescue. "Let me respond to that," he says. "What you say is *very* important. To create an effective movement, we do not need people from Moscow, we need student activists from all over the country. Our movement in the Soviet Union needs vitality. I'm speaking very frankly. And vitality comes from young people who understand the issues and have the ability to get excited and angry. I would love to see a *hundred* Soviet students come to Montreal." He is banging his pen on the table.

"We haven't yet gotten *perestroika* in the work of IPPNW in the Soviet Union," Lown continues. "And unless we have it, we will not be successful. The only way to have growth and development is to bring in an influx. We need students, from Kaunas, from Riga, from smaller places, to get involved in this movement first on a national level, and then on an international level. And we'll do everything we can in the central office to make this possible."

Kuzin continues to smile stiffly. The meeting ends. In the hall, I put an arm around Arnoldas and ask him if he knows the word "gutsy." He doesn't and I explain. "Yes, but I think maybe my words were to the sky," he says, looking discouraged. Yuri Dzhibladze is distraught. "It was not the right way, not the right time or place," he keeps saying. We are all upset and disheartened.

Arnoldas and the students from Leningrad and Riga do not go to Montreal. We are not even able to arrange for Zhenya, Volodya, Slava, or Olga to attend. The various Komsomol-controlled student SCPPNW committees in Moscow do not much care what other students do in their hometowns, but they definitely do not want to lose their ability to dole out the privilege of Western travel.

But the success of the Moving Mountains speaking tour in the United States helps sweep away these old monopolies. During three weeks in May 1988, we give more than 100 presentations to nearly 10,000 people in fifteen cities, and we reach a media audience of five million more. The seeds planted by the Moving Mountains tour fall into fertile soil. We help recruit a fresh generation of "medical student diplomats," and within a year, an array of new projects has sprouted, ranging from a climbing expedition in the Georgian Caucasus Mountains to eight reciprocal student exchanges between Soviet and American medical schools. The Kaunas medical students invite Americans and Canadians, including some with physical disabilities, to Lithuania for three weeks of kayaking and public talks. From this project spring a half-dozen new ones: a bicycling tour for blind Lithuanians and Americans, a joint program in rehabilitation medicine, a Minnesota canoe trip for disabled veterans of the Vietnam and Afghanistan wars.

Remembering the way our Russian-language fact sheets had evaporated on the streets of Kaunas, we pull together some funding to make more copies. Working closely with Yuri, Zhenya, Arnoldas, and others, soon we are producing new translations of articles on nonviolence, ecology, and global security, and loading up the suitcases of willing Americans traveling to the Soviet Union. As this project snowballs, it acquires the name "GOLUBKA," a Russian word that means both "dove" and "carrier pigeon." Within a year, thanks to a network of volunteer translators and distributors in both countries, we have built up a library of two dozen translations and delivered more than a thousand pounds of materials to the informal Soviet peace and ecology movements.

Gradually we realize that the lack of concrete information is only part of the problem; far more fundamental is a lack of belief that individuals can make a difference. As discouraging reports about economic woes, ethnic violence, and the failure of *perestroika* continue to dominate the evening news, many Soviets adopt a fervent pessimism that relieves them of responsibility to try to change the situation. In January 1990, our GOLUBKA team sponsors a three-day workshop on personal empowerment for forty young people in Moscow that directly addresses the question "Is there really nothing I can do?" Afterwards, one participant writes to Gail Straub and David Gershon, the American workshop leaders: "Cynicism and nihilism are deadly maladies that jeopardize the minds of the people in this country. You gave a powerful injection that neutralized these hazards for at least a small group of people and showed that these diseases could be curable." We decide to expand GOLUBKA's activities to include organizing workshops all over the Soviet Union on empowerment, ecological thinking, conflict resolution, and ethnic understanding.

In a country where buying shoes can occupy days, where ordering airplane tickets can take weeks, and where getting access to a photocopy machine is still nearly impossible, the logistical work required for organizing a workshop or any other public event is immense. Everything must be done on foot and in person. No workplace answers the telephone, no one seems to take messages, and there is not even a quick way to ship packages. Vast amounts of people power must be mobilized to make up for the inefficiency and lack of infrastructure. During preparations for the 1989 Lithuanian kayaking expedition, for example, one Kaunas student had to fly to Moscow to pick up publicity posters; another spent several days arranging for a factory to donate 600 candles for a peace lantern ceremony; another visited every newspaper office in town to spread word about a press conference.

Yet somehow, the work gets done. As our collaboration across the borders deepens in intensity, we become experts at circumventing the antiquated barriers that still block communication between our countries. We call each other in the middle of the night to get through on inadequate telephone lines. We develop an elaborate system of human *golubki* (carrier pigeons) to shuttle paperwork and letters back and forth. We accumulate lists of phone and fax numbers at the State Department and the Soviet Embassy, and learn the hard way never to take visas for granted. And somewhere in the midst of all this wrestling with permission and money, tickets and exit papers, we remember to remind each other why we are doing this. Best of all are our visits, too infrequent but treasured, when we can stay up until three in the morning dreaming new plans, listening to music, and running to the computer with inspiration.

Together we step over the invisible boundary of trust—trust between Americans and Soviets in our small GOLUBKA "flock," but also, no less significantly, trust between Russians and Lithuanians, Kazakhs and Georgians. Arnoldas and Yuri, for example, become such close friends and partners that their initial mistrust turns into a running joke. "I think your first impression of me was not quite positive," I once overhear Yuri tease Arnoldas. Arnoldas smiles and claims not to remember. "It's okay," says Yuri, suddenly turning more serious, "I myself would not have trusted who I was then."

As time passes, it seems hard to believe that we had once trembled to speak our little heresies and take what now seem such small steps, that it was once a breakthrough to hold an unsanctioned public meeting and pass out unapproved literature, that there was ever a reason for nightmares. Two months after the Kaunas wedding ceremony, the Lithuanian independence movement took to the streets, and soon open-air political demonstrations became huge and commonplace throughout the Soviet Union. In retrospect, the fear by which totalitarianism operates seems so unnatural and absurd that we can barely remember its existence. We have to remind ourselves that what felt like breakthroughs then *were* breakthroughs for that time, and that our actions were part of the process of change.

But our Soviet friends knew that fear intimately, as a companion from childhood, and even though they can now, with wonder and relief, view its corpse from a distance, they can also hear an occasional cackle from its ghost, and wake up in the night shivering at the thought that it could someday return.

"You are a power from outside," Arnoldas explains to me. "You show us that there is an alternative way to live, to act, to be. Now I am searching for inside power."

Once, not so long ago, it felt risky to visit Zhenya in her home, to sneak away from the Intourist Hotel and sleep on her couch after an evening of singing and conversation. Now I live in her apartment during each visit to Moscow. The children and neighbors are used to me, and the old women sitting on the bench by the front door return my *zdravstvuitye* (Hello) with grave, companionable nods. I help with the dishes and shopping, I use the telephone freely, and I often sit alone at the kitchen table late at night with a notebook, nursing my last cup of tea, staring at the illuminated fields of apartment buildings and trying to see what Zhenya sees from this window.

What would it be like to grow up in a country where the main newspaper is called *Truth,* although everyone knows it is full of lies? To take oaths you do not believe to organizations you know are hollow and corrupt, simply to live a normal life? To learn to cherish family and close friends as the only trustworthy things in life, and to sing, in the privacy of the home, Bulat Okudzhava's song:

How greedily the age craves
to discover a weak link in our chain!
Join hands, friends,
join hands, friends,
so we won't perish one by one.

Zhenya is ordinarily an extremely positive, cheerful person. When the fold-out couch breaks and the doors fall off the cupboards, she laughs. When the stores have no potatoes, she shrugs and buys cabbage. She is an expert at making lemonade when the universe hands her lemons. Always I have admired her ability to create joy in her life through her circle of friends, her music, her family, her trips to her beloved mountains.

Today she is different. "I'm in a bad mood," is all she says when we meet, as planned, at a metro stop. Something dark and unexplained shadows her face. An unpleasant experience at work, she mumbles, and I do not press her for more. We go to a store and buy juice, potatoes, cheese. The bag is heavy and we carry it between us as we walk on icy paths toward home. "You know, Gale, I don't know if you can understand how easy our life is here in Moscow," she says suddenly. "Here we can peacefully walk into a store and buy food. In the provinces they have nothing. They are living on canned fish and macaroni. They have nothing, absolutely nothing, to eat." We walk on in silence, the snow crunching under our boots. "This country is like a prison," she says at last, her voice hard. "Like a place where criminals must sit for punishment."

What do you say when your friend tells you this? The next day I will fly home to the United States. I will flash my blue passport and be gone.

As we step into the elevator, I speak, carefully, a statement rather than a question: "Things are better now than before."

"Yes," she replies, without changing her expression.

"Then there is reason for hope."

"Without hope," she says, smiling faintly, looking me intently in the eyes, "it is impossible to live."

The children almost knock us down with enthusiasm at our return, and the cat purrs against our legs. Soon we are peeling potatoes, writing last-minute letters, making plans for next time.

At the airport, I hug Zhenya and Yuri good-bye and say: "What a tremendous journey we have had."

"Lots of good stories to tell our grandchildren," Yuri replies with a grin.

"Yes, we'll sit around and talk about these strange things called borders that used to cause so much trouble and keep people apart."

And for a moment it sounds possible—it sounds like prophecy—we feel the currents of the present swirling around us, and a glimpse of that future appears.

At times our work seems full of an inchoate power. If we do our work well, this power whispers, then someday our children will indeed listen wide-eyed to fantastic tales of borders and wars, of missiles poised for catastrophe, of concepts such as "national security" that have the same distant, old-fashioned ring as "the divine right of kings." If we do our work well, then rivers and springs will run clear again, forests will soften our wastelands, the air will be cleansed and the laughter of children will become our earth's clearest song. If we do our work well, then the colorful skeins of tradition and culture on our planet will be preserved and woven into one tapestry, strong and warming to all peoples everywhere.

At times we are impatient. In the eyes of my Soviet friends I see that they may never live in a world that will allow them to travel, learn, and express their restless caring for the planet as much as they would like. Too often we still stub a toe on some ancient bureaucratic roadblock, or encounter some official squawking that we hold different passports and different rules apply. We are young, still, but time is going by, and we may never see the world we are trying to create.

Yet, in a way, we already live in that world. We strengthen and empower each other, pull each other through the hard times, refuse to believe in the borders others see. When our voices blend, something powerful and previously unspoken is heard. The threads between us shimmer and hum with hope.

There are nightmares, but there are also dreams.

In one, we are sitting around Zhenya's kitchen table in Moscow, drinking tea and talking into morning. We are five years older. Our Russian and their English have matched, and we talk easily in both languages about our children, about music, poetry, friends. We are laughing, remembering the times when our meetings were events that *Pravda* and the *Associated Press* felt worth reporting. We are remembering the sun creeping brilliantly over the shoulder of the mountain. The night has ended, and we are singing the ballad by Bulat Okudzhava that we used to sing to audiences, back when this was a dream.

> I'll bury a grape seed in the warm earth
> I'll kiss the vine, I'll gather the ripe bunches
> I'll call my friends together
> And I'll tune my heart to love—
> What else is there to live for
> On this eternal earth?

INDEX

INDEX

About the Author

GALE WARNER co-authored *Citizen Diplomats* and has written for *The Boston Globe, The Christian Science Monitor, Parade,* and *Sierra.* She is co-founder and co-director of GOLUBKA, a Soviet-American network that supports independent Soviet peace and environmental activists by distributing information and conducting workshops on ecology, empowerment, nonviolence, and global security. She lives in Framingham, Massachusetts.